*Athenian silver coin (ca. 460 BCE), identifying the city
with its eponymous goddess. The little* glaux—*the
round-faced, round-eyed owl—is Athena's special
emblem. Here, with a branch of the olive tree, her gift to
her beloved city, the association is emphasized by the
letters ATHE[nai].*

ATHENA

a biography

ATHENA

a biography

LEE HALL

ADDISON-WESLEY PUBLISHING COMPANY, INC.

Reading, Massachusetts   Menlo Park, California   New York
Don Mills, Ontario   Harlow, England   Amsterdam   Bonn
Sydney   Singapore   Tokyo   Madrid   San Juan
Paris   Seoul   Milan   Mexico City   Taipei

Library of Congress Cataloging-in-Publication Data

Hall, Lee.
    Athena : a biography / Lee Hall.
      p.   cm.
    Includes bibliographical references (p.   ) and index.
    ISBN 0-201-87046-0 (alk. paper)
    1. Athena (Greek deity)   I. Title.
    BL820.M6H35 1997   96-39464
    292.2'114--dc21   CIP

Jacket design by David High
Text design by Karen Savary
Set in 11.5-point Bembo by Octal Publishing, Inc.

123456789-MA-0100999897
First printing, May 1997

CONTENTS

ACKNOWLEDGEMENTS

The dedication of this book to Elizabeth Jastrow and Patience Haggard, great teachers, is minuscule recognition of their contribution to this work. I gratefully remembered their words and felt their presence throughout the research and writing of *Athena.*

I am grateful to the America School of Classical Studies in Athens, and to Dr. William Coulson and Dr. Robert Bridges (director and secretary respectively) for hospitality and assistance during my residency there; and for access to the splendid treasures of the Blegen Library. I am grateful, too, to Dr. Judith Binder for her companionable conversation and for her helpful suggestions.

The book was enriched by contributions from friends. I thank Paula Treder for her generous support, Margaret Horsnell for advice and encouragement, and Tracy Devine, Miriam Cavanaugh, Brian Hotchkiss, and Joan Davis for reading the manuscript in several stages. Ms. Davis also prepared the index.

The photographer for the American School of Classical Studies in Athens, Marie Mauzy, was a dependable and imaginative researcher; she negotiated the use of images from the archives of the ASCSA, the Agora, the National Archaeological Museum, and the Acropolis Museum in Athens. I am indebted to those institutions, and to the Hellenic Republic Ministry of Culture for illustrations. Laura Luckey also identified and acquired important photographs from museum collections: I thank her.

Kimberly Witherspoon, my agent, and her associate, Gideon Weil, furthered the book at every point in its journey from idea to publication. I remain appreciative to them; to Nancy Miller, the editor who acquired the book for Addison-Wesley; and to William Patrick, who improved the manuscript measurably with his suggestions and insights.

Lee Hall
South Hadley, Massachusetts

*Athenian silver coin (ca. 460 BCE), identifying the city
with its eponymous goddess. The little glaux—the
round-faced, round-eyed owl—is Athena's special
emblem. Here, with a branch of the olive tree, her gift to
her beloved city, the association is emphasized by the
letters ATHE[nai].*

SEVERAL BEGINNINGS

OUR BEGINNING: RACISM, SEXISM, AND CULTURE WARS

Athena's immortality—her ability to lay claim to the human imagination and symbolize deeply felt beliefs and aspirations—is evidenced by the heated arguments she attracts today from diverse camps in the culture wars. While it is appropriate that Athena should be courted and claimed by people passionately concerned with the festering issues of racism and sexism in our culture, it is equally appropriate that she be called upon to revivify the tenets of *civilization,* and to clarify her—and humankind's—unfinished business.

Athena does not belong exclusively to culture warriors of any particular stripe, nor to propagandists who bang and whimper for and against political correctness. Groups of both feminists and ethnocentrists claim Athena as their poster god. The feminists recognize Athena as the offspring of a prehistoric female fertility deity and claim her as a founding mother of the Great Goddess cult; the ethnocentrists argue that the Greeks appropriated Athena from her African roots, robbed her of her real identity, and assigned her to duty in the Olympian pantheon. Both feminists and ethnocentrists believe that Athena, along with her powers and symbolic portent, was taken hostage by white males, the power group that owns "Western civilization."

Athena belongs to any person interested in the meaning of history and the nature of humankind; both we and Athena—as well as civilization—are works in progress. And, of course, Athena's story, like our own, is shaped by human episodes of savagery and civility, war and peace; she was present in power struggles between the sexes; she employed her celebrated wisdom and skill as a strategist against the fumbling attempts of mortals and immortals to obfuscate the relationship between *might* and *right* in order to get their own way; and she helped humankind understand laws and customs needed to form communities, build and live in cities, and honor beauty and wisdom.

It is unarguably true that Athenian civilization, the presumed root of our own culture, was misogynistic in the extreme, that it limited citizenship and participation in "democracy" to a group of men, and condoned slavery. Over the centuries the flaws of Athenian high culture receded in the imaginations and data bases of scholars and laypeople alike. A romanticized version of ancient Greece took hold in textbooks and political rhetoric; that canonization of Greek civilization was as sterile as nineteenth-century white plaster copies of Parthenon sculpture intended to instill in viewers reverence for "our" culture.

But Athena, despite the failures and perversions that are cited in indictments against Western civilization, remains a symbol—sometimes charming, sometimes savage and corrupt, always powerful. Her precinct is the human consciousness; she represents the potential our species has to create an ideal state, to banish barbarism, and to ensure that the physical and spiritual resources of humans have optimum encouragement for development and expression.

Athena also symbolizes the obstacles that stand between us and a civilized state, and reassures us that they are as old as humankind's aspiration to be superior to other animals. While barbarity may wear new masks or answer to new names, it is still a demon in the human heart as old as mythology, as inseparable as dreams from the human mind; barbarity, Athena finally tells us, must be routed and replaced by wisdom and justice if we are to achieve civility.

We can know Athena as the handsome goddess of wisdom, war, and craft; we can know her as the resident of the Parthenon, that undisputed masterpiece of human architectural achievement built for her on the Acropolis in Athens, her special city and the birthplace of democracy. We can know her as the emblem of Neoplatonism and neoclassicism, two traditional cornerstones in our intellectual history. We can also know her as evidence of the Greek genius, and one of our most potent symbols for our concept and tradition of civilization. Yet this quintessential goddess of wisdom and civility began life in territory difficult to know—in the emerging consciousness of humankind in prehistoric millennia. Her first evidences appear in the relics associated with barbarian blood sacrifices, rituals, superstition, and fear. Moreover, this female deity—deemed by us to be high minded in the extreme—not only rejected absolutely the restrictions that gender placed on her individuality, her *persona,* but betrayed her sex in the power struggles among gods and men.

Athena's story has come to us through myth, most specifically through Homer's *Iliad* and *Odyssey,* and other ancient literary sources. Her long supernatural life weaves its way through the writings of the ancients, leaving stories of events of greater and lesser importance among mortals and immortals. She consorted with seductresses and rapists, monsters and mortals, heroes and cowards; and she knew pride and anger, triumph and failure, good days and bad. At times she was generous and helpful to mortals and immortals; at other times she was treacherous, vindictive, and dangerous. She did not live in the time and space measured by humans, but was known to be many places at once, to fly through the air and move from one place to another in an instant. She did not weep, eat, or bleed. And finally, unlike our fated species, she was immortal. She did not die.

In addition to the literature of mythology, there are images of Athena in sculpture, vase painting, gem carving, and other arts, dating from prehistoric times and including the great works of the Athenian Acropolis. In both word and image she appears sometimes as a maiden-goddess, sometimes as a warrior, and sometimes as an elder wisewoman; she appears in artifacts related to prehistoric fertility rituals, and may have had several manifestations—or lives—before she sprang from Zeus's head, fully armed, to become a major deity in the Olympian pantheon.

But Athena does not succumb to human constraints and consistencies: her story is composed of disparate parts that are not linked coherently by plot, theme, time, or rational concepts of cause and effect. Born of the human mind, Athena was shaped by magic and dreams, and by the deepest needs and longings of our species. It is not surprising, then, that, from a modern reader's or biographer's point of view, Athena's story is full of inconsistencies, incongruities, dangling effects without rational causes, abrupt action without lucid motivation, and illogical temporal loops and dizzying spatial swirls that defy the common sense of narrative sequence. But taken together, the various clear glimpses we get of Athena allow us to see her rising tentatively and at first shapeless from the fertile ooze of the most ancient human imagination, to watch her transformation in the expanding consciousness of mortals in different times and cultures, to see her rebellion against the limitations of gender imposed by ancient society, and to meet her as she measures the inherent conflicts between the individual and the just community.

I am grateful to the long line of storytellers, researchers, and teachers who have laid their insights alongside the works of ancient writers and artists. I have tried to remember throughout the research and writing of this book that, necessarily, I approach myth through literature and mute works of visual art. I cannot hear the stories sung or told. And I cannot see artifacts, even those in pristine condition, with the same eyes that etched the images into the Greek mind. I believe I benefit from the twentieth-century perspective in assessing the relationships between information and experience, imagery and language, and truth and fantasy. Even with my unavoidable twentieth-century mind-set, I have tried to be attentive to the unique contribution of myth to human understanding; I have granted myself permission to savor myth as story, and have acknowledged that a biography of Athena is, in the end, a literary conceit, a game or speculation that I invite others to share.

Notes at the end of the text are offered to aid the reader who wishes to explore Athena's territory in greater breadth and depth. Unless otherwise specified in the text, all dates are before the common era (B.C.E.).

IN THE BEGINNING, MYTH

In the beginning Athena was ritual and myth; her name, her attributes, her powers, and her presence in human consciousness evolved without regard to twentieth-century rational concepts of time and space, but in response to human perceptions and needs in those dark aeons before the discovery of agriculture. For an incalculably long period before history, she was a force among other forces; supernatural and natural were indistinguishable, and deities appeared in nature and were brought forth in the rituals human beings found to appease, petition, or thank the spirits behind all beings and events. As stories were told and spread, prototypes of Athena appeared and reappeared; the goddess's attributes became familiar, clearer, and more predictable for both the tellers of and listeners to stories. She was given a name, a particularity; *Athena* became the symbol of understood powers even as each teller and each region modified the stories to conform to new and changing needs of women and men in the prehistoric millennia.

With the invention and spread of writing after the Bronze Age, Athena was reinvented in literature; with the creation of history and the evolution of social institutions, she loomed as a civic presence. Like all deities in all cultures, Athena traveled across the barrier between myth and history, emerging from the dark corridors of the former to inspire and influence the latter.

Myth, the collective consciousness of a culture, enables people to agree about who they are, what they value, and how and why some individuals should be praised over others; myth hovers always in the background of political thought and action, of patterns of social behavior, and of the deep understanding of truths that permeates the arts and customs of a culture. Myth, like history or any other intellectual discipline, is a human effort to understand human life, and to find the reasons and causes behind events, to understand the significance of life and its driving passions: who are we and what will become of us? How did we get here, and what makes us good or bad, worthy or unworthy, lucky or ill fated? What forces shape our days, enlighten our thoughts, stir our hearts, or bring about change? Myth is composed of concepts and symbols that attempt provisional answers to these abiding human questions.

In the preliterate cultures around the Mediterranean, stories were told and retold, refined and embellished to fit the needs of tellers and listeners. With the appearance of the writings of Hesiod and Homer in about the eighth century, stories from the ancient oral tradition that had been more or less codified during the Bronze Age were transposed into the first works of Western literature; and through the rich and varied cache we today identify as Greek mythology—especially in Hesiod's *Theogony*—we begin to look behind history and science, to peer into the dark centuries before human beings created the alphabet and learned to write, and to imagine Athena's long gestation in human consciousness.

Those of us intellectually groomed by twentieth-century deification of rationality may be programmed to dismiss Hesiod's *Theogony* as weird or fantastic "fairy tales," but that would be a mistake. His description of the birth of the cosmos and the appearance of the gods should not be confused with history or science or with any other modern academic discipline. Hesiod, Homer, and their contemporaries had not separated myth from history, religion from science, or art from magic: they perceived and explained natural forces and human events in the stories we call "mythology" because they believed—had faith in—the precepts and symbols of mythology as matter-of-factly as we accept "scientific" explanations.

For eighth-century Hesiod and for us, Athena's story begins appropriately at the very birth of the cosmos, in Chaos—the dreadful abyss that existed before the gods had been born, before the earth had shape, before human beings had been created. In his *Theogony* Hesiod writes on a clean slate of nothingness, and he enlightens a fertile darkness.

IN THE BEGINNING, DARKNESS

According to Hesiod, in the beginning all was darkness; nothing moved or was thought. There was no earth and no sea, no firmament on which plants grew and creatures lived; there were no vapors and fluids, not even matter and void, not even dimension. Neither shape nor substance, neither time nor space existed; and there was no mind—immortal or mortal—to perceive or conceive that dark primeval nothingness.

Then, inexplicably, the cosmos stirred and Chaos spontaneously separated from Darkness; here is the first miracle and the first thought, the beginning of the universe and, with it, the "once upon a time" that would open the first chapter of the story that would eventually include gods and humans, and their intertwined fates.

No one knows how much time passed before Order struggled to exist and stirred Darkness to give up Chaos, which, although still without shape, contained all essences and principles of all things possible and impossible, all powers to be realized or unrealized. As Hesiod had learned from the old stories, Chaos was the protean force from which all else would issue; it was the Beginning and the End. But the separation of Chaos from Darkness was not a matter of simple division, not a clear split that yielded two from one. Rather, in the very moment of splitting, Chaos also released the Fates, divinities so powerful that they would never bow to the rule of other gods; they would forever possess a prior claim on the territories of the Olympian deities, would hold sovereign rights to ultimate power and to dominion over the singularity and destiny of all mortals and immortals. Once and for all the Fates took their places, and irrevocably portioned good things and bad into each life.

IN THE BEGINNING, EROS

At the same moment that Chaos issued the Fates, another ubiquitous force, Eros, was also turned loose in the cosmos. Powerful and unpredictable Eros held absolute power over sexual desire and love and, it is told, was so constituted as to be incessantly, compulsively, and forever striking immortals and mortals alike with his handiwork—lust and love. Even as Chaos and Darkness divided, at the very instant they separated into distinct entities, Eros took hold of them, infused them with sexual desire, and drove them to frenzied coitus. Their union was fruitful, and brought forth Night (Nyx) and Day (Hemera) and also produced Air and Erebus, and the Eternal Shades.

Eros swiftly brought about intercourse between Night and Erebus, a union that produced Doom, Old Age, Death, Murder, Continence, Sleep, Dreams, Discord, Misery, Vexation, Nemesis, Joy, Friendship, and Pity. Air and Day joined to produce Mother Earth, Sky, and Sea. Then Air and Mother Earth united to produce Terror, Craft, Anger, Strife, Lies, Oaths, Vengeance, Intemperance, Altercation, Treaty, Oblivion, Fear, Pride, and Battle.

BEFORE ATHENA: URANUS AND GAIA

Athena's good and bad traits, like those of the mortals who imagined her, can be traced to her progenitors as well as to her experiences. She issued from a family of supernatural beings as marked by their bizarre natures as by their powers; they were determined by fury and lust, given to conflict among themselves. The gods of ancient Greece had no pact with mortals, no holy writ promising humans rewards or punishments for specific behaviors, no commandments or proscriptions set in stone or memory to guide human beings in dealing with the gods. Mutable, volatile, and unpredictable in the extreme, the gods endured troubles and triumphs similar to those they imposed on people. The gods remained true to the mysterious and savage stuff of which they were made; no amount of mortal longing could imbue them with consistency, loyalty, justice, or compassion.

The first deity, Mother Earth, or Gaia, joined Darkness and Chaos, and gave birth to the god Uranus, the sky god. He immediately lusted for his mother, Gaia, rose above her body, overpowered her, and, against her will, mated with her; thus Uranus was Gaia's son and husband, and he was the god of light. As the sky over the earth, Uranus covered Gaia completely and ravished her repeatedly. In this beginning-of-it-all orgy of fecundity, Uranus poured fertile rain into Gaia's cavities and clefts, impregnating her continuously, causing her to give birth to grass, trees, and flowers, and to bring forth from her recesses all the beasts and birds, flowing rivers and glimmering lakes.

This, it is told, is how the universe began, and how Gaia ruled the earth and Uranus the sky; this is how they coupled, brought all life into being, and established the seasons and the rain.

THE FIRST RACE OF GODS

It is known that Gaia and Uranus were the first gods, the ancestors of the Olympians, Hesiod tells us, but they were undisciplined themselves and unable to control the powers, forms, and forces they possessed or created. After they produced the cosmos and everything and every being within it, they did not rest; rather, Uranus continued to embrace and copulate with Gaia at every opportunity. It followed that she received his seed and gave birth to a gruesome lot of flawed beings of unsurpassed strength and hideousness, a flock of god-monsters, physically powerful but psychologically dark and untrustworthy, including the first race of giants—the six Titans (Oceanus, Coeus, Crius, Hyperion, Iaptus, and Cronus) and the six Titanesses (Theia, Rhea, Themis, Mnemosyne, Phoebe, and Tethys); the three Hecatoncheires (Hundred-Handed Ones); and the three Cyclopes.

The gigantic Hecatoncheires (Cottus, Briareus, and Gyges) combined bizarre appearance with crazy ways; this set of weird offspring had a hundred arms and fifty heads apiece; they gushed destruction and dark disorder in all directions. Then Gaia and

Uranus, apparently unlimited in their ability to propagate oddities, brought forth the Cyclopes (Brontes [Thunder], Stereopes [Lightning], and Arges [Thunderbolt]), each with one large eye in the middle of his forehead, a threesome as strong and agile as they were fearsome and unpredictable.

Hesiod depicts Uranus as a barbarian, a gonad-driven savage without a glimmer of intelligence. But Uranus must have experienced a flicker of at least semicomprehension when he looked at his monster-children and saw their brutish strength and savage unruliness. He justly feared them and, regretting that the children of his loin had been born to see the light of day, he knew that it was only a matter of time until they joined forces against him and usurped his power. Uranus reasoned that he could undo what he had done; return to oblivion that which he had brought forth. So Uranus rounded up his grotesque children and unceremoniously reversed their birth by forcing them back into Gaia's body. He pressed them into the darkest and deepest recesses of Mother Earth, into a dungeon known as Tartarus, a place in the universe as far removed from Hades as the earth is from heaven. Ancient sources describe Tartarus as one of the elements of the universe (along with Eros, Chaos, and Gaia herself) and say that it is a dark void that exists deep beneath the earth and sea, enclosed in an impenetrable layer of night, a placeless region of nothing, the ultimate environment for the lost, the hopeless, the despairing. And so the Titans, entombed in their mother's body by their despotic father, suffered in awful and terrifying darkness.

GAIA'S REVENGE

But Gaia loved her monstrous children, and suffered with them. She despised Uranus for his brutal treatment of their offspring, as well as for his abuse of her and his continual sexual aggression. So, hatching a plot, Gaia persuaded the youngest of the first race of gods, Cronus, to rebel against his father. Under her direction, the younger god freed the Cyclopes. Well and good, responded Gaia, but Cronus must now take action against his father. Uranus must be prevented from resuming his old lecherous ways, Gaia persuaded Cronus.

Convinced that his mother was right, and armed with a sharp flint sickle supplied by her, Cronus followed her directions; he hid and waited for the lascivious Uranus to approach his mother in her flowery bed. In due course Uranus, fired by sexual desires and thinking only of immediate pleasure, drew near Gaia's recumbent body and prepared to satisfy his lust. At the moment Uranus moved down and covered Gaia, Cronus sprang from hiding, the flint sickle sharp and ready. Before Uranus could penetrate Gaia, Cronus cut off his father's testicles and threw them over his shoulder.

Of course, Uranus was immortal, and so were his amputated sexual organs. The severed and bleeding parts soared into the distance and fell into the sea, which foamed and hissed orgiastically and spewed out the beautiful Aphrodite, goddess of sexual love. This, it is said, is how Aphrodite was imbued with her irresistible allure and sexual cunning, her power over erotic desire and love among mortals and immortals; and this, it is said, is why she never showed the slightest taint of self-control.

But as the gory testicles flew over the earth, Uranus's immortal blood dripped onto Gaia's body, once again fertilizing her. From this bloody impregnation, she gave birth to an assortment of nymphs and divinities associated with nature, as well as the Erinyes and the giants, two sets of beings who would prove troublesome to the Olympians and who would challenge Athena's claim to power and wisdom.

Gaia, now free from Uranus, did not elect a life of restful celibacy, however, but quickly took another mate—one of her sons, Pontus, or Wave—and continued to spawn children, including the marine divinities Nereus, Thaumas, Phorcys, Ceto, and Eurybia.

CRONUS, FATHER OF ZEUS

While Gaia thus busied herself with what she did best, her son and deliverer, Cronus—Zeus's father and Athena's grandfather—ascended to Uranus's throne to rule the entire universe. In short order, however, son proved to be like father; Cronus, as brutal and tyrannical as Uranus, threw his brothers and sisters into Tartarus, where, he decreed, they would remain forever.

Moreover, Cronus proved to be as sexually aggressive a husband and ruthless a father as Uranus. Married to his sister Rhea, he rightfully feared that their children would inherit his lust for power as well as his savage strength. He decided to prevent his progeny from growing up, rebelling and overthrowing him; and so Cronus lay in wait for Rhea to give birth and, one by one, as the babies fell from his wife's body, Cronus ate them. With each pregnancy and with increasing horror Rhea watched helplessly as Cronus gobbled up her babies—the to-be-Olympian-gods Hades, Poseidon, Hera, Hestia, Demeter—and imprisoned them all in his dark stomach.

ZEUS IN THE BEGINNING

Rhea wanted to keep her children. When she knew that she was pregnant with Zeus, she sought advice from her parents, Gaia and Uranus. Just as Cronus had devoured her previous offspring, so the expectant Rhea feared that her husband would murder and eat the infant Zeus. How, she asked her parents, could she protect her child from her demonic husband?

Mother Earth and the sky god, drawing on a store of experience in domestic discord, pondered the problem and spoke to their daughter. Rhea listened to Gaia and Uranus, who suggested a scheme for saving the infant, and then followed their directions meticulously. As soon as Rhea gave birth to Zeus, she swaddled an infant-size stone in a blanket and meekly handed the bundle over to Cronus, telling him that it was his latest progeny. With no further formality, Cronus gulped the stone into his great stomach and immediately fell into a deep slumber.

While Cronus was sleeping off his heavy meal, Rhea spirited the infant Zeus to Crete and hid him in a cave—sometimes identified as Mount Dikte, sometimes as Mount Ida—where he was protected by male guardians, the warlike and priestly Curetes, who masked the infant's cries with their loud music, dancing, and singing.[*]

---

[*]Hutchinson, *Prehistoric Crete*. Later, according to these legends of the Cretan Zeus, the god was buried or allowed to sleep for long millennia under the peak of Mount Jouctas, where he remains.

On Crete the infant Zeus was rocked in a golden cradle hung between heaven and earth, and therefore invisible to Cronus. It is said that he was nursed by the goat-nymph Amaltheia, drinking her milk and protected by her warmth. The young Zeus grew stronger and braver every day. When he was old enough to be weaned, Amaltheia fed the young god the perfumed honey that bees made especially for him, and fondly watched over him as he played on the mountainside with the shepherds.

Zeus discovered during his happy childhood that Amaltheia's name—which means "the tender one"—described her perfectly. When he became a great god, Zeus honored Amaltheia by borrowing one of her horns to fashion the Cornucopia, or horn of plenty, from which endless good things flow. He also created in her image the starry constellation Capricorn.

But Zeus's paradisiacal life on Crete ended with his childhood. Inevitably Cronus learned of Rhea's deception and Zeus's existence on Crete, and set out to kill the almost-grown son who might fulfill the ancient prophecy and overthrow his father. Zeus, however, learned of Cronus's murderous intention and, eager to test his own powers as a god, disguised himself as a serpent and his nurses as bears. The ruse was successful, and was later celebrated by the young god Zeus, who created still more constellations, the Serpent and the Bears.

As Zeus grew to manhood, Rhea saw that he possessed a turbulent and lustful nature, not unlike that of his father. In an effort to prevent Zeus from bringing sorrow and pain to himself and others, Rhea ordered her immortal son never to marry. Infuriated, Zeus laughed maliciously and, as if illustrating his mother's worst fears about his nature, turned his anger into sexual desire. Zeus grabbed Rhea. She struggled against rape, and tried to thwart Zeus by turning herself into a viper. But Zeus merely laughed again; then he transformed himself into a male serpent and wrapped his body in a knot around the serpent Rhea, and raped her.

Thus began Zeus's history of seduction, rape, and marriage. In short order he fathered the Seasons with Themis; the Three Muses with Mnemosyne; the Charities with Eurynomne; and perhaps Persephone with the nymph Styx. Sometimes it is said that Zeus married Themis, Mnemosyne, Eurynomne, and Styx; sometimes, that he either seduced or raped them.

After Zeus and his sister Hera had been lovers for a long time—some say they were married—Zeus took a fancy to Metis, daughter of Oceanus, god of the river of the world, a stream that bounded both earth and sea. Some even say that powerful Oceanus, not Chaos, was the beginning of all things, that he was the original father and Thethys the original mother. Their daughter Metis—her name means wisdom or prudence or, in some interpretations, treachery—at first hid from Zeus, even changing her appearance to avoid him. But he was persistent and, whether by choice or force, she eventually bedded with him.

Although Metis is often identified as Zeus's first "wife," marriage did not exist in the sense of a legal or religious institution for gods or mortals; the word, as it appears in ancient writings, is little more than a synonym for seduction or rape. Irrepressible Eros struck without concern for the niceties of language: and a direct hit from Eros defied explanation or definition.

ZEUS, LORD OF THE UNIVERSE

When Zeus believed himself ready to take control of the universe from his brutal father, he turned to Metis, the wise one, for advice. Metis listened attentively to the ambitious Zeus and sent him to ask his mother, Rhea, to appoint him cupbearer to Cronus. Young men who served as cupbearers lived intimately with their masters, attending their physical needs and obeying every command, providing everything from sexual servitude to the preparation and serving of food and drink.

Rhea was fully aware of Zeus's dark purpose in becoming his father's servant. But she was secretly glad, for she had not forgiven Cronus for his brutality toward herself and her children. It pleased her to think that Zeus's rebellion would punish Cronus for his murderous ways. And so Rhea happily complied with her son's plot and installed him in Cronus's household.

The disguised Zeus was politely attentive to Cronus's whims and needs; he soon won the old god's confidence, and learned his habits well enough to use the god's daily rituals against him. When the time was right, when Cronus trusted him completely, Zeus turned again to Metis for assistance. They secretly placed powerful emetic herbs in the honeyed drink that Cronus received from his attentive young cupbearer. The old god took the cup in both hands, and drank greedily, emptying the cup in several gigantic gulps. But almost immediately the emetic herbs painfully twisted his innards. He began to vomit. Retching violently, he tossed up first the swaddled stone that he had eaten in the belief that it was Zeus, and then he vomited up Zeus's elder brothers and sisters—five of the immortals who would join Zeus to rule the universe from Olympus: Poseidon, Hades, Hestia, Demeter, and Hera.

Unhurt as they emerged, and grateful to be released from their cannibal-father's body, Rhea's children naturally looked on Zeus as their leader, transforming him in effect from the youngest of their mother's offspring to the eldest child "reborn" from their father's vomiting.

Now, with Zeus as their warlord, the Olympian gods declared war on their enemies, the Titans, who from the outset were clumsy warriors and blundering strategists. Their ruination was assured when they scorned the wise counsel of Prometheus who, in exasperation, then left their forces and sided with Zeus. The Titans chose Atlas, Prometheus's brother, as their commander.

The two sides fought bitterly for ten years, with first one side and then the other gaining temporary advantage, with first one and then the other claiming power over all of the universe. But the end of the war was not in sight; neither side seemed able to triumph. Then, with no prospect of a victory in sight for Zeus and his followers, Gaia came forward and held out to her grandson a means to the prize he coveted. She would give Zeus and his fellow Olympians a way to win the war, she bargained, if he would release her monster-children imprisoned in Tartarus by Cronus, take them into his camp, and let them use their monstrous strength against the Titans. Zeus agreed.

And so with Gaia's guidance, Zeus crept into the dark region beneath the earth, murdered the crone who kept the keys to the terrible dungeon, and freed the monsters—the Hundred-Handed Ones and the Cyclopes who became the Olympians' weapons for the destruction to the Titans.

In gratitude for their release, and before embarking on their campaign against the Titans, the Cyclopes gave powerful gifts to Zeus and his brothers: to Hades they gave a helmet that made him invisible; to Poseidon, a trident; and to Zeus, the thunderbolt. With these fine gifts in hand, the three brothers together possessed the means for overthrowing Cronus. First Hades, wearing his magic helmet, crept into Cronus's quarters and—invisible, of course—stole his weapons. Then, while Poseidon brandished his awful trident threateningly and diverted Cronus's attention, Zeus struck him with a powerful thunderbolt. The Hundred-Handed Ones, seeing Cronus's condition, renewed their battle against the Titans, and used their strong multiarms and hands to hurl enormous boulders onto their enemies with such force that even the mighty Titans fell right and left.

When the battle ended with Zeus triumphant, he spared the Titanesses out of courtesy to Metis and Rhea; but he banished all the male Titans, except Atlas, to the very ends of the earth; or, some say, to Tartarus. The one remaining free Titan, Atlas, was punished by being sentenced to hold the sky in place forever after.

And so, it is told in myths, this is how Zeus became the reigning god, the ruler of the Olympian pantheon—thunder thrower, cloud gatherer: this is how Zeus became lord of the universe. But there are other stories, too, about the rise to power of the father of Athena.

IN THE BEGINNING: PREHISTORY AND HISTORY

Long after Athena entered human awareness, and long after she figured prominently in the stories that passed among people as explanations of how things came to be as they were, myth was transformed into literature and thus given a location in history. But myth had never really existed outside the time and space and events of human life; it had always been a part of human existence, a tool for coping with the ordinary and extraordinary events of life. We may not know the names of the first storytellers, or where or how or when they lived; but by their stories we know that they once lived with the same questions and fears that plague us, that they hoped and searched for laws and order that would sustain society, that they were human beings very like ourselves in basic needs, desires, and mortality.

Both myth and history are ways of seeing and explaining human life; both are forms of human narrative that describe reality as it has been or can be known by people. But history and myth are based on quite different notions of what reality might be or might have been; and each requires a distinct set of intellectual tools as well as an underlying set of beliefs or assumptions deemed self-evidently true.

History, a branch of human knowledge derived from the analysis of events and records, depends first on observers and first-hand reports, that is, primary evidence. As an adjunct of writing, history is built around facts related to specific times and places and people; its stories tell us when and where they occurred, as well as by whom they were enacted or caused, and to what results. The recognition of the primary importance of *who, what, when, where,* and *why* informs the work of all historians however they as individuals may choose to navigate their craft under the rules of science or humanism, or some combination of the two sets of values. But in the absence of written documents, we turn to the disciplines of anthropology and archaeology to shed light on *prehistory.*

Archaeologists dig in the earth for answers to the same questions that impel historians, but they find information in material objects such as tools and artifacts, the remains of buildings and cities. Data inform inference, until preliterate people show themselves, utter their names, tell their stories. Our search does not begin at a single point in time or space but reaches as far back as we can imagine.

Archaeological evidence suggests that all of the gods acquired characteristic powers and essences as the concept of deity evolved; the gods were a presence among human beings involved in the sacrifices and rituals during the long dark period after our species stood upright, learned how to use fire, husband animals, plant and harvest crops, and build shelter against the elements, and gods were among mortals long before the creation of writing and history. Gods related to fertility of people, animals, and crops, to seasons and weather, to the life and death of all things, appeared to human beings throughout the ancient world from earliest times.

We do not know when or where humankind first experienced religious impulses and intellectual stirring; we cannot identify the moment of conception or birth of the gods. Being careful not to apply the tools of speculation too vigorously, we must probe behind written history, and dig from material remains the inferences and hypotheses that will help us glimpse, however provisionally, the several cultures that discovered the gods who would become the Olympian pantheon.

We customarily deal with periods in ancient history conveniently named to reflect technological achievement and to indicate the *stuff* from which we will try to read the stories of cultures that existed before writing, before history. But while we recognize the eras we know as stone, copper, bronze, iron, we must remember that other materials might just as well have given us names for still earlier periods, but they were fragile; and although we know that materials such as wood, textiles, and skin were widely used, objects made from those substances have rotted away and returned so completely to the earth that they have left little evidence of ever having existed.

In the continual contest with other animals for food, Neolithic humans had the advantage of stone implements and fire; they were efficient killers who could bring down animals larger and faster than themselves; and, unlike other animals, human beings could cook their meat before consuming it: raw flesh is the food of the savage; cooked meat the feast of a higher being, one worthy of god-given dominion over the earth and its plenitude. Ritual animal (and human) sacrifice probably evolved from the practices and beliefs of early hunters, with secular and practical acts of killing and eating becoming sacred; in time the actual killing—the eating of flesh and drinking of blood—was sanitized by symbol, which replaced actuality.

The quest of humankind for understanding of and power over the forces of nature, however, eventually led to agriculture, a brilliant concept then more related to magic and ritual than to scientific practice. Prehistoric farmers found that the earth received the seeds they planted and, with assistance from weather controlled by the gods, generously returned food for work invested in tilling and harvesting.

Stone Age people—in what must have been a mixture of observation and experiment—found and performed whatever magical rituals were efficient; they learned to speak powerful words, to sing songs that beguiled the gods, to dance in communication with the spirits; they learned what the spirits and gods liked, and they offered gifts. Ritual was utilitarian, not the gestures of lukewarm liturgy—and ritual did what was intended; the evidence was in available food, continual procreation among people and animals. The forces of nature were appeased and thanked; life was balanced by rituals that were repeated until they were regarded as sacred. If people failed to perform rituals, if they failed to please the spirits and the gods, woe fell upon them in the form of death, plague, pestilence, natural disaster, and they atoned for their failings. Over time, ritual was codified and humans found *religion.*

By the time the Bronze Age began in Greece, around 3000, the Olympian deities had taken shape in the minds and rituals of humankind: the gods and goddesses as we know them had been canonized, and Athena was a mature deity. By this time all of the gods had names; their powers and attributes were understood; and everyone knew and told or listened to their stories. Just as we cannot ascertain the moment when any one of the gods appeared to mortals and was named, we cannot determine when they took up residence on Olympia. We assume, however, that they had made their place known and that they had made their presences felt at the rituals and sacrifices, beliefs and fears, celebrations and thanksgivings of people who lived around the Mediterranean long before the appearance of the Bronze Age of mainland Greece, and very long indeed before their stories were first written by Homer and Hesiod in the eighth century.

IN THE BEGINNING, RITUAL

In the beginning, Athena was ritual. Or, at least, modern scholarship allows us to infer that Athena was known—by one name or another, as an aspect of a multifaceted deity or as a singular goddess—long before she joined the Bronze Age warrior-heroes of Mycenae on the mainland of what is now known as Greece.

Exploring the shadowy intellectual territory of prehistory, using an intoxicating blend of fact and supposition, contemporary scholars find one or many Stone Age Mother Earth goddesses, unnamed or known by many names. Although evidence partially supports recent hypotheses that a single Great Goddess was known and worshiped in Stone Age matriarchal cultures spread over northern Europe and the Mediterranean areas, available information begs for caution in interpretation. Granting that it would be wrongheaded to deny the incipient presence in prehistory of female deities who either evolved into Athena, Hera, or Artemis or who contributed to the realization of the characteristics, aspects, and powers by which we know them, it is still imperative that we proceed cautiously in those regions unmapped by language.

The Great Goddess is more than wish fulfillment for feminists in search of a cult. There *is* clear evidence that female deities were known and worshiped in the very ancient world. Moreover, numerous traditions among ancient writers root Athena in many places, and identify or allude to numerous and widely separated cults around the Mediterranean that continued to perform rituals and festivals in her honor long after she was identified with—if not solely owned by—the Hellenes. Most notably, her genesis is assigned to Stone Age cultures in Libya, Crete, and Mycenae.

The Libyan tradition survives through ancient writers who knew stories that convinced them that Athena appeared first, in her earliest recognizable form, in northern Africa. For example, the Pelasgians, ancient peoples who lived in the area of and around Greece, believed that the goddess was born in Libya beside Lake Tritonis; and that nymphs found her, knew her to be a goddess, dressed her in goatskins like the ones they themselves wore and nurtured her to maturity. Plato, too, assigned a Libyan genesis to Athena, identifying her with the goddess Neith, who reigned in a period before paternity was recognized,* when copulation may have been one of several orgiastic rituals rather than the socially sanctioned union that would form the basis for marriage, family, and kinship. During this time, it is speculated, pregnancies, childbirth, and children evidenced female power; the ability to conceive and bring forth life was magic, a power possessed by women. On the basis of that awesome power, it is further speculated that the oldest social order may have been matriarchal, a system that would have furnished a reasonable response to the deepest desire of humans to multiply and survive.

Other ancient writers say that Athena, after her birth in an unspecified place, somehow found her way to Libya, where she was reared; and still others say that she merely passed through Libya on her way to Crete, an island off the north shore of Libya, where she developed as a portion of the female deities identified with Minoan culture.

OTHER BEGINNINGS: ATHENA IN CRETE

Even if Crete cannot be recognized as the womb where Athena gestated, it supported an early culture that serves as a backdrop for her struggle for power and for her rebellion against her gender. Crete, an island wrapped by myth and history as well as the sparkling Aegean, emerges from archaeological evidence as an exception among the cultures of that region in the Stone Age. Unlike their warrior neighbors who honored male deities, the Neolithic inhabitants of Crete appear to have been peaceable and to have practiced rituals associated with a female deity or deities. The oldest legends suggest that a female deity came with the earliest

*Plato: *Timaeus* 5

inhabitants—probably migrants from Anatolia[*], and perhaps as early as 6000; but perhaps the people who settled on Crete discovered a goddess or goddesses in the soil and sea and sky of their new home.

Today Crete is a land of meadows and mountains, a honeyed land of fragrant wildflowers and humming bees, a welcoming and gentle natural garden of olives, vines, and cypresses. There is no cause to believe the island to be more beautiful or generous now than in the Stone Age, no reason to imagine that its mountains could have been less imposing, or its flora and fauna less luxuriant then than now. Rather, it seems certain to the modern visitor to Crete that ancient members of our species would have stood dazzled before the abundance provided by the earth, awed by the vistas afforded by mountains, and emotionally stirred by the protective yet darkly forbidding caves. Religious impulse may have followed naturally, and understandably resulted in the recognition of the earth as mother of all life; ultimately, we easily imagine, a deity was recognized, worshiped, and petitioned.

Today scholars read the available evidence of the early rituals—offerings, sacrifices, identification of sacred sites—as an indication of the marriage between our concepts of agriculture and religion. Those rituals, as read from the gem carvings and other artifacts that appear to record them, support the conclusion that the Stone Age inhabitants of Crete knew and worshiped female deities with great powers.

But caution is needed in weaving a tapestry from a few threads. The entire story of our species is bracketed, interspersed, and punctuated with *perhaps*. Perhaps the early Cretans continued or reinvented a form of goddess worship they had known earlier, something remembered and recounted from the past in Anatolia or Africa. Perhaps they found in Crete the ingredients and causes—such as awe in the presence of the island's beauty, gratitude for the rich supply of food—for a new form of religion, but, whatever the causative impulses or the particulars of rites and sacrifices, perhaps the goddess we now identify with the early inhabitants of Crete was, as we think, a multifaceted, omnipotent being with

[*]More often today called *Asia Minor*, Anatolia, in the ancient world referred to the Asiatic area of Turkey, a peninsula defined by the Black Sea on the north, the Aegean Sea on the west, and the Mediterranean on the south.

numerous aspects and epiphanies; perhaps there were several goddesses. We do not know the name or names by which she was
known; but we believe that she influenced every aspect of animal
and vegetable life, that she had power over every being and object
on the earth.

Although we can infer from archaeological evidence many
aspects of her existence, the goddess who appeared to Neolithic
tribes on Crete—unlike the Hellenic Athena of the Parthenon—
lacks for us the rational clarity and historical definition we associate with classicism and, therefore, with Athena Parthenos. Rather,
she hides behind centuries clouded by human and natural events,
many of them traumatic, and remains enfolded in the shadows of
preliterate millennia. She is mute, untouched by light from written documents; she is the dark female goddess revealed to us
through emotional empathy or through the painstaking peeling
and deciphering of layer upon layer of scientific evidence laid out
under the light of the great *perhaps*. Empathy alone is a heady
intoxicant if not toughened by rational steel, but scientific data are
lifeless without the breath of imagination.

Evidence of the goddess's life on Crete can still be found at
the sites of the most ancient sanctuaries identified with religious
practices—caves, mountains shrines, sacred groves, and the later
and more sophisticated shrines, or household altars, within the
Minoan palaces. In the very earliest forms of worship of the earth
as the body of the goddess, the sacred sites were probably located
in proximity to singular trees or rocks, or high on mountains, and
treated as points of actual physical contact with the goddess. While
images of mountaintop shrines, sacred groves, and blessed trees
appear on gem carvings, they are difficult to locate today in the
actual landscape and so elude the sharp-shoveled archaeologist.
Caves, however, remained visible and have welcomed twentieth-
century scholars with a wealth of objects and images, vestiges of
offerings, burials, and rituals.[*]

---

[*]The Cave of Skotinó, near Goúves, was where Briómartes, the Cretan Artemis
worshipped; the Cave of Psichró, was the legendary birthplace of the Cretan Zeus;
Mount Joúchtas and its hilltop sanctuary holds the cave in which Zeus sleeps; the
Kamares Cave was where the goddess of fertility was worshipped; and the ruins of a
temple on the hill of Anemóspila, contains evidences of human sacrifice.

From such evidences as these we infer that the goddess was *chthonic*—of the earth—and can easily imagine that her followers reckoned as her discontent the quaking earth, erupting volcano, and roiling seas. Similarly they may have rejoiced in her benevolence, and understood it to emanate from her own body. They may have believed that she took humans into her body's caves and crevices and sheltered them from the elements and other animals; that she nurtured all creatures; that she received the rain; that she recorded the changing seasons and responded; and that she took back into her body the dead in a final embrace, returning life to herself, the source of all life. And, after death, she gave life back again.

Perhaps in firelight, with shadows rising and falling, celebrants drank the ritual libation laced with dream- and vision-inducing herbs. And then perhaps they whirled in the sacred dances, caught in the music of pipes and lyre, their feet touching the body of the goddess, transmitting their rhythmic messages directly into the being of Mother Earth. Human euphoria invited the goddess to show herself by image or sign, and to bless and keep the worshipers through good and bad times.

In a nature-centered religion, it is not surprising to find that emphasis was laid not on the building of temples but on discovering the sacred places of mountain peak or cave, identifying magical trees or natural rock altars, and, later, on establishing a household or hearth altar.

Many scholars see the goddess of ancient Crete as composed of three identifiable parts, or personas, later to be separated and recognized as Demeter, Aphrodite, and Athena, or perhaps as Artemis, Hera, and Athena.

Religion is a late and sophisticated construct of the human mind. We have no religious documents from Crete, no evidence that their language contained a word for religion (as Greek did not until fairly late). Even so, from our position in history and language, we point to the relics that for us signify Cretan "religion" and view that culture's artifacts as evidence of a relationship to later Hellenic religion. In tracing the roots and various lives of the ancient deities, scholars commonly noted that early peoples *included* rather than *excluded* unfamiliar gods, and so welcomed gods brought by newcomers. This habit of fusing and recharacterizing gods, of adding a god or letting one fall by the wayside of consciousness, finally more or less stabilized with the canonization of the Olympian pantheon, but only after centuries of shaping and testing the immortals until they at last met the needs and answered the questions of mortals. Gods may appear suddenly, but they often arrive only after a very long gestation.

Scholars who study the objects of early Crete identify a young male consort—or is he a priest? her son?—attending the goddess. She is usually larger, more important, than the male figure; she occupies the dominant position in works of art; she, by her position and by the action depicted, controls the event in progress. Although no one can be certain of underlying theology or custom, some archaeologists and anthropologists have postulated that the numerous images of goddess–young male refer to fertility rituals, that the male god was sacrificed at the end of the harvest season, that he lay dormant through the winter and was resurrected in the spring. The theory is made more credible because the death and resurrection of the life-giving and life-sustaining god is a recurrent theme in religion.

Since legend gives both Zeus and Athena roots in Crete, it is tempting to cast them in the roles of goddess and consort, a relationship that would later be changed to accord with the social concept of male dominance that was clearly evident by the time of the Bronze Age heroes. At any rate, it is fair to believe that the all-powerful goddess had the status on Crete that Zeus would later be accorded in the Hellenic world: she was the ruling deity.

For all Stone Age people the earth's authority was supernatural: seasons changed under the direction of powers, forces, and deities. Knowing that everything came from the earth, the inhabitants of ancient Crete returned to the source some of its gifts: they offered first fruits from gatherings and from harvests, and they made blood sacrifices—probably human in the earliest times, certainly animal throughout the centuries. The pact with the gods to allow animals to substitute for humans as sacrificial victims helped define mortals as lower than gods but higher than other animals; and, taken in our terms, it represented a theological revolution.

Before a special class of priests or priestesses had developed, sacrifices and gifts to the gods were made by individuals at any spot deemed to be sacred—a cave, a mountaintop, a grove of trees, a particular tree known to have special powers; later, altars appeared around the hearths of huts as well as in the great palaces. Spontaneous fear, desire, gratitude, or joy could be recognized in private ritual: the goddess would hear and see. There were signs; gifted people—seers and prophets—could read messages and portents in the song or flight of birds, in stones or weather, and in strange and familiar events alike. A special class or caste of people formed to mediate between people and the forces and events of the natural world. Priests and priestesses took charge of rituals; their job was to appease the gods, to garner favor, to protect people in life and give them properly to death.

THE MINOAN PALACES

By about 2300, the great Minoan or palace civilization had flowered on Crete; its rich remains fascinate us and add another set of clues regarding Athena's earliest manifestation. For several thousands of years people on Crete seem to have lived in a comfortable and uneventful manner in the limestone caves that pock the island, or in dwellings made of mud brick; but, supported by prosperity based on the vine and the olive, and by production of pottery and widespread trade, they eventually built large, rambling structures such as those at Knossos, Phaestos, Mallia, and Kato Zakros. Everything, including the absence of fortification or any hint of military concerns, suggests that the Minoans lived a peaceful, sybaritic life despite occasional earthquakes that destroyed their palaces.

Even after destruction, they rebuilt the sumptuous, sprawling palaces; rebuilt the magazines of storage jars, *pithoi,* and filled them again with grain, honey, oil, and wine; they enjoyed papyrus-glazed windows, light wells, running water, and flush toilets. Between 1750 and 1450, Minoan palace culture flourished—even with the noticeable increase in Mycenaean influence from about 1500—until around 1400, when the great palaces were burned, whether as a result of earthquake or human conqueror. The remaining stones have not told us the secret of their collapse; we know the civilization almost entirely through its appealing, mysterious, sophisticated, elegant art.

In addition to the widely known frescoes of bull-vaulting, of handsomely coiffed and attired aristocrats, and of aspects of life and nature suggesting joyful mingling of pleasures—music, games, and sex—Minoan art included a variety of pottery styles, expertly worked and intricately decorated with bird, fish, flower, or geometric motifs; ivory and faience figurines—including the "snake goddesses"; delicate jewelry and splendidly decorated tools; and numerous carved seal rings and gem stones. And we see everywhere—painted on pots, carved into gems, freestanding as figurines—women in ritualistic roles; we call them priestesses. But that is our word; they stand before us, arms often upraised, eyes staring; they offer no clues as to their names or roles.

In the world of these ancient images, women dance and sing; they often seem euphoric, in a state that may have been produced by the poppy pod crowns they sometimes wear, or by other dream-making herbs. They raise their arms in salute or gratitude; they stand with trees or beside altars; they oversee or participate in animal sacrifices. Often snakes wrap the arms of priestesses or the goddess; snakes adorn their clothing, entwine their heads, and mingle with their hair.

The snake is also entwined in the story and attributes of Athena; she kept the snake as a familiar, as an epiphany, and as a sacred creature in her temples.

Early inhabitants of Crete may have believed that the kingdom of snakes enjoyed a special affinity with the gods; they seem to have known, for instance, that snakes, when called upon by the gods, carried out demands. Snakes came to people with messages; they stood as portents, executed miscreants, or indicated actions to be taken or avoided. In due time, gods were known to take the form of snakes in order to inflict good or evil upon mortals, and mortals were careful in dealing with snakes.

It was understood that in the proper order of things human beings walked the earth, and that snakes sunned themselves in safe places, or lurked in the dark crevices of a dwelling or coiled deep beneath the surface of the earth. Changed behavior on the part of snakes was noted, sometimes with alarm or fear, sometimes with eager anticipation of events to come: snakes, as everyone knew, were sometimes the goddess in disguise.

When on Crete intimations of earthquake ran like electric currents through the dens of semisentient snakes in deep caves, the reptiles uncoiled and slithered upward through hollows, from the shadows of caves, through cracks in the floors of huts and palaces alike. They appeared everywhere, writhing before mortals who tried to read the signs. What could the snakes mean? How should the omen be interpreted? What should people do? Should the mood be one of celebration, thanksgiving, hope and expectation, or fear and sacrifice?

Perhaps, they began to tell one another, the snakes were man-ifestations of the goddess herself; perhaps the snakes were sacred. Did they not, after all, destroy the insects and rodents who ate the stored grain? Should they—these epiphanies of the goddess—not be honored with offerings and rituals of appreciation?

When the big palaces were built in Minoan Crete, the god-dess was invited to dwell within them, and her protection and patronage were invoked at festivals and sacrifices, with daily rituals and offerings. Her tame snakes ate the cakes and honey provided for them inside the palaces and dwelt among the rows of giant ceramic storage jars containing oil, wine, honey, grain, and other riches.

THE MYCENAEAN CITADEL

We call them Mycenaeans and try to know them through the remains of their great citadels such as those found at Mycenae,

Tiryns, and Pylos. Homer called them Achaeans or Argives. We do not know what they called themselves. Their origin is as mysterious as their end. But most of the stories we identify as *Greek mythology* took shape in their Bronze Age culture; and they recognized Athena as a warrior-goddess, gave her the attributes by which we know her, and sought her counsel and power in war.

We now believe that human beings occupied the area we call Greece at least sixty or seventy thousand years ago, and that seafaring had developed as early as 9000 to support trade in flint and flint tools. The passage from hunting to agricultural life was made even more difficult because good pasturage was scarce, but Neolithic settlers in the seventh millennium found plains for their herds in Thessaly or Boeotia, and without the power of the plough, they tilled land. That fertility was a primary concern is attested by the large number of female idols—lumpy creatures with exaggerated breasts, huge buttocks; they are often taken as evidence of a widespread matriarchy, and of goddess worship.

The use of metal appeared, probably with still unidentified people from the north moving into Greece during the first half of the third millennium; stone houses were built and trade flourished. Over thousands of years the area was invaded, rarely peacefully, it appears, and rarely by groups with known identities. But successive waves of migrants from other areas brought technological innovation, new languages, and new gods—specifically a male deity associated with the sky. From this racial and cultural cauldron, the Mycenaean warrior culture was cast. Feudal barons ruled small settlements, their wealth derived from piracy and plunder as well as from agriculture and trade.

In 1876 the amateur archaeologist Heinrich Schliemann discovered graves at Mycenae that contained evidence of great wealth, power; here were chariots, armor, richly worked bronze swords, engraved gems, and a variety of gold objects, but not cult images, no indications of the religion of the culture. Other archaeological finds have included the enormous beehive tombs, *tholoii,* the Lion Gates, and remnants of thick stone walls thought to have been forty feet high. Numerous grave markers, *stele,* were found; typically they are decorated with depictions of sharp-featured, bearded men in scenes of hunting and fighting. From these scenes and from the high level of fortification that characterizes their settlements, we conclude that Mycenaeans were warlike and aggressive. We know that they controlled extensive areas of the Mediterranean, including shipping lanes, but we know little about the beliefs, religious practices, and social institutions of these people. The only fragments of their language—the Linear B tablets that are inscribed with an early form of Greek—consist of administrative records of crops, yields, and herds, as well as lists of goods to be sold, and tallies of textiles, pots of honey, and jars of wine shipped and traded.

Archaeological evidence supports our belief that the Mycenaeans rose to the height of their power between 1500 and 1300, and dominated the region with steadily expanding overseas trade, perhaps to the detriment of Crete. From about 1450 to 1400 a Mycenaean dynasty was actually established in Knossos. By about 1300, however, the Mycenaeans' hold on shipping lanes and commerce was challenged by pirates of uncertain origin. At about the same time fortifications around their centers of populations were strengthened, suggesting that they were threatened on land as well as at sea. By 1200 the Mycenaean culture had been laid to waste by invaders of unknown identity; the age of the heroes was over, and Greece fell into a period we identify as the Dark Ages, as much an indication of the limits of our knowledge as of the condition of life in the Hellenic world at that time.

According to historians of religion, the Mycenaeans venerated the northern sky god, a male deity; but, perhaps incongruously, they also appear to have taken the Minoan goddess home with them to their fortified citadels, and perhaps mingled her with the Neolithic mainland fertility goddess already familiar to them. Thus, in their accommodation or appropriation of the deities they encountered, the Mycenaeans welcomed a female warrior-goddess to their great stone fortresses, and there the name *Athena* was firmly affixed to her, along with her special attributes and powers. A Linear B inscription from this period can be read to mean Athena, or perhaps Athens.*

The Mycenaeans seem also to have appropriated artistic styles and skills from Crete, folding them so intimately into their own work that the two are often indistinguishable. Perhaps artisans from Crete had traveled with the goddess to Mycenae; perhaps they felt her company as they plied their skills for the pleasure and aggrandizement of the Mycenaean warlords; perhaps there was a special bond between the priests or priestesses and the artisans of Crete; and perhaps it is in this milieu that Athena came to be recognized as the goddess of craft and useful arts. Or perhaps the aggressive Mycenaeans simply stole from Crete what they wanted, and took home loot as well as the idea of the Lady of Athens. We cannot know precisely when, how, or why the Mycenaeans adopted aspects of Cretan culture, but we easily imagine the Minoan goddess, an aspect or manifestation of the early Athena, surrounded in Mycenae by Minoan-style pottery and jewelry and by frescoes on the thick stone walls of the citadels.

In Mycenaean citadels Athena was no longer merely one aspect of the ancient fertility goddess or a household deity; she was a vivid presence in these great halls, or *megara,* where drinking and feasting chieftains boasted about strength and courage, and planned their campaigns to conquer and plunder other people throughout the Mediterranean world. Among these swaggering mainland heroes, Athena got her shield, helmet, and spear, as well as her name.†

---

*It has been noted that her name is an adjectival form, meaning probably merely "of Athens," or, perhaps, "maiden of Athens," and it is uncertain whether she was named for the city or the city for its goddess.

† While the famous Linear B tablets give no indication of the attributes by which deities were known, they include the names of now familiar deities in the context of gifts or offerings to be delivered, perhaps in the form of taxes to temples or chieftains. In addition to Athena, Linear B texts include references to Hera, Artemis, Dionysus, and others.

Athena, in this process of transmutation, also adjusted to the requirements of the masculine, warlike heroes rather than the more domestic concerns of fertility and hearth. As the heroes recognized this powerful masculine-female goddess, they believed her to love them—heroes, men who would die for glory—as much as they loved her. In their presence, she acquired the masculine traits associated with battle and, in effect, became an honorary male. No longer one part of a multifaceted female deity, Athena was vividly defined, a protector of the masculine war culture dominant in the territory that would become Greece.

By the time the Mycenaeans dominated the Aegean and went to war against the Trojans, Athena was one of them; as they lifted their cups and voices to the glories of war and triumph, Athena was among them; she received the sacrifices and prayers offered to her. These Mycenaean warriors—the Achaeans of the *Iliad*—who asked her blessing, gave thanks to her for their victories and did not doubt her skill as a warrior, her power as a goddess: Athena was a warrior-goddess able to ensure the success of generals and knights-errant.

While it appears that the goddess of Crete had ruled the earth, the sky, and the sea, the later Athena of the Hellenes came to control only the earth; Zeus, the sky; Poseidon, the sea; Hades, the underworld. One of the most profound paradoxes in Athena's story emanates from this division of powers, this branching of separate identities from what was once a single deity, and the ultimate triumph of male over female, among the gods as within society.

The old struggle—as old as the cosmos, as fierce as that between Gaia and Uranus—was recast; some accommodation had to be reached between Zeus of the sky and Athena of the earth, between Athena with the powers of fecundity and war and Zeus with the powers of thunder and lightning. In the ensuing struggle men and masculine gods would take control, relegating women and female deities—with the exception of Athena—to women's work: Hera to protecting marriage, Aphrodite to entrapment through sexual allure, and Demeter to Mother Earth's tasks.

This shake-up and reorganization of deities occurred at the same time Athena was forging her new life in the Mycenaean citadels, as aspects of Minoan and mainland tradition began to meld, as stories moved toward myth and myth toward history. It has become almost a cliché to describe Minoan civilization as feminine and Mycenaean as masculine. Without trafficking in stereotyped gender characteristics, however, the difference between the two cultures may indeed pivot on the dominating sex in each and, alongside that factor, the dominating god. Words subjugated female "emotionalism" to male "rationalism"; stories made it clear that power—to say nothing of rich plunder and useful slaves—was bought with war and aggression rather than through peaceable harmony with nature; and myths gave dominance and glory to the "hero"—not to the ecstatic worshiper, not to the pious craftsworker, and not to the bearer of children. Myth gave *immortality*—fame—to men; it remained for history to enact the societal desires encased in myth.

During the time of the heroes of Mycenae, temples were built as residences for the gods. While the earliest, probably wooden, temples at Olympia and Delphi honored male gods, other cities—notably Mycenae, Tiryns, Aegina, Athens, and Troy—had as their center a temple to a goddess. Troy, like Athens, depended for protection on Athena, and even boasted possession of the magical *pallas,* the sculptured figure that had fallen from heaven and had been given a position of honor in their temple. This temple for Athena is the only one mentioned by Homer in Troy, as he describes how Hecuba brings her fairest robe as an offering to be laid on Athena's knees—like dresses that had earlier hung in the Minoan goddess's shrine.

By 1300 Athena stood with the Mycenaeans at the peak of their power. But soon thereafter, whether from external or internal forces, the Achaeans fell on hard times and were overpowered by the invasion of the Dorians, a northern people of mysterious origin. As they swept into the world of the ancient Greeks, the Dorians failed to capture Athens, by then understood to be

Athena's major citadel. This, it was said, proved beyond doubt her power as a protector of the city.

We know the Athena of the Homeric epics as a tall and hand-some strong woman, as a firm character who makes unyielding demands on other gods and on mortals, as a blazing intelligence and dazzling presence. But we know that in the course of her long life in human consciousness, she was not always so clearly defined. Many times over she adapted her appearance, her epiphanies, and even her powers and attributes to meet the requirements of the humans who reached out to her. As she moved toward establishing a presence in literature and history, Athena was adaptable in the details of her birth, flexible if not willing to be perceived as issuing from different regions and circumstances; she was eager to flatter or seduce many communities by encouraging or allowing them to consider themselves special to her.* Her mutability was further evidenced by her different epiphanies: she appeared as snake, as owl or other birds, or as a variety of mortals. Her pliability doubtless increased the geographic range of her domain and the power of her presence, and accounts importantly for her longevity in human awareness. While other immortals sometimes lost favor or became obsolete and; therefore, short-lived, Athena's varied birth sites and multi-epiphanies met the changing needs of mortals: her ubiquity added to her veracity, multiplied her presence and force. She could have drifted into the oblivion of mere memory in her manifestation as a household goddess, for example; instead she joined the warlike Mycenaeans and transferred her presence to their shrines on the Greek mainland.

In time Athena, like myth, would enter history not to champion the causes of her gender or demonstrate female power; she

---

*Athena had not only had many roots and many "births," she also had many "residences." Far from belonging exclusively to Athens, she had come from many lands, and was claimed by many citadels and cities. She was known to protect acropolises in general, and several in particular where she was the center of strong cults, including Argos, Troy, Smyrna, Epidarus, Troezen, and Pheneus. These ancient sites enjoyed the patronage of the goddess from early times; inhabitants celebrated her in images, festivals, and sacrifices, and knew her to dwell in a sacred precinct dedicated to her.

crossed over, as it were; as a male persona in female guise, she both glorified and solidified (or stereotyped) the traits associated with masculinity—rationality, cunning, bravery, brutality, strength of mind and body; she exemplified the manly virtues of wisdom and warlike aggressiveness. Then, later—some say it was because of her great affection for Athens—she showed herself to be maternal and nurturing, and to hold the people of Athens in special tenderness.

But before Athena can embark upon her journey with mortals from barbarity to civility, before she can be a presence in history, her relationship to Zeus, father god and lord of the universe, must be resolved: two deities cannot hold the same powers or occupy the same status in the minds of mortals. Zeus and Athena must establish their precincts, and must effect a relationship that will be honored by both mortals and immortals.

The Acropolis Museum in Athens houses this Archaic head from the pediment of the Old Temple of Athena (ca. 525 BCE)

ATHENA AND THE OLYMPIAN PANTHEON

ZEUS'S WARRIOR DAUGHTER

Athena's birth into the Olympian pantheon is not simply a matter of telling a magical story. The events leading to the birth, as well as its meaning, are subjects for discussion and dispute. Historians, archaeologists, and mythologists agree, however, that the supernatural physical phenomenon, the goddess's mythic entry into the Olympian pantheon, was a decisive occurrence. It not only fixed her attributes and powers in the Hellenic canon and established her identity and sphere of influence among the tribe of gods who recognized Zeus as their overlord, but it also carried theological and political significance for mortals.

Athena is a third-generation deity in the Olympian pantheon despite her previous life or lives as a very ancient goddess. Her birth from her father's body, however, marked her as a part of Zeus himself; it was as Zeus's daughter—not his colleague from Crete—that Athena joined Hera, Poseidon, Hades, Aphrodite, Apollo, Hephaestus, Hermes, Artemis, Dionysus, and Ares. While all of the Olympian gods shared the genealogy that began with Gaia and

Uranus, they were individuals marked by singular traits, passions, and bizarre quirks and obsessions. Olympus was not so much a familial as a theatrical setting for the newborn goddess; it was the stage from which Athena could define herself as a cosmic power.

METIS, ZEUS, AND ATHENA

Some say that Athena's story began with Metis.

Looking back, Athena's priests could see the history of her rebirth into the universe ruled by Zeus. It was a story, they said, that began when Zeus was a young god, when lust led him to the bed of his sister, Hera, and to that of Metis, his ally and mentor in taking the throne of Olympus and the overlordship of the universe. Some say he was married first to Hera, some say to Metis; everyone says he made love to both of them—as well as to numerous other mortal women and girls, goddesses, nymphs, and assorted creatures.

Gaia, learning that Metis was pregnant with Zeus's child, prophesied that the baby would be a girl and, therefore, inconsequential; but after the girl a second pregnancy would yield a boy. And that male offspring, in the tradition of his paternal line of Uranus and Cronus, would rebel against Zeus and take his throne as ruler of the gods and Mount Olympus. It was easy enough for Zeus to believe that his yet unconceived son might behave toward him as he had toward his own father: this form of succession after all, was the traditional model in the family business. But that did not comfort Zeus. He, like his father and grandfather, raged inwardly against the awful prospect of being dethroned.

The ruler of the gods was understandably reluctant to suffer a downfall resembling that of Cronus and, before him, Uranus. Like them, he decided to derail the prophecy. To prevent Metis from giving birth to the rebellious son who would overthrow him, Zeus loosed the savagery he had inherited from his forefathers. He could be cunning; he could be brutal. He could also be charming and seductive. Zeus would have his way.

And so Zeus, the most powerful of the gods, the god of gods, masked his ruthless intentions and spoke sweetly and seductively to the pregnant Metis, and drew her to his couch. Their love affair was long and ardent, it is told, and contained equal parts of lust and friendship. Zeus had relied on her wisdom in the past, and Metis had helped Zeus attain the throne of Olympus. But the finer points of fair play did not burden Zeus in his campaign to ensure his power; he intended to buttress his status and display his might at once, and he tolerated no challenge to his authority.

Compliant and pregnant Metis responded to Zeus's sweet ways, and lay ready to give herself again to the virile god. Zeus drew close as if to kiss her. But rather than make love to her as she expected, Zeus swallowed his hapless lover and her unborn child. Then Zeus, with Metis and the child she carried residing in his belly, boasted that he had full benefit of her immortal wisdom and counsel. Indeed, he bragged, Metis lived only as a part of himself; he had absorbed her powers, he contained all wisdom and would employ it for his own purposes.

But had Metis and Athena outwitted Zeus? Had he been tricked into taking their wisdom into his being? And had he been further tricked into giving birth to a female deity who would be identified with wisdom—the highest virtue, some would say, of mortal or immortal?

Whatever his plans might have been, Zeus was apparently unprepared for Athena's actual birth. Having swallowed Metis and her unborn child, perhaps he thought he had dispatched his problem. Instead, the child in time had grown to adulthood and was ready to leave his body, to emerge from his head, the seat of thought and wisdom. Perhaps she first knocked gently and asked to be let out. Perhaps Zeus ignored the tapping, and settled back into a nice nap in the warm sun and cool breezes of Mount Olympus. It is said that he woke suddenly from a snooze and began to bellow in pain. All of the other Olympians heard their master, dropped what they were doing, and ran to his side.

By the time the immortals had gathered at a safe distance and stood wondering what to do, more than half-fearing Zeus in his angry state, Athena was using all of her considerable force to pound the inside of the expectant father's cranium. His immortal brow near bursting, Zeus screamed. The earth shook with thunder and lightning. The Olympians drew back, and whispered among themselves.

Zeus roared, the sound of the thunderer's voice rocking the mountains the tearing the sky. Hephaestus, who was carrying his axe and limping to join the other Olympians, approached the great god and asked the cause of his pain. Zeus saw that Hephaestus carried his axe, and begged the god of smiths to split open his aching head and release the pressure. The other immortals, first curious and now concerned, watched as Hephaestus, eager to oblige, swung the axe, and split the great god's skull.

And Hephaestus, the sooty and misshapen blacksmith, stood transfixed in awe as a female deity leaped from Zeus's head. Some speculate that he welcomed into the community of gods a fellow craftsworker at that moment; others say that the smith-god fell immediately and hopelessly in love with the strong, tall, beautiful goddess Athena, the owl-eyed daughter of the lord of the universe.

ATHENA, BORN OF ZEUS

All of the gods stood round and watched the drama on Mount Olympus. Fully formed Athena, with a triumphant victory shout that shook the universe almost as resoundingly as had Zeus's labor-caterwauling, sprang from her father-mother's head:[*] she was commanding and beautiful, even then a radiant presence nearly equal to that of her parent. The awed and astonished immortals who witnessed the emergence of the eternal virgin goddess from her father-mother's head reported her to have been "fully armed and brandishing a sharp javelin." They said, too, that "Great Olympus was profoundly shaken by the dash and impetuosity of the bright-eyed goddess. The earth echoed with a terrible sound, the sea trembled and its dark waves rose."

---

[*]Her birth reflects the prevailing Greek pre-scientific conviction that male sperm—and therefore the male parent—had the dominant role in determining the offspring.

But, despite later designation of a summer birth date for Zeus's glorious daughter[*], Athena's emergence from the head of Zeus is not a fixed beginning for a chronology: her birth does not occur as the first in a logical sequence of events, does not even bridge neatly the chasm of disparities between her first life and her transmutation to the pantheon of Olympus. Her birth does mark, however, a critical moment in sexual politics; it was the downpayment on *patriarchy,* which would be bought largely at the expense of women and, as such, can be viewed only as a goddess's betrayal of mortal women.

Before Athena was born from the head of Zeus the father, it is told that she had already lived, made herself felt, perhaps even been named by the people who prayed and gave offerings to her; she had helped Zeus, nearly as his equal in battle, to take control of the universe. She had been a powerful deity for a long time, it was told, with an existence reaching far back into dark before memory. But gods do not subscribe to the laws of sequence made by mortals. Time inevitably refers to mortality itself, to the instant when there is no more time for a human: a trifle, at best, to the gods, and merely a dismissible instance of the inferiority of mortals.

It is among mortals, then, that Athena's previous life has meaning. In addition to material interpreted as evidence of her kinship with the goddess worshiped on Crete, people remember other legends of her previous lives and births, stories that persisted in ancient writings. There was even gossip that Poseidon was not Athena's uncle but her father. In this telling of Athena's origin, she turned against the god of the sea, for reasons not known, and beseeched Zeus to adopt her. He did so happily and struck a bargain with her, in which he called her his own dear daughter and acknowledged her powers as second only to his own, and she, in effect, became his ally in promulgating male dominance among the Olympians and mortals.

---

[*]Her birthday is given as 28 Hektombaion (July-August), the time of the Panathenaia in her honor.

Priests associated with cults of Athena, however, promoted a different version of the goddess's birth, and it has been stitched into the standardized genealogy of the gods, and into the stories of Hesiod and Homer. In this telling, Athena's arrival on Olympus and her birth solely from the body of a male parent is a brilliant work of imagination, and a supreme example of the diplomatic theology of inclusion of disparate gods, rather than the rational exercise of critically defining, of distinguishing and excluding, of saying that there can be only one, and if this one *is*, then that one is *not*. The gods had become many, their attributes confused, their powers overlapping and competing: in other words, they resembled mortals more than a little.

To tidy the roster, to clarify and reassert the power and order of the gods, a significant birth—a new beginning—was required. There could be no new leader: Zeus's lordship of the universe was unassailable. Zeus was wanton and perverse, erratic and mean spirited; he was driven by sexual appetite, and not especially concerned with governing his domain—except when he was challenged. But to challenge him, let alone overthrow him, would be to bring down the Olympian pantheon. Besides, save for rapes and tantrums, Zeus did not upset things: leave him on his throne, then, but add another layer of power, a more *thinking* deity.

The appearance of Athena and the new order in the house of the gods made things easier for mortals, allowed them to address specific gods, to know them in their particular sanctuaries, and to make sacrifices and offerings to them. When tribes or cities differed, they did not have to squabble over which side had the blessing of a single god; both—or all—sides were assured of at least one patron deity; and any one deity might receive the supplications of opposing sides. There were enough gods to go around, to appease and vivify all points of view among human beings.

We are not privy, however, to the bargain struck between the earliest manifestations of Zeus and Athena, nor to the manner in which mortals influenced or learned of the reorganization among the divinities. We cannot know why Athena agreed to be reborn as Zeus's daughter, or what she gained by agreeing to be subservient (although not always very much so) to a male overlord.

Some say that Athena, as a segment of an earlier goddess, had been Zeus's superior in the ancient rituals of Crete—perhaps his mother, sister, wife, or all three—and that she had been present at his annual death and rebirth. They say Athena had powers then over nature, fertility, and the household, that Zeus was subject to her control.

But she shed the trappings of the Cretan goddess before she appeared from Zeus's head in full armor: Zeus's daughter was instantly recognized as the imposing and powerful goddess of war; she was the Bronze Age goddess who favored the aggressive Mycenaeans.

When Athena stepped from Zeus's head, Metis or previous incarnations notwithstanding, she was the product of a male parent exclusively. She had not gestated in a female womb, had not been shaped or nurtured by enclosure in a mother's body. Although she was female herself, Athena's birth from a male parent signaled her rejection of the Hellenic perception of femininity and affirmed her solidarity with the warrior-heroes.

From the first moment she emerged from Zeus's head, Athena personified the masculine virtues of valor; she manifested in her being and held out for others the promise of glory—fame and immortality—associated with heroism in war. She let it be known that she was first among equals, immortal and nearly her father's equal in status among the gods.

Whatever else Athena's birth might have meant or established in human consciousness as the story was told over and over again, it signified the triumph of male over female, of the male divinity's ascendancy over the goddess; Zeus possessed ultimate power; Athena, although female in form, iterated the grandeur and heroism of masculinity. But Athena's retention of her female form, and her rebirth as the daughter of Zeus, was a theological transformation that made her subservient to him. We read that subservience as the symbolic birth of the role of women in Greek culture for, whatever else it might have symbolized, Athena's birth sanctified patriarchy; as a female, she would maintain power among mortals and immortals by asserting male virtues and prerogatives. Femininity was weakness; masculinity, power. In that miraculous rebirth, Athena crossed over the line separating the sexes, too; she was liminal, a male in female shape.

Stepping from Zeus's head, newly minted, the new girl on the block nonetheless brought her history with her in the familiar and identifying tokens of her millennia-long past—her snake, her owl, her helmet and spear. And so the reborn Athena, bringing mysteries from the past into the present of her birth, assumed a powerful position among the ruling gods. As the offspring of the overlord of the gods, the daughter born without the participation of a mother, Athena also clarified Zeus's role as husband and father. In what begs to be described as a vivid manifestation of uterus envy, female Athena made apparent male Zeus's authority over females. Her all-powerful father needed no female to produce a child; further, the female offspring was to remain a virgin, was to prefer no other male to her father: she was solely his. Athena and Zeus, in effect, had mocked and diminished the once revered female powers—conception, birth, nurturing. Or so it might have been thought. But Athena would prove wily, both more powerful and more headstrong than Zeus could have supposed.

By her rebirth she broke the chain of male-heir rebellion among the gods; with the physical characteristics of one sex and the psyche of the other, Athena was at once favored son and beloved daughter.

In this new arrangement of female and male deities, both father and daughter occupied uncontested territory among the other gods and the mortals, he as lord of universe and she as goddess of war, wisdom, useful arts, and cities. Nothing was written down for mortals to assist them in understanding the behavior or powers of the gods; no agreements were made or commandments graven in stone. Even so, everyone knew that an accommodation had been made, and storytellers knew the names of the gods, and they told over and over the legends about the sources and reasons for their powers. And the stories offered different explanations for the inconsistencies, infidelities, betrayals, lust, and envy among the gods; and always the old stories recalled how, without cause, the gods hated or loved humans.

Athena's birth from Zeus was more than just another trick the gods played on mortals; it was a brilliant amalgamation of earlier forms and new meanings, a spectacular coalescing of legendary events: it was the birth in humans' consciousness of a cosmology. Athena's overlord father dominated the universe, and his power was protected by a valiant warrior-son disguised as a loyal daughter, a goddess who also protected city dwellers.

But the stories make it clear that the greater power accorded to Zeus did not burden him with responsibilities that deterred him from his old whims and foibles, or from his predilection for sexual capers ranging from quasi-romantic seduction to savage rape. Nor, despite the father-daughter relationship between Zeus and Athena, did the relationship ensure Athena's total loyalty to the patriarch, especially during the Greek invasion of Troy.

HERA AND HEPHAESTUS

Hera, "who walks in sandals of gold . . ." according to Hesiod, was the child of Cronus and Rhea; and, like her brother-husband Zeus, she was as capable of desiring vengeance as she was cunning and capricious in meting it out to those who offended her or, as she perceived it, to those who violated the sanctity of marriage. While some claim that Metis was the first wife of Zeus, Hera insisted that she was his first, only, and complete wife; her passion for strict monogamy threatened continually to transform the "goddess of the white arms" from dignified wife to a cartoon nag and scold, a caricature of femininity.

However they may have been connected in their past lives, Zeus and Hera on Olympus were officially married. As the recognized consort of Zeus, Hera was called queen of heaven, and she proved jealous of her status as well as of her husband with the roving eye. No one—save perhaps Athena—doubted that Hera was great enough in her own powers to be Zeus's queen.

But no love was spent between Hera and Athena. The gray-eyed goddess knew that Hera could be as treacherous and spiteful as any stepmother. In addition, Hera continually spewed sanctimonious harangue, and set herself up as the model of chastity, a strident advocate of the duties and responsibilities of marriage. If Athena rejected femininity and Aphrodite traded in sexuality, Hera traveled another course altogether: she caricatured the wiles assigned to her gender, appearing as a demanding, jealous, and suspicious wife; an unrelenting nag; and a manipulator of immortal and mortal affairs.

Some say that Hera, to show Zeus a thing or two after he gave birth to Athena, marshaled her own generative powers and produced Hephaestus without benefit of male seed; others claim that the lame blacksmith was the son of Zeus and Hera; almost everyone says that Hera was little burdened by the tenderness of motherly love toward the infant. Whatever his origin, Hephaestus was to play a special role in Athena's life, and, like her, there is disagreement about the relative place in time of his birth. Some stories tell that Hephaestus was born after Athena, but some tell how he participated in her birth.

Everyone agrees, however, that when the infant Hephaestus appeared, Hera hated the very sight of him: he was misshapen, with a deformed leg: he was ugly, a sin in the Hellenic mind as dark as beauty was brilliant. It is said that Hera took one look at the misshapen infant and refused to suckle him and, disgusted at his appearance, threw him away to perish.

Pitched from Mount Olympus by his mother, baby Hephaestus landed in the sea, where he sank into the province of the sea nymphs Thetis and Eurynome. They took pity on him, and kept him with them in the watery depths for nine years, protecting him from his mother and the other gods, and patiently teaching him the arts of metalcrafting. All the while that he practiced his craft, growing ever more proficient at the forge, he nursed his resentment of his mother's rejection of him.

In time he found a way to ply his craft to punish Hera for casting him into the sea. Driven by dreams of sweet revenge, the smith-god designed and fabricated a marvelous throne, golden and irresistible in its material and execution, and sent it to Hera as a gift. But it was actually a beautiful and enticing trap, a snare engineered to complement Hera's vanity and avidity. Hephaestus knew his mother's weaknesses. As he planned, she gazed admiringly on the wonderful construction; she thought it a suitable throne for the queen of heaven. And so proud Hera sat on the throne, thinking what a grand figure she would appear to the other Olympians. But suddenly great metal arms shot forth, enfolded her, and held her prisoner. No amount of struggling and screaming, of twisting and cursing, freed her.

Only Hephaestus, her long-ago rejected son, could release her from his intention; only the magic of a lame and misshapen son could restore to his unloving mother her dignity and freedom. Hephaestus exulted; Hera raged. Hephaestus, deeply satisfied with his work, withdrew to the sea world and waited.

When Hera learned the origin of her imprisoning throne, and the power Hephaestus held over her, she was furious. But reason came to her through the clouds of her anger, and she called to him in a tone of motherly authority; she ordered him to appear before her and open the trap. But Hephaestus had no love in his heart for his mother, and he refused her pleas. It is said that he even laughed.

Another of Zeus's children, Dionysus, god of drink, took pity on Hera, however, and went to Hephaestus to urge him to release his mother. Hephaestus was unmoved by the pleas and reasoning of Dionysus. He was firm in his resolve to leave Hera imprisoned, he said; but, under the urging of Dionysus, Hephaestus said yes, all right, he would like to share the cup of wine. And so Dionysus poured a generous cup for the smith-god and wished him well-being. And then he poured another cup. And yet another.

When Hephaestus became drunk on the wine provided by Dionysus, the god of wine asked him to hand over the key that would unlock the throne that held Hera. But Hephaestus was not so drunk that he had lost all his senses. He demanded a bargain: only after he secured an invitation to live on Mount Olympus and to take his rightful place among the gods did he hand over the magical key.

So Hephaestus had his way and moved to Mount Olympus; and that, it is said, is how he came to be there on the day Athena was born. Hephaestus and Athena soon developed a special bond, whether based on mutual affection (there would be gossip about the smith-god and Zeus's virginal daughter), mutual dislike of Hera, shared interest in arts and crafts, or all these points of agreement combined.

Pallas Athena

The epithet *Pallas,* although the name of several ancient figures, including a particularly gruesome monster, also means merely "maiden." Two stories weld the term to Athena.

One ancient story suggests that perhaps Athena was fathered by the monster-giant Pallas, and honored her origin by taking his name as one of her more common epithets. It is a legend clouded by time and tellers, and complicated by the existence of several different creatures named Pallas. The one purported to have been Athena's father, however, was a winged monster, perhaps with the legless body of a goat affixed to a gargantuan serpent's tail: details are lost and confused, of course, as stories are told over and over.

It is agreed, however, that this monster Pallas was as loathsome in character as he was gruesome in appearance, and that he was filled with lust for Athena. One day—some say this was during the battle between the gods and giants—he crawled behind several giant rocks and lay in wait for the young Athena. As she strode by, helmet and spear in hand, the ghastly creature fell upon her in lust and tried to rape her. He misjudged his prey.

When Athena resisted his advances sternly, Pallas insisted that it was his right to have sex with her, saying that he was her father, an argument presumably intended to induce desire on her part. But the monster Pallas had not reckoned on Athena's quick temper and fierce protection of her virginity any more than he had calculated the power and effectiveness with which she would express her defiance.

The young goddess blazed with fury. She turned on the monster, killed him on the spot, split him open from end to end, and flayed him. Taking as trophy his tough, scale-coated hide, she made her famous aegis. Proponents of this story insist on its credence by pointing to Athena's adoption of the name Pallas and the eternal presence of her aegis, as well as the shield's ghastliness. It is, after all, well known that the mere sight of the aegis defeated heroes and turned back armies.

But both the name and the hide-shield call up other stories that explain their presence in Athena's life on the basis of entirely different events. And, in the end, a more likely story explains Athena's preceding her name with the epithet *Pallas*.

The title *Pallas Athena* may recall and clarify the goddess's alleged Libyan interlude, and the great affection she held for a companion. According to one legend, Zeus sent Athena soon after her birth to Libya to live in the palace of the lake god Tritonis, and to be reared with his young daughter Pallas. The two youthful goddesses soon became fast friends and comrades in adventure; they had no use for the primping ways of adolescent girls, but adopted the life of soldiers, schooling themselves in military discipline and the skills of war. It is told that the two wrestled, hunted, and played war games, as free and exuberant as callow wild creatures.

One day they armed themselves with sticks and stones for a game of battle. It was their custom to practice the virtues and disciplines of heroes. On that day, however, the mock fight got out of hand, and the goddesses became angry and began to fight in earnest. While Athena's attention was diverted, Pallas, almost as strong and agile as her Olympian playmate, raised her stick to deliver a mighty blow. Athena, who often failed to mitigate her great strength or to curb her proclivities to anger, raged back at her friend, and lunged.

Zeus, watching from heaven, sought to intervene by placing a shield between the two girls; but the father god fumbled and only blocked Pallas's blow, thus enabling Athena to strike and kill her beloved Pallas.

Realizing what she had done, Athena ran grieving and howling across the earth; then, half-crazy with grief, the goddess thundered into the mountains to mourn her action and the loss of her friend. Athena's weeping made the earth tremble and the skies darken. Falling upon the earth, the young goddess looked up and through her tears saw in a fallen tree trunk the likeness of her lost friend. She rose and brushed away her tears.

Always in possession of artistry and skill with materials, Athena tore away the wood that obscured the image she had seen, and thus freed a likeness of Pallas. This primordial creative act made Athena the patron of carvers and sculptors, all of whom, forever after, hoped to see beauty lurking in material and, with the assistance of their patron deity, hoped to free with their clever hands the nascent form concealed in inert material.

Athena set her carving of Pallas on a throne beside Zeus on Mount Olympus and decreed that the figure would forever possess magical properties to protect anyone who sought safety in its presence. No one would be denied her help and protection, Athena vowed, who drew near the figure of Pallas and prayed.

The statue remained beside Zeus's throne, almost ignored by the thunder thrower and the other immortals. Then, one day, while sitting beside the image of Pallas, Zeus was roused by the sight of Electra, one of the Pleiades, and decided to ravage her on the spot. But as Zeus pounced upon Electra, she slipped his grasp and ran to the statue of Pallas; she fell prostrate before it and begged it to save her from the rapacious god. Zeus, in furious pursuit, was not to be deterred from his conquest. Never mind the figure of Pallas. Zeus ripped Electra's hands from the statue, threw her down, and raped her at the foot of the statue.

His lust spent, Zeus was annoyed by the statue's conscience-twitting presence, and threw the pallas from heaven. It fell to earth and landed within the still-unroofed temple of Athena being built in the city that would become Troy. The Palladium, venerated in Troy, assured that city of Athena's protection—or so the people thought until the goddess turned against them in their war with the Achaeans, the Trojan War of Homeric epic.

But before that terrible betrayal and the destruction of Priam's house at Troy, people everywhere knew that the figure of Pallas, imbued with Athena's spirit, brought good fortune to those who touched it. Copies of the wooden Pallas—and sacred stones resembling it, a second generation of the magical sculpture—were sought by those who wanted Athena's beneficence, and were often housed in sanctuaries or temples dedicated to the goddess. In time people in many cities claimed to have the real, or original, Palladium, saying always that it had fallen from heaven, and saying always that it was a promise of protection for Athena.

ATHENA, ZEUS, AND DIONYSUS

Athena's birth and Zeus's official marriage to Hera had done nothing to change the patriarch god's randy ways. Eternally exercising his prerogatives as ruler of the universe, Zeus appeased his sexual appetite whenever and with whomever he chose, impregnating all those he seduced or raped.

Hera was not the only sister Zeus bedded; he also seduced Demeter, his sister who held powers over the earth's crops. From intercourse with Zeus, she bore Persephone, her only child and the focus of her intensely tender mother love. Persephone, half-sister to Athena, grew happily to young womanhood on Mount Olympus, and rivaled her handsome mother in sexual allure and in charm.

When her uncle Hades fell madly in love with the beautiful young goddess, and demanded from Zeus an opportunity to rape her, Zeus gave his permission. Then the brothers hatched a plot. Zeus agreed to allow his brother to abduct Persephone and have his way with her. Zeus then sent Persephone to a lovely meadow, where she was quickly distracted by the abundance of beautiful flowers. As she picked lilies and narcissuses, it is said, the earth opened and Hades swept his niece into the underworld and onto his couch.

Demeter heard Persephone cry out and rushed to find her. But there was no sight of the girl, and no mark on the earth, no clue to indicate where she had been or where she might be. Nearly maddened by worry, Demeter roved the earth for days and nights without sleeping or eating or bathing; in her misery she caused a great blight to kill crops all across the land, and she brought about a severe drought that threatened all life on the earth. Zeus, recognizing that Demeter's grief was making the earth sterile and all beings sad and barren, ordered Hades to return Persephone to her mother.

But Hades objected. He had, he argued pettishly, abducted Persephone with Zeus's complicity and, further, he quite liked her and he wanted to retain her in the underworld as his wife. Moreover, he pointed out, she could no longer return to the upperworld, for he had made sure that she had eaten the seeds of an enchanted pomegranate, making her forever the goddess of the underworld.

Zeus considered the dilemma, saw that Hades had secured Persephone for himself, and decreed a compromise. Persephone, he commanded, would divide her time between the earth and the underworld. Meanwhile, Zeus had noticed Persephone; indeed he saw that she lived up to Hades' praises of her beauty and charm. Perhaps the plight of the earth brought about by her abduction to the underworld simply called her to his attention for the first time, or perhaps Zeus realized that his brother Hades desired Persephone, or perhaps the lascivious god of gods merely responded to his daughter's much celebrated beauty and charm. Whatever the motive that stirred Zeus, it is well known that he began to desire Persephone for himself. After all, it did not take much to arouse Zeus; in no time at all, he burned with desire for Persephone. It did not matter a whit to him that she was his daughter, and the wife of his brother: he wanted her for himself.

And so, when Persephone returned to the upperworld, Zeus grabbed and raped her, impregnating her with Zagreus. Hoping to keep his indiscretion from Hera, and feeling a warm fondness for the child of the delightful Persephone, Zeus enlisted the assistance of the Curetes in hiding the infant. He ordered them to protect Zagreus as they had protected him deep in a cave on Crete.

But as the Curetes leaped about and made great noise to mask the child's cries, just as they had done for the infant Zeus on Mount Dikte, Zeus's enemies, the barbarous Titans, learned of Zagreus's existence and of Zeus's affection for the child. The Titans waited until, at last, the Curetes slept. Then the Titans lured the child away from their encampment, offering him toys and baubles, such delightful items as bits of wool and golden apples.

When Zagreus realized that they were kidnapping him, he struggled bravely, transforming himself into a fast horse with sharp hooves, a roaring lion, a snarling tiger, an enraged horned serpent, and a snorting bull. But the Titans overpowered him in his bull disguise and, grabbing him by the horns and hooves, set about tearing him apart and eating his raw flesh.

Athena heard the cries of Zagreus, however, and rushed to find him. By the time she located the gory feast, only the child's heart could be salvaged. She took it in her hands and quickly delivered the still-living organ to Zeus, who, perhaps out of affection for Persephone, wanted to save Zagreus and to render him an immortal. But first, and in great anger, Zeus struck the Titans with thunderbolts, killing them all. Then he took steps to restore Zagreus to life.

While the infant had been still in his mother's womb, Zeus had taken still another lover, Semele, the daughter of Cadmus and Harmonia. Now he went to her with the bloody and still-beating heart of Zagreus. He persuaded her to swallow the organ, the essence of Zagreus, and regenerate him as if he were an embryo within her body. This Semele did, eager to please her lover.

But poor Zagreus was doomed yet again. Hera, knowing that Zeus had been making love to Semele, hatched a plot to punish her faithless husband and his lover. With sweet words and cajoling ways, Hera succeeded in gaining Semele's confidence, and in convincing her that she should ask her mysterious god-lover to appear before her in all his majesty and glory. Zeus had disguised himself when he lay with Semele, but, in the heat of passion, he had promised her anything she desired. And sly Hera knew this.

Zeus, now outwitted by Hera, was trapped. When Semele asked to see him in all his majesty, he was forced to keep his word, and so he materialized before the young woman with his blazing thunderbolts. Semele of course could not withstand the blast of the lightning that accompanied her lover, and was burned to death immediately.

Once again the heart of Zagreus was rescued, this time from the ash heap that had been Semele. And this time the still-beating heart was stitched into Zeus's thigh, or loin. When the child was reconstituted and reborn, he was named Dionysus.

Dionysus and Athena, half-brother and half-sister, linked by their births from the body of their male parent, were separated by opposing attributes: he, born full grown from his father's loin, promoted orgiastic and ecstatic religious experiences; she, born full grown from her father's head or mind, emblemized wisdom and rationality. He, although male, was a soft and insinuating seducer; his feminine characteristics appealed to women. She similarly manifested masculine traits and attracted heroes. Each was more clearly defined because of the presence of the other; as opposites they created—or made available—conflicts among mortals, between males and females; they enacted the universal conflicts between reason and emotion, mind and body, orgiastic ecstasy and cool clear wisdom; just as Athena and Dionysus were born from different parts of Zeus's body, they stood on opposite sides of the chasm separating savagery from law.

THE GIGANTOMACHIA AND HERACLES

Athena fought on the side of the Olympian gods in the Gigantomachia, a terrible war with the giants, the winner to have and hold power over the whole universe. She fought zestfully beside her father, enjoying the pitch of battle as well as the spoils of triumph. But it was not an easy victory, even for Olympian gods. To defeat the gruesome spawn of the earlier race of gods, the Olympians had to have special assistance from heroes, and one particular hero—Heracles*—was blessed by Athena's attention and assistance.

The giants, born from Gaia after she was impregnated by Uranus's blood spilled upon her body when Cronus cut off his father's genitals, resembled human beings in their upper bodies, but they had serpents' tails instead of legs, and were hirsute and unruly. They were barbarous and disgusting creatures, and all the

---

*Heracles, the subject of many stories concocted over a long period of time, is perhaps the best known and most popular hero from the ancient world. He is associated with three major categories of legends: The Twelve Labors, The Exploits, and a series of secondary adventures.

more dangerous because they were also were dull witted and violent. But Gaia, who had repeatedly shown herself capable of loving even her most ghastly children, recognized the giants despite their unwanted genesis in her body and despite their monstrous nature and appearance; she loved them as best she could.

Even so, it was not the mother's love so much as the love of her children for battle that impelled Gaia to use the giants as weapons of revenge against Zeus. She had nursed her burning fury at Zeus since he had locked the Titans into the dark recesses of her own body, Tarturus, and kept them there. Bursting with the pressures of the Titans deep within her, Gaia appealed to the giants to do what they did best—fight; specifically, fight to free the Titans. The giants needed little encouragement to roar into battle, to bash and batter any being in sight; and so, with Mother Earth urging them, the giants made war on the gods.

The resulting war, in which gods resembling humans went up against terrible monsters, was a thunderously brawling and sprawling battle that tested the nastiness of the giants as well as the might and wiles of the Olympians: Who would rule? Would the universe be controlled by deranged monsters whose collected physiognomies cataloged all the possible faults, ugliness, and ills that might befall man; brutish creatures still shackled to Chaos? Or would all existence be ruled by Olympian gods, resplendent beings resembling humankind perfected; immortals who, in being and significance, possessed form?

Zeus is said to have known for a long time that he would have to rid the universe of the giants one day, and that he had been warned that the giants, being the offspring of Uranus and Gaia, possessed powers older than his own. It had been established that even though the giants were not immortal, they could not be killed by the gods alone. To dispatch a giant, it was ordained that a god would have to have the assistance of a hero, a mortal, and that a giant would have to be killed twice simultaneously—once by a god, once by a hero.

And so Zeus selected a mortal woman, Alcmene, and used her to produce a mortal son and hero, Heracles. But before Zeus noticed Alcmene's mortal perfection and took her to breed his offspring-ally, she was betrothed to a mortal and fully intended to marry him and live monogamously with him. Zeus knew that she would not willingly oblige him by bearing a son to serve as his personal weapon against the giants. So the god wasted no time on persuasion or courtship; he tricked Alcmene and, unwittingly, she became his mortal concubine and the mother of the mortal hero-son he needed for battle.

On the very day that Alcmene was married, Zeus contrived to send her husband away on a warrior's mission before their union could be consummated. And so, on the night Alcmene expected the husband's return, Zeus disguised himself as the home-coming warrior-husband, and appeared before Alcmene. Believing Zeus to be her husband, home from battle and hungry for his wife's companionship, Alcmene took him eagerly to the marriage bed.

Later, after Zeus had made love to Alcmene and departed, the real husband arrived. He stood before his wife, a warrior home from battle and eager to love her. Alcmene, surprised by her husband's second ardent approach to her, asked if he did not remember making love to her earlier in the evening. When he said that he most certainly did not, both husband and wife knew that something was amiss.

Tiresias, a prophet, then appeared to them in their confusion, and explained to the couple what had happened, and that Alcmene had been impregnated by Zeus. The newly married couple fell into each other's arms, and into bed together, where they consummated their marriage and swore fidelity to one another.

Later, when Alcmene prepared to give birth to twins— Heracles, the son of Zeus, and Iphicles, the son of her mortal husband—Zeus boasted among the gods that his soon-to-be-born mortal son would rise to great power.

But Zeus had not reckoned on Hera's reaction to his bragging. Furious at yet another infidelity on Zeus's part, outraged by the merest thought of another child fathered by her husband, Hera punished Alcmene. She sent the god of childbirth, Ilithyia, to make the birth as painful and difficult as possible. Ilithyia positioned himself outside the laying-in chamber and used a powerful charm that worked so long as he kept his arms, fingers, legs, and toes crossed.

When Alcmene was exhausted and near death from painful labor, her maidservant wondered if Ilithyia might be frustrating the birth. She knew this was so when she spotted the oddly contorted figure outside the chamber and, to break his spell, the loyal maidservant tricked the spell caster. She cried out in a delighted voice that her mistress had already given birth. Ilithyia fell to the trick, ran to see for himself if a child had been born to Alcmene, and so uncrossed all his parts and undid the knot of himself and the spell of the charm. In revenge against the maidservant, Ilithyia, it is said, turned her into a weasel and threw her into the wild world where no one ever trusted her again.

When the twins were born, Alcmene and her husband placed them lovingly in a cradle, not knowing which son was of the god's seed and which of their mortal union. Hera, watching from heaven, had not yet had her revenge on Zeus, and spitefully plotted to destroy Zeus's offspring in his cradle. But Hera—as confused as the parents of the twins—did not know which child was which. That was a minor detail: Hera sent two serpents to the cradle with instructions to kill Zeus's mortal son.

The poisonous serpents slithered into the room where the children slept and slid silently into the cradle. As the serpents prepared to strike, Iphicles woke and screamed in terror. But the infant Heracles, unafraid, rose up in his cradle, grabbed the serpents by the head and twisted them to death, thereby revealing to his mortal parents that he was the son of Zeus.

Some say that Alcmene's husband hated Heracles, the token of his wife's debasement by Zeus, and immediately upon identifying him threw him onto a mountainside to perish. Accordingly, it is said, Athena was protecting her father's interests and keeping watch over the infant. But just as she saw an irresistible opportunity to further her father's plan, to protect the child he wanted and needed, she also relished the opportunity it provided to humiliate Hera. Athena despised Hera as thoroughly as Hera detested Athena; their mutual hate, although sometimes banked in the ashes of necessity or sweet good form among the gods, was never far removed; each gladly seized prospects for causing the other distress, indignity, or loss of influence with Zeus.

And so Athena, perhaps smiling to herself, went to Hera with soothing words, and suggested that they take a walk together on the mountain where she knew the infant Heracles lay. As they drew near the baby, Athena picked him up and handed him to Hera. Someone must have made a dreadful mistake, she said, to have put such a fine infant on the mountainside to perish. And look, she said to Hera, he is hungry. Hera, as Athena had intended, grew interested in the strong, handsome baby boy.

At Athena's suggestion, Hera took Heracles to her breast to suck. The infant drew on her breast with painful force, however, and Hera threw him from her, spewing milk into the sky. This, it is said, was the beginning of the Milky Way. And this, it is further said, is how Athena, Zeus's faithful daughter, tricked Hera into giving suck to Zeus's mortal child, thereby giving Heracles immortality.

Then Athena, knowing Zeus's plan for the child, returned him to his mortal parents, who promised to care for him. The infant Heracles, having already shown himself to be brave and strong enough to exterminate the deadly serpents, soon displayed as a youth the heroic virtues by which he would become known. He was powerful and good humored; he was compassionate and generous. But, being the son of Zeus and of a mortal woman, he had serious faults: a vicious and short-fused temper, and physical appetites almost rivaling those of his divine father. Athena watched over him, knowing that he was destined for both glory and grief.

One mortal man so admired the strength and virtue of the young Heracles that he determined to claim him as a son-in-law. He kidnapped Heracles, it is said, and kept him captive for fifty nights and days, requiring him to sleep with a different daughter each night. Another chronicle suggests that the daughters were sent all together, and that Heracles made love to every one of them in a single night, pleasing them all, and impregnating all fifty of them.

But it is also told that his endurance as a lover was equaled by his other physical skills. A muscular man of average stature, Heracles' weapon of choice was the bow, and he was a deadly marksman who outshot all of the other bowmen of the region. He also bested opponents in wrestling and spear-throwing. Before he reached manhood, he became the subject of legend when he caught and killed a lion with his bare hands.

While still an untested warrior, and not yet called upon to join Zeus in battle against the giants, Heracles practiced his battle skills at every opportunity. During one of the many ongoing wars between neighboring communities, Heracles was angered by injustice done to his native city by marauding warriors from an enemy city. As Athena watched and encouraged him, Heracles laid a trap for the foreigners. When, laden with spoils, they made their way home through a narrow mountain pass, Heracles waited until they were tightly packed into the confines of high rock walls. Then he leaped from hiding and single-handedly attacked them; driven by fury, he soundly trounced the lot. Not satisfied with the punishment he had dished out, however, Heracles then lopped off their noses and ears and hung the amputated parts around his enemies' necks. He sent them home—the living, disfigured and disgraced, carrying their dead instead of booty and displaying their own ruined parts rather than plunder.

Athena watched her half-brother with delight; he was, to her way of thinking, deliciously savage and a glorious warrior. She applauded his derring-do aggressive spirit and his reckless bravery; to her eye he possessed a stylish and effective manner of rendering vengeance to his foes. He was a hero, and worthy to fight on the side of the gods.

As Athena would often do thereafter to support a chosen hero, she descended from heaven, praised Heracles and inspired him; she also armed him splendidly, and assured him of her support in his continuing battles. His subsequent feats in battle became legend, but his uncontrollable temper resulted in cruelty and tyranny to his enemies as well as to his family: a mercurial hero at best—and still despised by Hera—Heracles required

Athena's steady attention as they prepared to fight side by side against the giants.

But if Zeus had been preparing for the inevitable clash with the giants, so had Gaia. She had generated special herbs to render the giants immortal, and to make them invulnerable to attacks by mortals. Zeus learned of Gaia's plan, however, and took immediate action. He ordered Helios (the Sun) and Selene (the Moon) not to shine; and he ordered Eos (Dawn) to remain abed. In the impenetrable darkness of the long night that resulted, Zeus summoned Athena and together they traversed the world, finding and expunging Gaia's magical herbs. Zeus recognized in Athena the ally he needed in the upcoming battle—a splendid warrior who possessed the wisdom and cunning of Metis.

And so both sides were ready for the battle, each with its strengths and angers whetted in anticipation of the fight, each with special powers. In the Burning Lands, a place called Phlegra where the giants lived, the war began. The giants hurled whole mountains and gargantuan rocks at the gods, and then darted at them with burning torches made of the largest trees in the world. Heracles rose to meet the advancing giants, and shot one of them, Alcyoneus, with a poisoned arrow. But the giant could not be killed within his own homeland. Effortlessly, Heracles took hold of the wounded monster and dragged him off his native soil, where he died.

Another giant, Porphyrion, unable to expend his lust in battle, turned toward Hera, intending to rape her. Zeus, outraged, hurled a thunderbolt at Porphyrion as, simultaneously, Heracles pierced him with an arrow. He, too, fell dead.

Athena, delighting in the pitch of battle in her own right, threw the island of Sicily on the fleeing giant Enceldaus, and imprisoned him eternally under its weight. It was such an enjoyable feat that she encouraged Hephaestus to repeat it with the giant Mimas, and to bury him under a heavy layer of molten metal. Such comradeship was sweet to the goddess Athena, as was the clash and savagery of battle.

Some say that it was during this battle that the giant Pallas tried to rape Athena, and that it was during an interlude in the

fighting that she killed and flayed him on the battlefield, trium-
phantly displaying her aegis as her just spoils. Perhaps this is so. By
all accounts, Athena enjoyed the battle enormously, and joined
Zeus in celebrating the end of the Gigantomachia.

Now, of course, Zeus claimed to be the undisputed lord of
heaven, ruler of Mount Olympus, god of gods, thunder thrower
and mountain shaker. But not even Zeus could control all things.
If he had had his way, the universe would have remained solely
the province of immortal gods, and human beings would not
exist. But other forces were at work, among them his own daughter, clever Athena.

Athena, virgin goddess and daughter of Zeus, was recognized by her helmet and spear.

ATHENA, GODS, AND MORTALS

ATHENA'S WILL

Just as everyone recognizes the images of Athena created by Phidias, so everyone knows the stories of how that same Athena came to be recognized in her full glory as an Olympian deity, to be accorded a position in the cosmos second only to that of Zeus, and to be widely known for her gifts to and dealings among mortals. But the goddess's arrival on Olympus did not guarantee her the immediate respect and the recognition of power that she required.

There was a time, in fact, when Zeus seemed to forget that Athena had brought her own ancient powers to her Olympian throne. He expected her, once reborn as his daughter, to acknowledge that she derived her power solely from him, the father god, the thunderer, the ruler of the universe. For a while Athena all but ignored Zeus's bluster; she played along with his strut and bombast, and gave heed in most instances to the protocol required of one in a subservient position. But her maidenly good manners in dealing with Zeus merely encouraged him to take her for granted, and to assume that it was his prerogative to rule her in the same manner that he ruled the other gods. Vaunted up with self-importance, emboldened by his victory over the Titans, Zeus let it be known among the Olympians that he was the source of all power, and that if he could give, he could take away.

Athena thought herself to be at least as clever as Zeus; indeed, clever enough to obscure from him her superior intelligence. And so she set out to establish her separateness, her individuality, and what she deemed to be an appropriate association with and influence on Zeus. In a series of events involving both gods and humans, Athena quietly rebelled against Zeus and claimed her territory among the immortals, validated her attributes, and displayed her special rights as Zeus's daughter and as a singular deity.

Her loyalty as the daughter who had assisted Zeus in the Gigantomachia had helped him affirm his power in the cosmos, was celebrated widely among the gods. But her fellow immortals failed to recognized the degree of independence that Athena reserved for herself. And so she became the deity who defied Zeus—some say she betrayed him—by assisting in the creation of mortals.

ATHENA AND MORTALS, ANOTHER BEGINNING

After Zeus and his allies had defeated the Titans, and Zeus had imprisoned the losers in the terrible Tartarus, Prometheus, who was gifted with foresight, had counseled the Titans to be patient and use cunning. But the Titans were not subtle beings, and so they had rejected their brother's sage advice, an insult to Prometheus that caused him to throw his lot in with Zeus and help him in the ensuing battle.

By the end of the war, however, Prometheus despaired of the flawed and despotic nature of the Olympian gods, and believed they should be shamed by lesser beings who would nonetheless display nobler characteristics. Wanting to give shape to his vision of justice and morality, and knowing that Athena was interested in—if not fully committed to—order and equity in the cosmos, Prometheus sought the goddess's help. She quickly agreed to help Prometheus; it is not known if she did so merely to defy Zeus, or if she saw in human beings the potential for enacting her ideas of wisdom and beauty. Perhaps Athena merely liked the idea of adventure. At any rate, she helped Prometheus go against Zeus's wishes, and together they created human beings.

Taking clay he found in Boetia, Prometheus modeled human figures, exercising great skill in shaping them into individuals. Then Athena breathed life into each of the first group of new beings. Even though mortals eventually consisted of both male and female beings, as did the gods themselves, the first humans were exclusively male. It seems not to have occurred to Athena to create mortals in her own image, or perhaps she so thoroughly identified with the male that she believed men were as much like her as like Prometheus.

Of course, storytellers wrapped ambiguity around the creation of mortals, insisting in their tales that men and women had already existed. Perhaps that is true; perhaps the mortals who had existed before Prometheus molded the Boetian clay were, like the Cretan Zeus and Athena, earlier forms of the same beings; perhaps they were the first and second races of men described by Hesiod; or perhaps Prometheus remade a known form. Or perhaps this all happened during an epoch when everything occurred at the same time, when supernatural principles obtained, and when the natural laws of time and space did not force events of mortals and immortals into rigid sequence.

But Zeus was not interested in the details surrounding the creation of mortals; from the beginning he frowned on Prometheus's creation, and found fault with human ways at every occasion. The universe did not need these creatures; they would interfere with the gods, who wanted nothing more than to behave forever like spirited and pampered infants. Zeus watched the new creatures fumble; he noted their imperfections and weaknesses; he carped and grumbled until he was no longer able to stand the sight of men upon the earth. So, it is said, Zeus decided to starve all of them, to withhold meat from the race of mortals.

Prometheus rose to the defense of human beings, however, and persuaded Zeus to allow men to eat meat, but only the inferior portions of animals, and only after appropriate recognition of the superiority and ubiquity of the gods. When Zeus agreed to this arrangement, Prometheus promised to let Zeus select which portions of an animal would belong to men and which to the gods. In what would become the model for ritual sacrifice, Prometheus killed an ox, butchered it, and divided its body into two packets. He placed the choice portions of meat in the stomach, and he wrapped the entrails in glistening fat. He laid the two bundles before Zeus and asked him to choose the portion that would forever belong to the gods.

Although wary of Prometheus's cunning ways, Zeus chose the fat-wrapped bundle, expecting it to be the good meat. But he was fooled and thereby deprived the gods forever after of good meat; moreover, by his choice, Zeus determined the nature of ritual sacrifice. From that time onward, mortals offered the bones and fat of sacrificed victims to the gods, and sent columns of smoke into the heavens to appease and petition the gods; mortals, indebted to Prometheus, kept and feasted on the meat.

Doubly angered by Prometheus's hateful creation and then by his trickery to protect them, Zeus schemed to be rid of mortals once and for all. He decided to withhold fire from humankind, and so to relegate them to life closer to that experienced by wild animals than to the immortals, to condemn them to darkness, cold, and raw meat. If they were to live, Zeus decided, they would live forever as savages scrambling for survival.

Again Prometheus defied Zeus, and once again turned to Athena for help in outwitting Zeus. Athena again agreed to help Prometheus, even though her actions clearly opposed the wishes of her father. Those who praise Athena as a dutiful and unfailingly loyal daughter neglect this story; others say her cunning assistance to Prometheus was outright treachery against Zeus. If Athena and Zeus, by her rebirth from his head, had redefined sexual politics, Athena now inaugurated her efforts to help people overcome savagery.

Everyone knows that Prometheus could not have stolen fire without Athena's assistance. She led him by a secret passage into the sacred precinct of Mount Olympus; then she took him to the fire Hephaestus kept in the forge in his shop. As Athena kept watch, Prometheus hid the coals in the stalk of a giant fennel, crept silently away from Olympus, and fled to earth. There, Prometheus gave fire to human beings: it was the gift that would separate humans from the other animals on earth and give them dominion over their environment.

But Prometheus, still possessing prophetic gifts, also knew the great sadness that lay before the human race, and he felt pity for creatures condemned to struggle to stay alive. To prevent humans from suffering lives of continual lamentation and cheerlessness, Prometheus deprived the race of the ability to see into the future. If they could not know what awaited them, then they had the capacity to hope.

Now Zeus detested the mortals even more. They were offensive to him in themselves and, to make matters worse, they were ugly evidence that he did not always get his way. And the more he saw of people, the sorrier he thought them to be, and the more he yearned to punish them for merely existing. He could hardly stand it when he looked down on the earth and saw the detested people warming themselves by fires, lighting their huts and caves, and cooking their meat. But Prometheus's wisdom in denying mortals prophetic powers added insult to Zeus's injury. There they were, he saw, unsullied by vision of the future, and therefore with the capacity for hope. Zeus knew in an instant that the flickering lights that dotted the earth had been made possible by Athena and Prometheus, and that they had also made it possible for the miserable lesser beings to surpass the pain and suffering of a given moment in the belief that their lot would improve. Infuriated, the cloud gatherer stewed in anger and plotted against those who displeased him.

But even in his overwrought state, Zeus did his best to ignore Athena's role in what he viewed as an outrage against himself, and turned his full rage against his former ally in the struggle against the Titans. Zeus ordered Prometheus chained to an enormous mountain. And he decreed further that every day a great eagle would swoop down—some say the eagle was Zeus himself—and rip out and eat Prometheus's liver. But Prometheus, being a Titan, was immortal: each day the eagle tore out his liver and ate it, killing Prometheus. But each night Prometheus came to life again and, the following day, he was tortured anew by the rapacious eagle.

Zeus liked to see the punishment he inflicted take its toll, make its mark. While he savored the agony he had heaped on Prometheus, Zeus was annoyed that his victim would not stay dead, and that he even refused to admit that he suffered. But in time Zeus grew bored with the Titan's plight and decided to rid himself of the irritation he felt. He threw a thunderbolt at Prometheus, and blasted him and the mountain into Tartarus.

Prometheus spent a long time in that banishment: no one can tell how long because those measurements were neither made nor recorded. But it is known that he was released only when Zeus needed the prisoner's skill in knowing the future and offered him a bargain. Then in exchange for his freedom, Prometheus warned Zeus not to marry Thetis—a goddess who had beguiled him—lest he produce a son who would overthrow him.

Although Zeus was grateful for the intelligence provided by Prometheus, he had still not forgiven him for creating humans, and, what was more, Zeus had not found a way to punish those hateful creatures for existing and, worse, for hoping each day that life for them would be better for them. Knowing well the torture and cruelty—as well as the irresistible allure—of sexual desire, Zeus decided that *women* would be an excellent eternal agony for men.

It would be perfect, he decided, to turn Eros loose among mortals, to cause them to burn with the same lust that gripped him, and to give them no lasting antidote for sexual fevers. The best punishments, Zeus knew, were those that took advantages of their victims' vanities; the most excellent punishment caused not only pain but humiliation.

Zeus gleefully summoned Hephaestus and Athena, both skilled craftworkers, and ordered them to create a woman to be set among men. Athena was as ready to assist Zeus as she had been to lend her energies to Prometheus, as ready to cause pain to mortals as she had been to help create them, as eager to play a joke on them as to bless them with the gift of fire. Athena, like the other gods, had no binding commitment to mortals or to abstract concepts or laws that might govern communication between mortals and immortals. Like Zeus, Athena acted on her whims or, worse, turned her rage or irritation into action against the real or imagined cause.

The woman created by the gods was to be named Pandora— "all gifts"—and was to be tantalizing to men. Oh, yes, Zeus decreed, Pandora was to be exquisite, irresistible. No mortal man would be able to keep his senses when in the range of her charms. And she would pass on to future generations of women the same characteristics that made Pandora desirable and devastating to men.

So Hephaestus skillfully modeled a woman of great beauty out of clay. Athena breathed life into her, and dressed her in enticing clothing befitting the tastes of the goddess of weaving, embroidery, and needlecraft. Aphrodite supplied her with hormones akin to her own; sexual allure would boil and foam in *woman* as the sea had boiled and foamed when Aphrodite rose from the severed genitals of Uranus. The goddess of sexual desire then schooled Pandora in the wiles of seduction and anointed her with irresistible sexuality. When she was further taught how to employ treachery and guile to get her way, Pandora was given a streak of mischief and another of sly curiosity. When she was a perfect and compelling mixture of allure and danger, Zeus sent her to Prometheus's feckless brother, Epimetheus.

Now everyone knew that Epimetheus did not possess a full helping of ordinary intelligence; in fact, people laughed at Prometheus's brother. Fool, they called him, and gullible, and even downright stupid.

The gods gathered around Zeus to watch and laugh as hapless mankind was punished. It was a perfect joke, a clever subterfuge that turned on using the victim's own vanities and failings to victimize him. It was the ultimate comeuppance, and it was exactly the style of mischief the gods delighted in inflicting on mortals. The Olympians even embellished Zeus's clever spite: they provided the innocent Pandora with a treacherous dowry.

The gods sent Pandora to earth with a beautiful sealed casket that contained all evil and bad fortune that might come to human beings; at the very bottom, they hid hope. Yes, they told Pandora, the casket was hers, but she must not open it. Ever. And so she promised that she would treasure the closed casket, and the gods winked and nudged one another, knowing that human nature included strong components of curiosity and greed, and that both characteristics made them vulnerable to the tricks and punishments the gods might want to inflict on them.

That Prometheus had warned Epimetheus not to accept gifts from Zeus was common knowledge among the gods. But the immortals thought that merely made the trick more delicious: slow-witted Epimetheus was unlikely to remember or heed his brother's counsel under any circumstances, but, they guessed, he would be absolutely witless in the presence of Pandora. He would be smitten, rendered helpless, and, by his own actions, would bring the curse of the gods down upon him and his kind.

Of course, the gods were right about Epimetheus. He was completely enchanted by Pandora, completely in her thrall, and unable to think of anything else. He stood by grinning as her curiosity about the box's contents grew. When she could stand it no longer, and began to tinker with the lock, Epimetheus made no move to stop Pandora from opening the casket. When she had barely cracked open the lid the terrible contents of the casket rose before the startled and frightened couple, and began to fall upon them. As Epimetheus and Pandora clutched each other in terror, all of the physical and spiritual pains that could afflict mankind flew out of the box and surrounded Pandora and Epithemeus—plague, pestilence, woe, sorrow, and grief rose before them, as did death, or mortality, the eternal reminder that the gods ruled and people made do with what they were allotted. Great dread filled the hearts of Pandora and Epimetheus, and their breath was taken by fear.

Those ancient and irrefutably powerful immortals, the Fates, did not intervene as the dark torments then spread quickly across the earth, dooming humankind to unceasing labor, to illness, to strife, and to certain death. Pandora and Epimetheus, realizing too late what they had done, hastened to slam the lid. But they were no better at controlling damage than they were at avoiding it. Alas, only hope was trapped forever in the box. Hope cried to be let out in order to compromise the woes that had been set loose on earth, but Pandora and Epimetheus were now suspicious, and kept the lid tightly locked. And so hope, locked eternally within the enchanted casket, whispers lies to human beings, telling them that tomorrow will be better, that things cannot get worse, that the road is smoother around the next bend, and that all clouds are lined with silver. It is said that only the faintly heard lies of hope prevent the whole race of mortals from mass self-destruction.

Athena looked upon people and their plight. Perhaps she was amused. Perhaps she felt pity, and contemplated changes to benefit humankind. But what can mortals know of a god's plans for them? After all, Prometheus made it impossible for them to know the future.

WHO ARE THESE MORTALS?

The gods, blessed or cursed as they were by their own intrigues and power struggles, could not avoid the trials and triumphs of people. As gods, of course, they had the power to appear to mortals, seize tight control over them, and function as despotic rulers over weaker subjects. Gods could also remain aloof, intercede in human affairs as it suited them, give people the illusion of freedom—another trick!—and jerk them up short, humiliate, torture, or kill them at whim; gods could leave people suspended in hope, let them search for meaning in their short and brutal lives, and dish out rewards and punishments whenever it suited them. What the gods decided to do cannot be known; but there are accounts of what happened to mortals after they were created by the gods.

Gods and people, irrevocably joined, would have to find ways to live together—would have to reconcile the differences between women and men, to accept rule from a leader, and to determine if the leader's power arrived as an inheritance, was won through might, or was given—by gods or other people—in recognition of ability or as a reward for achievement. The universe of gods and mortals proved a fertile atmosphere for the planted seeds of the cultural wars, and of sexual politics; Athena would cultivate the noxious weeds of sexism as well as the tender hybrid of civilization. Perhaps Athena spent aeons studying the mortal creatures that struggled on the earth, and considering their ways and what should become of them; perhaps she saw what Hesiod reported in *Works and Days*.

Hesiod recounted the creation and development of humans that he had learned from the old stories. People changed, he says, and as they changed so did their relationship to the gods. Surveying the early history, and nature of mankind against the background of the creation of the universe and power struggles of the gods, Hesiod suggests that humanity's lot is full of woe and torment, with fleeting pleasures and whispering hope puffing up expectations that can only be dashed. Mortals, after all, are fated to suffer and die; the gods have taken no responsibility for them, have established no rules of conduct or thought that will guarantee immortal beneficence to mortals.

But things had once been better, according to what Hesiod had heard. Himself a hardworking farmer who struggled to scratch a living from reluctant soil, the ancient writer looked back nostalgically to what he imagined to have been better days for humans. He may have repeated stories he had heard of preagricultural bee-goddess-worshiping tribes when he described the first mortals as living an Edenic life, laughing and dancing, eating the readily available fruits and the honey that poured freely from trees, drinking milk from goats and sheep. He describes a matriarchal society that lived in harmony. Those people never grew old; for them, death was merely a prolonged and pleasant sleep. These first men existed during the reign of Cronus, he writes, and were known as the golden race. Although these blessed and innocent mortals disappeared, their spirits lived on in music and justice, according to Hesiod.

Then, he says, the golden race was followed by the silver race, a divinely created race of bread eaters, men dominated by their mothers. Although they lived as long as a hundred years, these grain-growing men were rude and ignorant, Hesiod tells us. Zeus ruled them, and must have considered their pacific ways an inadequate compensation for their failure to sacrifice to the gods. This, it is said, is why Zeus summarily destroyed the entire lot of bread eaters.

The peaceable grain-growing, bread-eating race was soon replaced, however, by another unsatisfactory lot of mortals, meat eaters who dropped upon the earth like fruits from the ash trees. Probably shadowy evocations of the earliest Hellenic invaders, these Bronze Age nomads are depicted by Hesiod as warlike and cruel; they armed themselves and fought one another savagely until the gods expunged them with a deadly epidemic.

The next, and fourth, race of mortals were also warlike—perhaps the warrior-kings of the Mycenaean age—sired by gods on mortal mothers. They became the great heroes at Thebes, formed the expedition of the Argonauts, and fought in the Trojan War. When they passed from the earth, they went to live in the Elysian Fields.

Finally, Hesiod recounts, the fifth and present race of mortals appeared, a reckless, unjust, mean-spirited, ignoble lot. Hesiod called this group the iron race, and may have modeled them on the Dorians, who used their iron weapons to destroy Mycenaean civilization in the twelfth century. Hesiod notes disdainfully that they are incapable of heroism, being victims equally of their carnal drives and their innate malice.

And so, however they may have been created, there were mortals and immortals in the universe, and they needed to know how they were alike and how different. Athena, who had helped create both men and women, took special interest in their nature and their activities on earth. She, along with the other gods, set about competing for veneration by mortals; she, and the other Olympians, already possessed absolute power over the frail creatures who had been set upon the earth to survive or perish.

ATHENA AND POSEIDON

Athena, having asserted her independence among the gods, looked now to affirming her rule over the best part of the earth and, with it, to winning completely the hearts of the best people in the world. She looked down on the great hill where her cult worshiped her in Athens, and was confident that hers was indeed the best part of the earth and that her worshipers were the best of all the mortals.

But her uncle Poseidon had been appearing around the Athenian Acropolis, flexing his powers for all to see, showing off and making a terrible roar. The sea god was, Athena thought, trespassing in her precinct; but what should she do? She thought for a long time, and knew many things.

She knew that as humankind had worked to husband and gather the riches of the sea and earth, they had turned to different deities for help; they had recognized the power of and given praise to different gods. It was no different from the gods' manner of operation: everyone knew that different groups of mortals found favor with different gods, made offerings and sacrifices to them, and sought their protection. Sometimes the gods, preening and strutting, lured mortals to worship them; sometimes the gods threatened and punished mortals into submission, or merely withheld from the grasp of mortals that which they most wanted.

Gifts meant power; both gods and mortals understood that givers and receivers exchanged claims on one another. And, in the case of Athena and Poseidon vying for control of Athens, both gods stooped to bribery, to gift giving to win favor among mortals.

All Athenians down to the present day know that Poseidon, Athena's uncle, was never satisfied with his control of the sea, that he was jealous of Zeus's domain and continually sought to extend his own power and range. Of course, Poseidon coveted Athens, even though a shrine to Athena existed on the Acropolis, and mortals in Athens made sacrifices and left offerings for her there. Some say that the city was named for the goddess; some claim it was the other way around, that Athena so loved the city that she took its name. But from the earliest times, she had made her presence known to the people who dwelled near the Acropolis.

Greedy and barbarous Poseidon ignored the tradition of Athena's special relationship to the city, however, and claimed it for himself. He appeared on the Acropolis, thrust his trident into the great rock platform in Athens and drew forth a saltwater spring, mighty evidence of his strength and of his presence in and claim on Attica, the region including and surrounding Athens. Some insist that when the wind shifts in a certain way they hear still the angry rush of seawater far beneath the surface of the Acropolis. It is, they say, Poseidon's roiling.

Athena respected her uncle and, despite a long-standing difficult relationship with him, tried to show deference to the mighty god of the seas. But it is well known that she was irritated by Poseidon's invasion of what she considered her territory. She may have pretended indifference, even inattention; but she was cleverly waiting for the right time and circumstances to reclaim her city.

The time came when Cecrops ascended to the throne. Knowing that King Cecrops was devoted to her and that he made generous sacrifices to her, Athena decided to reassert her proprietorship over his earthly kingdom. She appeared and tenderly planted an olive tree on the Acropolis. It was a wonderful tree, of course, with fine fruit that yielded a near-magical oil. Athena saw that the people admired and enjoyed her gift, and so she waited for Poseidon to make the next move.

In short order the outraged Poseidon railed against Athena and demanded loudly that she engage in a battle for possession of Attica. Let's have it out, he bellowed. Let's see who is the stronger god.

Before Athena could accept Poseidon's call to battle, Zeus ruled that his brother and daughter must not fight, but must put their claims before a divine court. Although most of the immortals appeared divided according to gender, with the gods supporting Poseidon and the goddesses backing Athena's claim, Zeus refused to take sides. Unable to decide among themselves, the jury of immortals asked Cecrops to give evidence. Without hesitation the great king sided with Athena, insisting that her gift was the better, more practical one.

Everyone knows that this was how Athena became patron goddess of Athens. In seeking preference over Poseidon, the goddess did exactly what mortals were expected to do when seeking her favor: she offered a wonderful gift.

Poseidon, however, was a sore loser. Furious not only with Athena but with the mortals who sacrificed to her on the Acropolis, he crashed huge waves across the plains of Attica. Athena, it is said, stepped matter-of-factly over Poseidon's swirling waters and took up residence on the Acropolis. But Athena had a practical streak to match her wisdom; she recognized the need to assuage Poseidon's immortal rage. And so, it is told, that is why she agreed to another compromise—if not betrayal—in the realm of sexual politics: Athena agreed that the men of Athens would no longer be allowed to bear their mother's names as they had in the older matriarchal society; and she conceded, too, that women should be stripped of their right to vote, thus laying the foundation for citizenship to become an entirely male prerogative in Athens, thus sanctioning the misogyny that marred Athenian dreams of civilization.

But Athena had what she wanted: she had splendid Athens. And she had work to do among mortals and immortals to extend her power and to perfect her domain. Perhaps she considered then how she might make all people and all places as marvelous as Athenians and Athens.

ERICHTHONIUS

It has never been possible to say whether Athena loved Athenians more than they loved her; everyone knows that the goddess chose Athens and that Athenians chose her. Of course, Athena was venerated among Athenians; and of course all mortals and immortals alike recognized that the goddess possessed her own tremendous, sometimes terrible power, that she was important enough to stand beside Zeus. Enthroned high among the Olympians and celebrated by them for her intelligence, Athena had displayed a masculine love of aggression, war, cunning, and wisdom. True, she was visibly female; but she boasted that she had not been born from a female womb, boasted that she was the daughter solely of her father. Moreover, counter to the mores and the emerging social structure of mortals who honored her, Athena militantly rejected sex, marriage, and childbearing. Her frightening aegis, the thick breast-shield she wore, was never mistaken for a bustier; it did not enhance her breasts but, rather, tasseled in snakes, hid her femininity behind masculine armor. She strode about heaven and earth with her aegis, her helmet, her spear and shield—a formidable warrior.

She spoke for Zeus, and mortals and immortals obeyed her. She was the acknowledged daughter-son of the father god; she was an honorary male. Unbeknown to the Olympians and Athenians alike, however, Athena had a strong maternal component. She hid it from everyone, perhaps even from herself, until she had occasion to show her tenderness for her city and her people. That is why Athenians like to tell the story of Erichthonious.

The story began with Hephaestus and Athena. Hephaestus, they say, was the father of Erichthonius; and Athena, although not his physical mother, looked upon him as her child.

Everyone knew that Hephaestus shared Athena's interest in the arts and crafts and that the smith-god, like the goddess of weaving and craft, promoted excellent workmanship and fine design among mortals as well as the gods. While Athena particularly furthered weaving and pottery making, and is even credited with inventing the vase, Hephaestus worked metals with fire and hammer. Neither Athena nor Hephaestus wasted affection on Hera, and both demonstrated loyalty and respect to Zeus. The tall, athletic goddess and the limping, sooty smith-god were often seen together, talking or sharing information on craft.

Some say that Hephaestus had fallen in love with Athena immediately upon cleaving Zeus's head open and releasing her, and that he had wanted to marry her. But Athena, they say, rejected marriage, and loved Hephaestus as a companion, much as she loved men as companions in adventure and comrades in war.

The other gods, a gossipy lot with more than a little tendency toward viciousness and meddling in the affairs of others, looked for any evidence of amorous activity between Hephaestus and Athena. That too-masculine Athena, they said, she is proud and arrogant; she thinks she is better than the rest of us. But, they assured one another, winking at implicit prurience, she is Zeus's daughter. We know how he is. And she is no better than we are; she is probably not a virgin at all.

Athenians who tell the story of Erichthonius are careful to point out, however, that Athena ignored the other deities and steadfastly remained a virgin. But, they say, that is why her special relationship to Erichthonius and to Athens is all the more miraculous. For Athens, they say, Athena showed *motherly* instincts, and let the mortals and immortals think what they wanted.

Athenians bragging about Athena's great love for them and their city begin their story by telling how Athena went to the lame god of the forge and requested that he make splendid new armor for her. This he did. And when she returned to his shop to fetch her handsomely fashioned breastplate, shield, and helmet, Hephaestus was overcome with longing for Athena. He forcibly embraced her; she resisted and as he struggled to rape her, he ejaculated on her leg. She grabbed a piece of wool, wiped the semen from her thigh, and tossed it out the shop door, where it fell upon the earth which, being Gaia, was immediately made pregnant.

When the child from Hephaestus's seed was born, Gaia handed him over to Athena to rear. Athena named him Erichthonius, combining the words for wool (*eris*) and earth (*chthonos*). Perhaps Athena was not comfortable with her motherly response to the infant; perhaps she wanted to hide the child from the other gods. Whatever her reason, Athena gently placed the child in a beautiful basket, closed and fastened the lid, and gave the basket to the three daughters of Cecrops, king of Athens, for safekeeping. Although Athena ordered the young women not to look inside the basket, curiosity overcame their good intentions.

Two of the girls—Pandrosos and Herse or, perhaps, Aglaurus and Herse—disobeyed. Some say they lifted the lid and saw a terribly formed child, half human and half serpent, inside the box; others say that they saw a properly formed human baby wrapped in ghastly guardian serpents. Whatever they saw, the two girls went instantly mad, partially from the sight itself and, no doubt, partially from fear of Athena's likely reprisal for their disobedience.

Maddened, the young women, who lived on the Acropolis in the house of their father, ran screaming from their home. They threw themselves off the highest point of the Acropolis and dashed themselves to death on the rocks below. Athena at that moment was flying back from a mission to bring a giant rock from a distant source to add to the fortifications of the Acropolis. A crow, eager to win the goddess's favor by bearing tales, intercepted her and told her of the double suicide.

Athena was so distraught by the news that she dropped the great rock: it is known today as Lycabettus, and from its peak affords an excellent view of the Acropolis and the Parthenon. Then Athena struck out at the crow, it is said, and forbade it and its kind to ever appear on the Acropolis. Some even say that crows had been white until that moment, and that Athena turned them black and gave them harsh voices because they carried dark tales.

Athena flew quickly to the Acropolis and retrieved Erichthonios from the house of Cecrops and took care of him. Some say that she placed him in her temple; some say that she tucked him inside her aegis, and let him snuggle against her breasts. Athenians will tell you that she loved him dearly, and that she protected him until he grew to manhood. With her help, he became the king of Athens, made the cult of Athena official, and led the people of the city in festivals and sacrifices in her honor.

It is said that Erichthonius invented the four-horse chariot, with Athena's inspiration, because, being half snake, he was unable to walk and needed a speedy form of locomotion. Others say that he shed his snake end while protected within the goddess's aegis. But all agree that he was represented by pet snakes in Athena's temple on the Acropolis.

A PROUD AND JEALOUS GODDESS

Athena was not content to be Zeus's daughter, or even second only to the thunder thrower in power; she was not even satisfied by her sovereignty in Athens. She wanted it known universally that she was a cut above the rest of the immortals. This pride, it is said, caused her to compete with gods and mortals alike, caused her to consider herself the best, and to take a competitive, spiteful, even revengeful, stance toward those who challenged excellence.

Athena's pride provoked her equally well known and universally feared temper, and sometimes led her to do things people did not want to include in their stories. This, perhaps, is why confusion exists about the origin of her powerful aegis, causing some to say that it was given to her by Zeus; others that she made it from the skin of the giant Pallas, after she slew him; and others to insist that she made it from the skin of Medusa the Gorgon.

There were three Gorgons—Stheino, Euryale, and Medusa. They were once great beauties, and celebrated far and wide for their golden good looks, their long rich tresses, their feminine charm. But Medusa took Poseidon as a lover one night in Athena's temple, and lay with him near the altar.

Without even bothering to think *how dare she,* Athena turned her wrath on Medusa and immediately transformed her into a monster as horrible as she had once been beautiful. Freudian interpretation proposes that Athena, in a temper tantrum of take-that-you-cunt, punished Medusa's pollution of a sacred precinct by transforming the beautiful woman's face into a nasty caricature of female genitalia. After Athena had worked her powers on the Gorgon, she was a winged misshapen creature; her teeth were so large that she could not close her mouth and her ugly tongue lolled on her coarse lips. Snakes, like pubic hair, wreathed her face: woe to the penis that ventured near. In addition, anyone looked upon by Medusa was immediately robbed of any possibility of sexual activity and was turned to stone.

But even the terrible punishment Athena inflicted on Medusa did not empty hate from the goddess's heart; she held a grudge, waited, and looked for opportunities to punish Medusa further.

When she heard that Perseus—a son of Zeus—intended to slay Medusa in order to gain permission to marry the woman of his choice, Athena pledged her assistance. She transported him immediately to Samos, where he saw images of the three Gorgons displayed, and memorized the appearance of Medusa. Never, Athena told Perseus, look directly at Medusa, for her powers are terrible. If her gaze touches you, you will be turned to stone. You must look only at her reflection, Athena instructed; and with that she gave him a highly polished shield to serve as a mirror.

But before Perseus could go to Medusa's lair, he had to get magical winged sandals to make his trip possible, and he had to get from the Stygian nymphs a satchel in which to carry Medusa's severed head. Only the Gorgons' sisters, the three Graeae, knew the whereabouts of the Stygian nymphs. And the Graeae themselves were bizarre creatures, with only one eye and one tooth among them.

Now sped on his mission by Athena, Perseus went to the Graeae—the gray ones—at the foot of Mount Atlas; he crept up behind them and, before they could even smell his presence, he snatched the one eye and one tooth from the sister who possessed them at that moment. He spoke to the Graeae: if you want your tooth and your eye, you must tell me where I can find the Stygian nymphs. So, of course, they told him.

In short order, while Athena watched, Perseus collected all the magical implements he needed and then flew to the den of the Gorgons. Among stones that once had been men, the Gorgons slept. Perseus, careful not to look at Medusa, but only at her reflection in the shield given to him by Athena, moved toward her quietly.

Athena guided Perseus's hand; with one mighty stroke he cut off Medusa's head. The winged horse Pegasus, the fruit of Poseidon's seed, flew from her dead body.

Perseus quickly put the ugly head out of sight in the satchel he carried and escaped before Stheno and Euryale could capture him.

Later, of course, Athena invented a golden bridle and gave it to Bellerophon (who, according to some, may have been Poseidon's son) so that he could control Pegasus. Poseidon's gift—the horse—was like the sea god; he was wild and unmanageable. But, like the sea, he was beautiful, Athena thought, as she exercised her superior intelligence and devised the means for mortals to capture and control the splendid beast. Yes, Athena thought, intelligence harnesses brute power; and she looked at her work with pride, knowing that no other god could match her, and knowing that she had done something important in the eyes of immortals and mortals.

Athena was proud of her skills and, more than a little vain for having invented pottery and weaving, she expected mortals to honor her gifts and her mastery of useful arts. Everyone—with the possible exception of poor trusting Arachne—knew that Athena was a bit smug about her famed skill as a weaver and jealous of her role as patron of weavers. She was as celebrated among the gods for her weaving as Hephaestus was for his metalwork, and was much praised for making Hera's beautiful veil and headdress, a combination of fine weaving and intricate embroidery.

But the goddess's pride in her craft slipped into the abyss of jealousy, it is told, when she learned that a princess of Lydian Colophon had brazenly claimed for herself greater skill as a weaver than that associated with Athena. The princess Arachne was confident of her artistry and of Athena's justice, and so worked day and night at her loom. She produced a magnificent tapestry on the subject of the love affairs of the gods, and spread it before Athena for her judgment, innocently expecting praise from the goddess.

But Athena peered carefully at the fine fabric for a long time. She could find no fault with it. It was work that she herself would have been gratified to have done. Enraged by the perfection of the work, Athena spitefully turned Arachne into a spider and condemned her to spend eternity spinning webs with the fibers excreted from her own fingers.

And then there was the matter of Tiresias, another instance when Athena felt that she had not been accorded proper respect. Look what Athena did to Tiresias! One day, it is told, the young son of Athena's friend, the nymph Chariclo, happened accidentally upon the goddess as she was bathing in a clear pool. Athena felt his eyes upon her, swung round, and splashed water onto his face and blinded him.

When his mother appealed to Athena to reverse her harsh punishment of Tiresias, Athena refused: gods do not admit that they have been wrong. But either regretting the severity of the penalty she dispensed or out of respect and affection for Charilco, Athena compensated Tiresias for his loss of sight. She imbued him with inner sight, the ability to see into the future and to understand the language of birds. In time Tiresias became famous for his prophecies, and was often called upon by mortals to make clear messages and portents sent from the gods.

*Athena, Hera, and Aphrodite presented themselves
before Paris, each wanting to be judged the most
beautiful. Athena proud and dignified, perhaps
appeared as she is depicted in this relief sculpture,
the "Mourning Athena" (ca. 470-450 BCE).*

part four

EROS AND ERIS:
MARRIAGE AND WAR

EROS AND ERIS

Athena, like all of the other gods and all mortals, shaped herself, found her nature, and claimed maturity in the process of dealing with lust and strife, Eros and Eris. Everyone knows that Eros and Eris were close allies, and that they were almost continually together hatching mischief; everyone knows that Aphrodite and Ares joined them, and that the foursome enjoyed inflicting pain and havoc on the other divinities as well as hapless mortals. No wonder that Aphrodite, Eros, Ares, and Eris chummed about, causing havoc, laughing at the pain and woe they inflicted on the other divinities and on poor hapless mortals. A foolish and dangerous lot, Athena thought.

Eris—some say she was the daughter of Night, others that she was the sister of Ares—was an awful and bloodthirsty goddess of discord and brawling. Athena considered both Eris and Ares more than half crazy; they were both monstrous (even by Olympian measures) in their insatiable desire for brutality and carnage. They were as insatiable in their lust for savagery and lawlessness as Aphrodite was for sex.

While Athena displayed her own brand of savagery throughout the Trojan War, she made no secret of the repugnance she felt for both Ares and Eris; she proudly distinguished her style of warfare from theirs, saying that she, unlike the despicable Ares, used strategy, not demented brutality, to win battles.

Athena was also at odds with another of the most ancient forces, Eros (Lust), who, according to Hesiod, was the most beautiful of the deities, as irresistible as his ally Aphrodite. Eros was as old as the earth and Tartarus, born with them of Chaos. A powerful force among both deities and mortals, Eros was incapable of pity and, when eventually armed by Zeus with a strong bow and unfailing arrows, brought about great havoc and misery throughout the universe. He was lovely and irrepressible, a thoughtless and unreliable child with a driving craving for mischief. But militantly virginal Athena, unlike her lecherous father, successfully deflected arrows that lust-promoting Eros might have aimed at her. The warrior-goddess largely ignored Eros; even sometimes she seemed to pretend that he did not exist.

The ubiquitous presence of Eros and Eris inspired the creation of institutions intended to formalize and make predictable—if not control and make acceptable—their powers. The institution of *marriage,* whether between gods or mortals, is intended to reign in Eros; similarly the conventions of war veil the savage Eris in euphemisms such as honor and courage.

Without Eros and Eris, gods and mortals might have avoided the Trojan War, might even have learned to live together in the universe without strife. Eros and Eris created the riptide of mischief that erupted into that terrible war between the Greeks and Trojans. Four stories tell it all.

Bluntly put, the Trojan War did not begin in assemblies and diplomatic negotiations or, as Homer would have it, solely in the illicit union of Helen and Paris. But that gruesome war did have its beginning in the institution, the idea and public celebration, of marriage—and sumptuous beds prepared by Eros and Eris for three specific marriages, those of Zeus and Hera, Peleus and Thetis, and Menelaus and Helen. In these sanctioned unions, as well as in the infidelities that bracketed them, Lust and Strife combined handiwork; conflict was aroused and fortified by sexual desire. Marital conflict produced winners and losers, and brought about spite and aggression, possessiveness and jealousy. Compassion exiled, the love-war games escalated.

Warriors boast of honor and bravery, and say that a man will not be forgotten if he is successful in slaying his enemies; winners are heroes and are rewarded with license to rape and pillage. Winners take immortality, too: they live to tell the stories of the great battles and their great triumphs; they write their names on history's slate.

Eros and Eris put a snarling mask on *honor* as they shoved and pitted one partner against the other, and as they made the three marriages tournaments of frail yearning for peace and comfort flailing against angry self-centeredness. Eros and Eris, never fully subdued by the institutions of war and marriage, cross back and forth between their respective territories, knitting together the burning passions they stir up and blurring the distinction between sex and war. It delights them to convince mortals that might makes right, that honor and victory reward brute force, savagery, barbarity. The human contests set in motion by Eros and Eris resulted in no winners; the losers, however, include justice and civility. That alone impelled Athena to hate them.

Eros and Eris saw to it that the passions defining the three marriages—Zeus and Hera, Peleus and Thetis, Menelaus and Helen—erupted like wildfire, and spread destruction over the earth, strife among the gods, and grief and sorrow throughout humankind. Eros and Eris are never far apart.

ZEUS AND HERA

Despite their habitation of the paradisiacal sphere of Mount Olympus, Zeus and Hera hardly set the standard for a marriage made in heaven. The old stories tell that Eros and Eris were unseen partners in the marriage of the king and queen of heaven; tell that the brother and sister who became husband and wife were bound by conflicting passions for power as well as by the bonds and vows that grew from youthful lust. Their marriage, from its beginning, was pushed and shoved, shaped and fixed, by Eros and Eris.

Reigning on Olympius, the two showed themselves to be jealous, spiteful, and cruel to one another. Zeus, despite his power over mortals and other gods, was himself continually overpowered by lust, and was more cunning and vigorous as a sexual predator than as a proponent of justice or goodness among either mortals or immortals. Although Zeus gave Hera bountiful cause for her suspicion, jealousy, and resentment of him, she burlesqued the role of the aggrieved wife; she had no parallel in her bitching and nagging.

Both Zeus and Hera came from an early race of gods, divinities with more power than self-control, driven by unnameable passions, devoid of purpose other than immediate gratification of irrational impulses. No wonder that Hera, coming from that family tree, had an unpredictable, unstable streak; some say that her vanity exceeded only her meanness of spirit. But those are the same gossipy gods who cluck disparagingly over her rejection of her son Hephaestus because he was lame and not very handsome; and they are the ones who, no matter how hard they try, cannot understand the relationship of Hera and Thetis. After all, the rumormongers chatter, Hera adopted Thetis, a sea goddess, and loved her tenderly; Hera even reared her on Mount Olympus. But when Thetis returned to the sea, she and her sister Eurynome, without so much as a glimmer of loyalty to Hera or respect for her feelings, rescued Hephaestus when Hera pitched him into the water.

But Thetis, loyal to Hera or not, continued to be grateful to her foster mother and to love her until, in collaboration with the other gods, Hera attempted a revolt against Zeus. That, in Thetis's mind, was inexcusable. But, living beneath the sea, perhaps Thetis did not realize what a bully Zeus had become.

In fact, Zeus had become a near disgrace among the gods. Not only Hera but all of the gods had tired of his strutting arrogance and childish pouting, his chronic state of sexual arousal. Encouraged by Eros, Zeus raped and seduced whomever, whenever, and wherever he chose, irritating the other gods not so much because he raped—after all, that's what males did—but because he had no respect for the wives, daughters, and sisters (the property) of others. Under sway of Eris, Zeus took what he wanted; he bullied the other gods until they could no longer tolerate him. So they plotted against him.

Hera, Poseidon, Apollo, even Athena—all of the gods except Hestia—waited until Zeus lay sleeping, then stole his thunderbolt and hid it. With that mighty weapon out of the overlord's reach, the gods quietly surrounded their father and ruler; then they pounced on and bound him with leather thongs that they secured with a hundred hard knots. Zeus cursed and bellowed; he strained against the bonds and swore to kill his captors instantly. The gods merely taunted him and laughed; they walked away, confident that they had overpowered the thunder thrower.

But Thetis was watching from a distance, and she was outraged by Zeus's predicament. As the gods turned away from the bound Zeus and began to squabble over who would succeed him as ruler of the universe, Thetis summoned Briareus, the hundred-handed one, who used his many fingers simultaneously to loosen the knots and free Zeus. The king of the gods reckoned that Hera had led the plot against him; he grabbed her, clasped strong golden bracelets around her wrists, and hung her from the sky; he tied heavy anvils to each of her ankles. When she cried out in pain, the other gods dared not rescue her and risk Zeus's wrath.

Zeus, after a while certain of his victory over the other gods and of his power as the ruler of Mount Olympus, let his wife hang in the air until he extracted from her a promise to remain obedient to him. Only when he was satisfied that the other gods had learned not to try his patience again did Zeus free Hera. He then punished Poseidon and Apollo for their part in the plot by sending them to assist King Laomedon in the building of the city of Troy; and he pardoned the other immortals, including Athena, chiding them for their weakness in being persuaded by Poseidon and Hera to act against him.

Yes, Zeus thought, it was Hera, that hateful nagging wife, who had instigated the betrayal. The bonds of the marriage, he knew, were more constricting, more painful, than the leather thongs. But his power was intact; Thetis—now there was a fine and loyal woman!—had seen to that. He was in her debt.

PELEUS AND THETIS

With order restored on Mount Olympus, Zeus took another look at the sea nymph who had rescued him from his treacherous wife. At first glance he was merely grateful for her loyalty; then he was smitten by her beauty. At about the same time, Poseidon also took Thetis's measure and found her attractive; what was more, he thought a sea nymph would be the perfect wife for him in his underwater world. Meanwhile Zeus, easily contrasting Thetis with Hera, had decided to jettison Hera and marry his beautiful rescuer. Eros and Eris saw a delicious brawl in the making.

But before the brother gods undertook an all-out war for the favors of Thetis, they were persuaded not to marry her because of a prophecy that a child born to her would overthrow his father, a fate neither of them wanted.

When Zeus learned Thetis's secret from Prometheus, he then decided that Thetis must be rendered harmless to him, that she must be married immediately and, of course, that she should be united with someone else; indeed she must be married to a mortal so that no god would be overthrown by the fated offspring.

Hera, too chastened by her painful punishment to assail Zeus for his lingering passion for the sea nymph, knew that the only reason he had not bedded Thetis was his fear of the prophecy that her son would overpower his father in the same way that Zeus had brought down his father, Cronus. When she learned that Zeus had decreed that Thetis must be married immediately, the overjoyed Hera set about planning a lavish wedding for her foster daughter and former rival.

In due course it was decided that Thetis would marry Peleus, a mortal much admired by the gods for his bravery and intelligence. But it was also decreed that Peleus first would have to catch the sea nymph, a difficult task at best. Thus the undaunted mortal hid behind a bush near the opening to Thetis's favorite cave; Eros gave him strength and filled him with sexual desire. Soon the lovely sea nymph appeared, naked and riding on her dolphin. When tired of playing among the waves, Thetis entered the cave to nap in its cool shade. Peleus took her in his arms and held her as tightly as he could, but she was sea-slick; she struggled fiercely and turned herself into fire, then into water; but still Peleus clung to her. She became a lion and, finally, a serpent; still Peleus held her in his arms. Thetis even became a slippery squid and squirted ink on Peleus, but still he clung to her. At last, clutched as she was by the stouthearted mortal, Thetis's heart stirred. As Eros and Eris closed ranks, Thetis stopped struggling, softened in Peleus's arms, then returned his caresses; they joined in passionate lovemaking.

It was not their union, however, that was to influence the course of the Trojan War. Rather, the causes of the war—both those that impelled mortals and incited the gods—were set in motion at the wedding feast of Thetis and Peleus, and by the actions of Eros and Eris.

Hera invited all of the immortals except Eris to the wedding feast of the beautiful sea nymph and the admired mortal. The gods assembled near the centaur Chiron's cave on Mount Pelion and, seated on twelve golden thrones made by Hephaestus, the Olympians celebrated the union of Thetis and Peleus. It was a splendid occasion. The Muses sang, and Eros, never more enchanting, swayed to their tune; the Nereids danced on the ribbons of music; and the Ganymedes, charming in manner and appearance, poured nectar all around. Even the wild centaurs appeared and, behaving themselves for once, prophesied good fortune for the couple. Hera then lifted a bridal torch high into the night sky, and Zeus—now free of lust but still harboring tender feelings for Thetis—sanctioned the marriage, gladly giving Thetis to Peleus.

The wedding gifts were wonderful. Chiron had cut a supple ash tree on the summit of Mount Pelion; Athena hardened and polished it; and Hephaestus forged a blade that turned it into the most magnificent spear anyone had ever seen. The gods outfitted Peleus in golden armor, and Poseidon gave him two immortal horses, Balius and Xanthus, as swift and strong as their sire, the West Wind. All of these fine warrior's accoutrements would be passed on to the couple's son, the splendid but doomed Achilles, who would take them with him to the bloody war on Ilium's plain.

Meanwhile Eris—who never liked to be far away from Eros—loitered in the shadows at the edge of the wedding festivities, sorely irritated that she had not been invited and annoyed that the divine guests were untouched by discord. Seeing Hera, Aphrodite, and Athena, their arms linked companionably, chatting and laughing together, was too much for Eris. Such a peaceable good time was unbearable for her; how dare these foolish goddesses wallow in harmony, she fumed to herself. Those three bitches, she growled silently, should be feuding; they should be hissing and clawing the air, sniping and digging at one another. Eris plucked a golden apple from her bag of tricks, inscribed it "For the Fairest," and rolled it toward Hera, Aphrodite, and Athena.

Hapless Peleus, knowing neither the source of the beautiful apple nor for whom it might be intended, fetched it and held it out to the three goddesses. Perhaps Eris caught Eros's eye at that moment and winked.

Each of the goddesses thought the apple was for her. Of course.

EROS AND ERIS PREPARE TROUBLE

Hera knew very well that sometime earlier Zeus, overtaken by Eros, had disguised himself as a swan in order to rape Leda. And all the gods knew that the daughter of that union, Helen, hatched from an egg and grew up in the palace of her foster father, Tyndareus, the king of Sparta, to be the most beautiful woman in the world. While still merely a child, Helen showed signs of becoming a perfection of female beauty, and the most desirable woman that men could imagine. It is told that Theseus stole and raped her when she was but ten years old, and that her brothers rescued her and returned her to her mortal father's home, where she grew even more beautiful, even more bewitching, as she matured.

When it was time for Helen to marry, princes from all over ancient Greece courted her, bringing great gifts to her father. Hoping that Tyndareus would approve, hoping that Helen would admire them, they boasted of their prowess in war and in hunting; they bragged about their deeds and wealth, and about their fame among humankind. Tyndareus received these young aristocrats who would eventually distinguish themselves on the battlefield of Troy: Diomedes, Philoctetes, Idoemeneus, Patroclus, Menestheus, Ajax and his half-brother, Teucer, and others—all of the heroes, in fact, save the one who married Helen—Menelaus—and perhaps the greatest hero of them all, Achilles.

What a lovely time for Eros and Eris; more than enough lust swelled the egos of the suitors; aggression seemed inevitable. The trouble-making comrades moved among the would-be husbands, punching up envy and hate here, fanning the flames of lust there.

This well-stirred brew by Eros and Eris made a dicey situation. Tyndareus saw that it would take very little to set the heroes to fighting each other, and that hell itself would break loose if even one temper overflowed its bounds.

But then Odysseus, who would become Athena's favorite hero, stepped in. Showing the cunning that Athena admired and the cleverness that would forever be associated with his name, Odysseus, although too poor himself to contend for Helen's hand, appeared and joined the throng of suitors. He did not presume to court Helen; instead the ambitious fellow saw an opportunity to improve his own lot, and to get the wife he wanted. Quickly establishing himself as a leader, he then took the role of prudent matchmaker. The diplomatic Odysseus persuaded King Tyndareus to give Helen to the richest of the Greeks, King Menelaus. Although Menelaus had not presented himself in the contest for

Helen, he was represented at the Spartan court by Tyndareus's brother-in-law and Menelaus's brother Agamemnon.

Hear me, Odysseus said to Tyndareus. Odysseus knew that the Spartan king feared the mayhem that the rejected suitors might cause when one was chosen and many rejected; he knew that Tyndareus had been meticulously showing no preference for one prince over another. I will tell you, Odysseus bargained, how to keep peace among the suitors if you will promise to help me marry Penelope, daughter of Icarius. Tyndareus gladly accepted wily Odysseus's offer, gathered the would-be sons-in-law, and, as instructed by Odysseus, made them swear to protect the marriage of Helen to the chosen prince, whomever he might be. To sanctify the pledge, moreover, Tyndareus sacrificed a horse and required the suitors to stand on its bloody parts; then the suitors rejoined the horse's parts and buried the body. This ritual done and peace assured, Helen appeared and held up the crown with which she would wreathe Menelaus in the marriage ceremony.

And so Menelaus married Helen, became king of Sparta, and lived with her in the splendor of his rich palace. There, it was told the world, Helen's beauty increased along with her grace and charm; she was dazzling, spectacular; she was more to be coveted than all of Menelaus's gold and jewels and fine metal objects.

As the gods feted Thetis and Peleus on the slopes of Mount Pelion, purple-robed Helen poured wine for Menelaus; perhaps they smiled across the table at one another and discussed the guests they would receive and the hospitality they would offer. They were rich, and they knew the protocol and sacredness of hospitality. Perhaps they did not see Eros and Eris, uninvited guests, come near, hover, and nod to each other. Perhaps they could not comprehend that their beautiful dream would soon drop into a nightmarish abyss.

But Eris and Eros had joined in crafting and putting in place another piece of the perilous puzzle years before, when Hecuba, wife of King Priam of Troy, was about to give birth to Paris. Although numerous signs and portents appeared to warn that a child born that day in Troy would bring ruin to the city, Priam was unable to kill the newborn babe himself, and commanded the herdsman to destroy the child. But neither could the peasant Agelaus bear to slaughter the child outright, and so left him on the mountainside to die, where a great sow bear found him, suckled him, and kept him warm for five nights and five days. When the herdsman discovered the infant alive and thriving, he took it as a sign from the gods, and took him home and reared him as his own son. To prevent Priam from being suspicious, he slaughtered a dog and presented its tongue as evidence that the baby had been destroyed.

Paris grew into an astonishingly beautiful young man, with an abundance of strength and courage. Although he appeared to be a peasant, Paris soon became the lover of Oenone, nymph and daughter of the river Oeneus. When not enjoying the sensual delights set before him by Eros, Paris gave himself to the bucolic pleasures of hunting and herding with Oenone, or he amused himself and others by pitting bulls against one another. In time Paris became famous as the owner of a particularly fierce bull. One day he challenged all comers, promising to crown with gold any bull that might defeat his own champion. Ares turned himself into a bull and defeated Paris's beast. Even when Paris discovered the god's subterfuge, he honored his promise, and good-naturedly crowned Ares. The gods—who of course had been watching Ares' joke on Paris—were impressed by the young man's impartiality and fair-mindedness, qualities that fit him, they decided, to settle the argument among Hera, Aphrodite, and Athena. He could, they decided, hush the squabble and award the golden apple to the fairest.

And that is how it came to be that Hermes, closely followed by Hera, Aphrodite, and Athena, appeared to Paris on Mount Ida and summoned the handsome young man away from his cattle. Zeus orders you, Aphrodite told him, handing him the golden apple, to judge impartially which of the three goddesses is the fairest.

Paris hesitated. How, he asked, can a peasant herdsman make so great a determination? But Hermes and the three goddesses told Paris firmly that he could not disobey Zeus. He was, they assured him, to use his own intelligence in making the decision and awarding the golden apple.

Again he demurred, asking how a mere mortal could decide among three deities. But the goddesses themselves then assured him that they would abide by his decision and that they expected him to be honest.

And so, one at a time, Paris examined the goddesses. First he drew Hera aside. She turned before him, displaying her admirably proportioned body, her splendid white arms, her graceful posture. And the divine Hera offered Paris a bribe. If he chose her, she promised, she would make him the richest man alive, and lord of a vast dominion.

Then Paris examined Athena. Some say that all the goddesses disrobed for Paris, but most believe Athena removed only her helmet and lay down her shield and spear. Listen to me, Paris, she said rather bluntly and without posturing before the herdsman, choose me and I shall make you the wisest of men, and a great warrior as well.

But Paris thought of himself as a sportsman and lover; he had no interest in being a dull rich man or a great warrior. He kept his thoughts to himself, however, and called Aphrodite to him, and grew flustered as she drew close to him, as she let her warmth brush his body and filled his ears with her soft flattering words. Handsome Paris, she whispered, I am beautiful, am I not? And desirable? She smiled. Choose me, magnificent Paris, and you shall have a wife who is second only to me in appeal and beauty; you shall have a wife who matches you in beauty and grace. Bolstered by Eros, Aphrodite described Helen to Paris, saying that the Spartan queen was fair-haired and had delicate features, and that her beauty was the result of her parentage—noble Zeus in swan form and the lovely Leda.

Why, Aphrodite recalled for Paris, Helen had caused one war while merely a child, and had attracted all of the richest suitors of Greece when she was ready to marry. That marriage, she said, would be of little consequence to Helen once she met Paris. And,

Aphrodite added, she would arrange the meeting and attend to the circumstances to ensure the outcome she promised. She swore solemnly to Paris that she would deliver to him the most beautiful woman in the world.

As Eros and Eris congratulated themselves and rejoiced, Paris made his judgment with no further deliberation, and handed the golden apple to Aphrodite. This, Eros and Eris whispered, was as it should be: a perfectly splendid brawl was in the making!

Hera and Athena, who had hated each other in the past, now joined forces in an ever greater shared hate, plotting punishment of both Paris and Aphrodite. With Eris near them, they immediately broke their promise to abide by the decision and went into seclusion to plot the downfall of Troy, the city that had spawned Paris. No amount of spilled blood would be sufficient to wash away their hate.

Never mind that Troy was also a city with a temple to Athena, a city whose people believed her to be their protector. Athena wanted that city, its citadel, and all of its people destroyed. Nothing else would right the wrong that had been done to her.

Eros and Eris could hardly contain their glee when Aphrodite, a goddess with whom they had true affinity, smiled at Paris and set about keeping her promise to him. What were conventions, mere rules, in the presence of sexual desire?

HELEN AND PARIS

Aphrodite contrived to have Paris reunited with his family in Troy, taken into their fold, decked out as the prince he was by birth, and sent on family business to visit King Menelaus in Sparta. As Eros and Eris applauded her wiles, Aphrodite caused King Menelaus to greet Paris, offer him the hospitality of his household, and then almost immediately leave on a trip to Crete.

The rituals of hospitality in Greece included not only food and drink as lavish as the household could afford, but also baths and sweet oils to restore the traveler's body, entertainment by musicians and bards, and a leisurely exchange of stories and details of genealogy over cups of wine, and all offered and taken in a such a graceful manner as to turn strangers into friends. An excellent host would organize a feast and offer sacrifices to the gods; he would include the guest in petitions for help and in thanksgiving. The guest, having given himself into his host's keeping, would take leave only with his host's permission; and upon leaving the host's house, the guest received valuable gifts—fresh clothing, food and wine to sustain him on the next phase of his journey, weapons, bowls, tripods, perhaps horses.

Stranger and host were measured by each other and by all others who witnessed their behavior: good manners were displayed and rewarded in the guest-host relationship. A graceless guest was as despised as a miserly host, while a charming guest was soon friend in the house of a generous host.

Handsome Paris, abetted by Aphrodite, violated the code of honor that obligated the guest to his host. Behind Menelaus's back, Paris absconded with Helen. And Helen—her husband's property, an ornament to his rich palace—stole riches from the Spartan treasury and took them with her to give to Paris. The disgraceful twosome, their tarnished dowry in the ship's belly, sailed off to take pleasure in each other's arms, spending their first night together on an island visible from the peninsula of Sounion.

When Menelaus learned what had happened, his emotions churned and confused by Eros and Eris equally, he traveled immediately to Agamemnon's citadel in Mycenae, and pleaded with his brother to raise an army and lead it against Troy. That entire city, Menelaus cried out to his brother, must be made to pay for humiliating me and for dishonoring my home. But Agamemnon tried to calm his irate brother, and insisted on first trying to retrieve Helen through diplomatic maneuvers or, that failing, to get restitution for her loss. With Menelaus's reluctant agreement to try peaceable means first, Agamemnon sent an envoy to Priam to ask for Helen's return to her legal husband. But Priam claimed innocence—Paris was, so far as he knew, blameless—and sent the messengers home empty-handed.

Menelaus and Agamemnon, their sense of honor heightened by Eros and Eris, then sent messengers to all of the suitors who had desired Helen but had sworn on the bloody parts of a sacrificed horse to protect her marriage to the prince of her choice. Honor had been offended—the honor not only of Menelaus but of all the men who had taken the oath.

As Menelaus, accompanied by the heroic old cavalryman Nestor of Pylos, went throughout the land and recruited leaders for the expedition against Troy, preparations for the war were also under way on Mount Olympus. There, too, Eros and Eris were about their nasty business; they were mightily pleased to see Athena and Hera not only keeping a blind eye toward their mischief but, on their own, scheming and recruiting other gods to participate in the obliteration of Troy.

*This early sixth century BCE small bronze
figure of Athena Promachos—champion,
defender—is the precursor of the famous
"Bronze Athena" by Phidias, a colossal
statue that rose from its base on the Athenian
Acropolis, and could be seen by
sailors offshore.*

p a r t   f i v e

WARRIOR-GODDESS

ATHENA, WARRIOR-GODDESS OF THE *ILIAD*

Little is known about the great Greek poet Homer, who is credited with the creation of the *Iliad* and *Odyssey,* save that he was a poet of enormous talent. Both works are thought to be based on an oral tradition of stories about heroes and a glorious past. The Hellenes who heard recitations of the epic poems adopted Homer's version of their past as their *history,* with aristocratic families customarily tracing their ancestry to the gods and to the heroes of the Trojan War. Archaeologists—beginning with nineteenth-century amateur scholar Heinrich Schliemann—offer evidence that Troy existed, and that there was a Trojan War; they argue relentlessly, however, about details of the actual war and its relationship to passages in the *Iliad.* But, finally, we must recognize that the *Iliad* and *Odyssey* are works of art—of the imagination—and not works of historiography: we do not study Homer for information about the lives and events of real people in a real place; rather, we read these wonderful poems to explore the human mind and heart, to enjoy fascinating stories.

The *Iliad* does not tell how the war ends, or how Troy is sacked. In the brief time covered by the poem, however, Athena's

role as warrior-goddess is a potent factor in deciding the outcome
of the war, as well as which heroes will survive and which will
gain glory in battle. Again and again, Athena swooped down from
heaven to intervene, to participate, to inspire, and to shape the
outcome of the war. Consistently, and in cahoots with Hera, she
cajoled, sweet-talked, and manipulated Zeus to favor the Greeks
over the Trojans; she bided her time, deceived mortals and
immortals alike; when simple strategy seemed insufficient to get
her way, Athena resorted to trickery and lying. Geared up in splendid armor, driving her chariot, giving her battle cry, she inspired
the heroes, and she herself fought whenever she had the opportunity. From the moment Paris issued his fatal judgment, it had to be
Athena's war. She was bent on vengeance throughout and, con-
fronting the handiwork of Eros and Eris among the gods and on
the battlefield of mortals, Athena savored every drop of spilled
blood and every opportunity she had to send up her terrible bat-
tlecry. In the end, it was still her war; she had her revenge over
gods and men.

Athena had to win. It was a matter of pride to put Aphrodite,
the bitch, in her place. Zeus showed no interest in curtailing
Aphrodite's escapacles; he seemed to enjoy her sexy caprices
among mortals and immortals. But Athena wanted to smack her
into her place, once and for all; Aphrodite should not be allowed
to turn the cosmos into a frenzied rutting pit.

So grimly determined and so passionate was Athena that she
did the unthinkable: she tempered her customary bluntness in
deference to diplomacy, and took Hera as an ally in the struggle
for dominance over Aphrodite. Hera, for her part, despised
Athena even more than she loathed foolish Aphrodite; Athena,
after all, was the beautiful and ever-present evidence of Zeus's
independence and infidelities; she was, Hera thought, a power-
hungry and arrogant creature who thought and acted too much
like a man. Snooty virgin, Hera sniggered, not likely to catch a
man with that wretched spear and shield and helmet. But Hera
needed Athena for the very characteristics she mocked, and for
her influence on Zeus. Very well, a bit of hypocrisy would oil the
machinery of necessity.

Mortals alone could not have brought about the bloodshed; the powerful gods could have intervened to alter the course of events; but the gods set out to cause the war and, far more than mortals, they wanted the Trojan War to serve their own vested interests. Some say Zeus wanted to torture all mankind; some say Aphrodite breathed hot desire into men and let her companions, Eros and Eris, stir it to bloodlust. Some say the gods were merely bored and wanted the spectacle of war. Everyone knows that the gods used the frailties and squabbles of humans as a pretext, that they drew together the strings of cause and knotted them and pulled until the pressure was too great for heroes to withstand. There was nothing to do but go to war. But it was as much a civil war among the gods as it was a test of honor among the mortals, and the heroes were doomed or given glory as the gods disposed.

Athena, who wanted more than revenge on Aphrodite and precious pretty Paris, was much like the heroes she loved; the war gave her opportunities for glory and for plundering the powers and attributes of the other gods. Athena would leave the Trojan plain richer in power, the undisputed warrior-goddess who, in the end, won Zeus to her way of thinking.

And at the end of the Trojan War, after dispensing justice as she saw it to the surviving heroes, Athena turned in a different direction. But that is the story of the *Odyssey,* and it comes later.

ACHILLES, PRINCE OF SULK

Now looking down from vaulted heaven, Hera saw Achilles and Agamemnon squaring off to kill one another over a girl, a concubine. Although she hated Zeus's gray-eyed daughter, Hera put on her best face and called Athena. Please, she said, you know how to handle heroes. Fly down to earth and prevent these two from killing one another.

And so Athena appears first in the *Iliad* to undo the nasty work of Eros and Eris, to prevent a fight-to-the-death between Achilles and Agamemnon over a slave girl, over which hero would own a concubine. Agamemnon, forced to give up his concubine Chryseis, declares that he will take Briseis, slave to Achilles. But

Achilles balks. Briseis, he rages is rightfully his: he captured her after killing her father; why should Agamemnon be allowed to take her away from him? Achilles, swearing to kill Agamemnon, drew his sword.

Just then Athena, grabbed Achilles by his fiery hair, stopped him in his tracks. She could have communicated in a much less dramatic way, could have entered his mind and spoken to him; he knew her voice. But Athena wanted to make her commands very clear, unforgettable to the raging hero. She, let him not forget, was in charge. Her terrible eyes blazed; she held the hero's hair tightly and looked into his handsome face; only he could see her.

Achilles, half god himself, stood his ground and looked into Athena's eyes unafraid; he met her fierce gaze. Why have you come? he demanded. Do you want to see Agamemnon put to death?

But Athena's clear gray eyes burned away the hero's impertinence and gripped his soul; Achilles listened to her words. I have come to check your rage, she told the maddened Achilles; do not kill Agamemnon, but threaten him. Have patience, she counseled, and one day great honor will be laid before you; your justified outrage will be compensated.

Achilles, despite his bitter anger, obeyed Athena; he put down his sword as the goddess returned to join the other immortals on Olympus. Then, turning away from Agamemnon, Achilles raged toward sulk; if Athena would not let him kill the scoundrel Agamemnon, his goddess mother would find a way to help him get the revenge he deserved.

And so Achilles called his mother, Thetis, from the depths of the sea and beseeched her to put his case before Zeus. Why, he asked her, should your son suffer this humiliation, this loss, at the whim of Agamemnon? He reminded Thetis that she had boasted often of having saved Zeus from the other gods, and that the thunder-hurling god of gods owed to her his power and position. Go to him, Achilles begged, and kneel before him and grasp his knees; remind him of all that you have done for him; and ask him to let the Trojans pin the Greeks against their beached ships.

Hearing her son and sorrowing for him, Thetis rose on a crested wave, went to the bronze floor of Zeus's temple, knelt before the thunder thrower, and grasped his knees. Zeus had just led the immortals in a long procession to Olympus, and now sat gazing down on the world. He frankly did not care who won the war, so long as the heroes from both sides were annihilated, so long as he could watch them tearing one another to bits and dying awful deaths in the name of glory.

You rule the world, Thetis told Zeus; let the Trojans take victory after victory until the Achaeans return Briseis to my son. Let Achilles have honor and glory.

Zeus remained silent, unmoved; perhaps he did not hear. Thetis prayed to him, imploring, Bow your head in assent.

Although Zeus had favored the Trojans, Hera's nagging for him to support her precious Greeks had brought dread into his mind. So fate hung suspended in the mists of Zeus's indecision. And already all of the gods were lining up on different sides in the conflict, using the foolish mortals to get even with other gods, or to win some silly point or other. Why did things have to be so complicated; why couldn't the gods watch the war among the mortals; why couldn't they enjoy the spectacle of bloodshed? Why did *gods* have to get involved with *men*?

Zeus, irritated and snappish, spoke sternly to Thetis. You will drive me to war with Hera, he told her, and that would be worse for me than what the mortals do to one another. Hera promotes the Greeks and, already, she chides and abuses me for favoring the Trojans.

But then the tenderness Zeus had once felt for Thetis flooded his heart, and he remembered his gratitude to her. And so Zeus bowed his head as she had prayed he might, and reminded Thetis that he had thereby given his solemn and unbreakable promise that he would see Achilles to revenge and to glory.

Zeus's promise to Thetis complicated things for Athena. Victory for the Greeks would not be as simple as she had planned; she would have to employ strategy, be diplomatic and devious; she would have to fill Zeus's ears and heart with sweet reason.

ACHAEAN HONOR

Achilles, meanwhile, sulked on the shore near his ships. He played music and recited poetry for his friend Patroclus, and steadfastly refused to battle the Trojans. Agamemnon and the other Greeks knew the ancient prophecy as well as Thetis and Achilles did: victory over the Trojans would come to the Greeks only if Achilles fought and won glory. He, then, although the son of an immortal sea nymph, would die a hero's death and be celebrated eternally for his great deeds. He could escape an early death only by leaving the shore of Ilium, returning to his home, living a long and boring life; but then he would drop into dark death and be forgotten.

The Achaeans looked at the mighty Trojan citadel and thought themselves doomed. If Achilles would not fight, they told one another, the war was impossible. Resigned, then dejected, they prepared to take their long ships and sail homeward.

But Hera was not about to let the war end in this stalemate, nor was she willing for the Greeks to tuck tail and run, or to let the Trojans escape the destruction she had in mind for them. Zeus's white-armed consort, seeing the men of Argos about to abdicate, turned again to Athena. Zeus's daughter and wife were joined in one common interest—the total annihilation of the Trojans they hated. Working together they had set the Greeks against the Trojans and, still working together, they were determined that they would use the Achaean mortals to expunge the Trojans from the earth.

When Hera pointed out that the Greeks were preparing to sail home and leave the Trojans alive and well in their rich and fortified city, Athena again flew down to earth. Like Hera, Athena detested all of the emblems of her humiliation—Helen, Paris, and the entire Trojan race. Burning with hate and lusting for revenge, Athena prepared to strengthen the hearts of her chosen warriors.

Her owl eyes lit with pleasure at the thought of the battles to come, Athena found Odysseus among the ships. He, Athena knew, was given to extravagant boasting and lying, but he also possessed the traits she admired most in mortals—cunning and courage. Unlike his comrades, Odysseus preferred to remain and fight; and he, the goddess knew, was a strong and persuasive leader whose nimble tongue served well his sharp mind; he could think better than other men, and he could speak to the souls of men and turn them to his will. Yes, Athena would work through Odysseus, would motivate him to gather his men again to the Achaean cause, and to her cause.

And so Athena moved close to him and spoke into his mind so that only he could hear her. Is this right, Athena's voice asked Odysseus, this fleeing from battle, leaving Helen a trophy in Priam's house, giving glory to the men of Troy? Don't give up, the goddess of war urged Odysseus, but move among the troops. Use your powers to persuade them with winning words to leave their ships beached, and prepare to fight and be heroes.

Odysseus knew Athena's voice. Fired by her words, he ran among the other men and spoke as the goddess had directed; soon Odysseus filled the Greeks with visions of glory and plunder, and persuaded them to stay and fight the Trojans. With Athena as inspiration, Odysseus whipped up the courage of the men. When an insubordinate commoner resisted, Odysseus beat the man; the soldiers laughed and cheered Odysseus. Thrilling to the surge of courage mounting within the Greek army, gray-eyed Athena stood close by Odysseus, giving him inspiration as he marshaled his forces. She caused the men to listen attentively to their leader. And Odysseus spoke cunningly. Yes, he cried out, brave men must stay and fight. What man—what hero—would run away from the hard contest of war, who among the Greeks would relinquish his honor in soft and inglorious retreat? Yes, they must fight; they knew the alternative, he reminded them. Any one of them who lost courage, who tried to escape war, would be killed and left for carrion birds and feral dogs.

Satisfied with Odysseus's good work, Athena watched the armies amass like swarming flies in a barn. She stood near, savoring the preparations for battle. Heralds summoned the armies into formation, battalions gathered; Agamemnon stood at the fore of the long-haired Achaeans. Prepared for battle, their war cries rang across the plains. Athena strode among the ranks like a seasoned

general; her tasseled armor glinted in the sun, her eyes fiery
with the thought of battle, her shield flashed like lightning and
dazzled the troops like the sun itself. Not all of the Greeks saw
their goddess-champion, but all of the men felt her presence and
their hearts filled with fighting fury; there would be no turning
back now, no stopping these fierce warriors. The prospect of
battle excited them as it did Athena; the journey home was forgotten. And so Athena's warriors covered the plain, and their
bronze shields caught the sun and flickered like a forest fire.

But Achilles, on whom the outcome of the war turned,
moped near his ships and made music; his men played in the surf,
and his immortal horses—Poseidon's wedding gift to his father—
peacefully munched parsley and clover from the marshes, as unin-
terested in the rage of Achilles as in their chariots that rested
under tents.

TROJAN HONOR

On the other side of the plain, the Trojans inside their stout walls
gathered near their temple to Athena. They were confident that the
goddess's palladium, the ancient wooden image of Athena that had
fallen from the sky and been given a place of honor in the temple
dedicated to Zeus's powerful daughter, assured them of the warrior-
goddess's protection. They, Athena's people chosen to house the palladium, would be victorious.

So the Trojans assembled before their general, Hector. They
did not know, however, that Athena had turned against them, that
she had left their temple, rejected their offerings, and deafened
her ears to Trojan supplications. Athena, in whom they placed
their trust, plotted a holocaust for the entire Trojan race.

But the brave Trojans, like the invading Achaeans, prepared
for battle; they, too, envisioned victory, rich spoils, and immortal
glory; they, too, knew, however, that many brave warriors would
meet black death and descend into the underworld. And so
Hector's men checked their war gear, buckled on greaves and
breastplates, hefted spears, and waited for their general to lead
them against the long-haired Greeks.

But Hector, a respected and tried warrior of great valor, was also happily married and a new father. He did not thirst for blood, and detested his foolish brother, Paris, for his wanton ways and for setting in motion the war that would destroy many men on both sides. Hector, akin to Athena in his love of strategy, still sought a diplomatic solution and a way to avoid further bloodshed.

Hector went to Paris and saw Helen's pretty husband preening in his soldier garb, watched him throw a leopard skin across his shoulders and a bow across his back. Hector drew near as Paris hung a sword at his hip, hoisted two sharp, bronze-tipped spears, and stood ready for mortal combat. But Hector knew that Paris was more lover than warrior, and knew that the vain sportsman justly feared Agamemnon as a fighter and Menelaus as an outraged husband. Those two men, both Hector and Paris knew, wanted nothing more than to confront Helen's abductor in battle—he whom they regarded as adulterer and outlaw, a violator of the sacred laws of hospitality. They were as fierce, everyone said, as they were lacking in compassion; and their lust for revenge multiplied their wrath, magnified their strength. Everyone knew that Agamemnon and Menelaus had brought many ships and an invading army to Ilium's shores; they had come to hack Paris to pieces, and to strew his body before hungry dogs and carrion birds.

As Paris primped in his warrior finery, his brother Hector sneered at him. Beauty, he called Paris, and a seducer who ruins women. Paris, taunted Hector, you are hardly a man; you are a strutting vain fool, the butt of Achaean jokes; you are only a pretty face on a hollow man; you are a coward.

Thus goaded to grandiose gesture, Paris offered to fight Menelaus; the winner of the duel would get Helen and her riches, and would be a glorious hero. The armies would watch, Paris proposed, and cheer their man on, but not engage in battle; the war would end.

It was the solution Hector sought. The Achaeans accepted the challenge, and both armies exulted in an arrangement that would forestall the agonies of war, the certain pain of further bloodshed, but would ensure honor to the side represented by the victor.

And so Athena watched as mortals attempted to end her war, to blunt her weapon against the Trojans. Not only would Zeus abort the battle, so would these ridiculous mortals. Athena watched Paris and Menelaus square off and draw lots. When Paris was chosen to hurl his spear first, Athena watched the weapon hit Menelaus's shield and saw the point of the spear break. She heard Menelaus pray to Zeus and remind him that he sought revenge for wrongs done him by Paris. When Menelaus hurled his spear, the sharp weapon penetrated Paris's shield and tore his shirt, but inflicted only a slight wound. Paris dodged death.

Athena continued to watch as Menelaus ran forward to attack Paris with his sword, but the weapon shattered. Menelaus cried out to Zeus, accusing the god of interfering. Then the wronged husband and host lunged again at Paris, grabbed the crest of his helmet, stunned him with a blow, and began to drag him off to the slaughter. As Paris's helmet strap cut into his throat, choking and strangling him, Aphrodite flew down to the battlefield, broke the strap, and rescued her favored Paris. Menelaus was left dragging only an empty helmet, storming in anger and frustration as Aphrodite's darling Paris skittered to safety. Athena watched, growing ever more angry and annoyed.

Athena fumed as she watched Paris return to Troy and take Helen to their large carved bed and make love to her, while Agamemnon stood on the battlefield and claimed victory for the Achaeans and demanded the winners' spoils and the surrender of Helen and all her treasure.

Blistering with anger, Athena returned to Olympus. There was thinking to do, and plotting.

ATHENA, LOVER OF WAR

While the war stood still on the Trojan plain, the Olympian gods assembled and considered what to do next. Zeus was now forced to see that the gods had made a mess of mortal affairs: Hera and Athena, on one side, protected and promoted the Achaeans; Aphrodite, on the other, threw her powers behind Paris and the Trojans. Zeus did not want to face the wrath of any of those goddesses, but their continuing conniving and interfering with mortals threatened the unity of his pantheon, threatened his peace. The war between the Greeks and Trojans was becoming a civil war among the gods; Zeus had to put a stop to it or, he realized, lose power.

Despite Aphrodite's intervention to save Paris from Menelaus's murderous wrath, the god of gods proclaimed Menelaus victor in the duel. Then Zeus pondered the situation further: should the grisly war continue or should the gods hand down peace to the opposing armies? But even as the most powerful god considered the situation, Hera and Athena huddled together and schemed to continue the war until Troy was destroyed.

Hera, annoyed that Zeus would even consider peace, confronted him and demanded that he support her in her vendetta against Troy. Order Athena down to the killing ground of the Trojans and Achaeans, she urged, and let her use her cunning to cause the Trojans to break the truce.

Although Zeus had promised Thetis that the Trojans would be empowered to punish the Greeks for Agamemnon's humiliation of Achilles, he was weak before Hera's demands. He bowed his head in assent.

Athena relished the mission and, like a shooting star, plummeted into the midst of the armies. The men on both sides saw the showering sparks of her arrival, and wondered what the sign from heaven meant: war or peace? survival or black death?

Athena, with Zeus's blessing, winged to earth to carry out the cunning business of inciting the war and the eventual triumph of the Greeks. She disguised herself as a soldier, fell in among the Trojans, and approached the archer Pandarus. She removed his good sense and put visions of glory in his mind, making him vain and foolish.

Shoot an arrow at Menelaus, Athena tempted Pandarus, and win the gratitude of the Trojans; be famous, she coaxed, and a hero among all men. Kill Menelaus and send him to his pyre, she urged; bring grief and tears to his comrades.

Foolish Pandarus, his heart fired by Athena's wily words, launched a razor-sharp arrow toward Menelaus.

But Athena, queen of fighters and as duplicitous as she was shrewd, rose invisibly before the target, intercepted the killing arrow with her own hand, and caused it to merely graze Menelaus. She did not want Menelaus killed. So Athena saw to it that the wound was superficial, but that dark blood spewed forth, stained his muscular thighs, and showed the world that the Trojans had broken the truce.

Agamemnon howled in outrage. Summoning help for his wounded brother, the general of the Greek armies swore revenge on the Trojans. They had broken the truce, Agamemnon roared, and Zeus would not tolerate their treachery.

But red-haired Menelaus attempted to calm his brother. See, he said, the wound is superficial and the men should not be alarmed. But Agamemnon's outrage could not be stanched as easily as his brother's wound; he went among the long-haired soldiers, inflaming hatred of the Trojans, spurring them toward war. The Trojans, he commanded, must be beaten, their city razed, their wives and children taken into slavery. Zeus, he proclaimed confidently, would be on the side of the Achaeans, and the Trojans would be left for the vultures. As the soldiers chewed Agamemnon's words among themselves, the general went to the leaders of the armies, and one by one whetted their appetites too for war and for victory.

Athena, pleased with her success, returned to Olympus to watch the Greeks slaughter the Trojans.

GODS AND WAR

But other gods, too, now prepared to exercise their powers in the war. Ares, god of war, knew a good thing when he saw it and he saw killing fields spread between the opposing armies. He cared not a whit for one side over the other, but he hungered for carnage and he was Aphrodite's lover, and so swore to fight with the Trojans.

Athena detested Ares, their shared enthusiasm for war notwithstanding. Ares had no sense of honor or glory; he promoted only cruelty and savagery. Athena, although certainly not above nearly fiendish brutality when it suited her purposes, preferred victory through cunning and strategy. But seeing that Ares had entered the war on the side she wanted destroyed, fiery-eyed Athena summoned Terror, Rout, and Eris to aid the Achaeans; and

Eris, in turn, summoned her favorite colleague Hate onto the battlefield. Unruly and undependable, these immortal energies of war prepared to aid the Greeks—at least for the moment.

Now urged by the gods, the armies clashed shield against shield, and the earth rocked with the roar of battle; the ground streamed blood. The men on both sides threw themselves into the savage work of war. Athena, blazing with power, hurtled through the carnage, encouraged the Argives, inspired slackers, to maul their enemies. At day's end, the warrior-goddess looked with deep satisfaction at the dead from both armies, strewn side by side across the plain of Ilium, their faces hidden in the dust.

ATHENA AND DIOMEDES

But after the dark night a new day came, and Athena renewed her war work and her determination to see the Trojans exterminated. She went to Diomedes, son of Tydeus, and set him ablaze with heroism, his shield and helmet glowing like a great star. She pitted him against the brothers Phegeus and Idaeus, well-trained Trojan soldiers, the sons of a priest of Hephaestus. The goddess of war caused the brothers' spears to miss Diomedes, who then plunged his own spear through Phegeus's chest. Idaeus leaped forward to protect his dead brother's body from mutilation and to fight Diomedes. But, probably on a signal from Athena, Hephaestus swept Idaeus from harm's way.

Athena saw the violent and disgraceful god Ares smelling blood and preparing to step into battle on behalf of the stunned Trojans. Athena set aside her loathing and approached the savage god gently, took his hand, and spoke wise words to him. She flattered him, quietly lauded his reputation as a destroyer of mortals and fortresses, as a god reeking of human blood. She coaxed Ares away from the battle and persuaded him to let Zeus give honor to the side he chose. Let us, she quieted her brutal brother with guileful words, leave matters to the father, and not incite his rage.

Then Athena, certain that she had outsmarted Ares and lured him away from savagery against her heroes, sat beside the river Scamander and watched the Argives and Trojans batter and slash one another. As the goddess watched hero rip hero, she saw the victors of each hand-to-hand battle strip the fallen bodies and pile up booty. It was the custom, both the right and reward of the victor.

Athena also watched with satisfaction as her inspired champion Diomedes whirled about the battlefield, hacking and piercing his enemies. His native strength amplified by her inspiration, Diomedes appeared to be everywhere at once, slashing down and spearing his enemies. When Pandarus, the excellent if easily beguiled Trojan archer, shot Diomedes, the arrow pierced his right shoulder and splattered his armor with blood. Pandarus exulted in his hit and, screaming for his comrades to move in and attack, the Trojan quickly prepared to kill Diomedes.

But Diomedes, knowing that he was favored by Athena and thus protected, ordered a companion to pull the arrow from his shoulder; he rose then to give a heart-stopping war cry and to pray aloud to Athena, so that his comrades and enemies alike would know that he fought with the goddess at his side. He asked the daughter of Zeus to hear him, and to stand by him as she might stand by her own father in the heat and blood of battle. He asked Athena to grant him a favor—to bring Pandarus into range so that he might kill him with a spear. He reminded Athena that the Trojan archer had attacked him when he was off guard, and that now he was boasting that he had killed Diomedes.

Athena heard his prayer, and readily invigorated his limbs and feet, added strength to his fighting hands, and stood near him. Courage, she urged, and fight! She assured Diomedes that she had implanted new courage in his chest, and that she had given him the ability to distinguish a god from a mortal and thus avoid doing battle with a god. Avoid the deathless gods, she told Diomedes, all save one. If Aphrodite should appear, Athena commanded mischievously, Diomedes should stab her with his spear.

Athena, her eyes bright with war excitement, soared away, leaving Diomedes like an angry lion stoked with new strength and courage. Ecstatic with Athena's inspiration, Diomedes charged back to the front lines and attacked the Trojans; he stabbed and hacked his enemies, zestfully ripped life from them and then their armor and weapons from their bodies.

Pandarus recognized the armor and special visor that Diomedes wore, and realized that his arrow had not killed the

Argive hero. In plain view Diomedes now fought like a god. Although Pandarus knew that he was not a god, he recognized Diomedes as a mortal raging with the confidence of one protected by a god. Diomedes had escaped the house of death, Pandarus comprehended, because Athena favored him.

Infuriated that Diomedes should be given such unfair advantage, Pandarus and the royal Aeneas, son of Aphrodite and Anchises, raced their chariots toward Athena's favored hero, intent on hacking him down. As they rushed toward him, Diomedes waved aside comrades' pleas that he give ground, and stood to face battle with the oncoming Trojan charioteers. Fighting strength steady in his chest, he refused to shrink. Athena, he believed, would not let him flinch. And so Diomedes ordered his comrades to prepare to capture the Trojans' strong pure-blooded horses, the best stallions under the light of day.

Pandarus whipped his horses forward, taunted Diomedes for bravado, and flung his spear hard at the son of Tydeus. Diomedes, unhit, shouted back and hurled his bronze-tipped shaft at the Trojan archer. Diomedes' confidence in his goddess was well founded. Athena guided her hero's spear and drove it hard into its target; it split Pandarus's nose, shattered his teeth, smashed his jaw, and cut out his tongue at its root. As the archer fell dead from his chariot, Diomedes and his comrades captured his rearing horses, excellent spoils made available by Athena.

Aeneas, expecting the Argives to drag away the shattered corpse, sprang from his chariot and straddled the body of his fallen friend. But Diomedes lifted a giant boulder—one that men nowadays could not begin to lift—and easily hurled it at Aeneas, striking him and breaking his hip. The Trojan fighter fell in a faint as black as night. He would have been killed on the spot, but Aphrodite stepped in and rescued her wounded son.

APHRODITE, SEX, AND WAR

Aphrodite, born from the hissing sea that rose up around the severed genitals of Uranus, radiated sexual allure and physical lust: she was a gonadal force unsullied by cerebral deterrents. Athena hated her, and considered the goddess of love to be as barbaric as Ares;

both incited the basest instincts in mortals, and both loved the company of Eros and Eris.

Athena, aloof and contemptuous of the goddess of love, watched Aphrodite fly down to the battlefield, cradle her beloved son in her arms, wrap him tenderly in her splendid robe, and flee away with him.

But Athena knew that Diomedes was not to be robbed of his prey; he pursued the goddess and her son. Certain that Aphrodite was a coward—unlike Athena and the other mighty gods who accompanied men into battle—Diomedes recalled Athena's command. He dove through the fighting lines, rushed the goddess of sexual love, lunged at her, and thrust his bronze spear at her wrist. Athena's hero gouged Aphrodite's immortal flesh, releasing the ichor that flows instead of blood through Olympians. It is well known that the gods, who eat no bread and drink no wine, are bloodless and deathless; but it is also known that they can suffer wounds and experience pain.

And so it was with Aphrodite, who cried out in pain and fear and dropped her son. Apollo quickly rescued the wounded Aeneas, while Diomedes, inspired further by Athena, shouted war cries and moved to attack Aphrodite again. Is it not enough, the Argive screamed at the goddess of love, to lure women to their ruin? Must you also lust for the carnage of war? As if speaking for Athena, Diomedes mocked Aphrodite, who whimpered with pain until Zeus heard her and sent a messenger to fetch her home to Olympus.

But Diomedes, even though filled with courage from Athena, was only a foolish mortal, and it was known that men could never win in combat with the gods. And so he turned back and left Aphrodite to the gods.

Athena and Hera mocked Aphrodite's cowardly whimpering. Then they taunted Zeus. Athena sneered: Did Aphrodite, insatiable goddess of love, expect the gods to believe that she had been wounded in battle? Had she not really just been going about her usual sneaky business of rousing men to pant and lust? As for the wound—the silly wound on her silly limp wrist—had Aphrodite not merely pricked herself on a golden pinpoint as she stroked the beautiful gowns of one or more hapless women?

Zeus listened to Athena's mocking, called Aphrodite to his side, and reminded her of her role. War, he told her, was not for her, but for violent Ares and cunning Athena. She, he said, should attend to bringing about lust and longing; she should devote herself to intrigues involving sexual love and marriage.

Zeus, by delimiting Aphrodite's sphere of influence, perhaps inadvertently allotted to Athena a greater role in warfare and, ultimately, in the male world of power and politics.

ATHENA AMONG THE HEROES

Aphrodite was a piffling matter in warfare. But while she was whining and whimpering before Zeus, Athena saw that, in her absence from the fighting, Apollo and Ares had put new courage and lust for war in the Trojans' hearts, and had inspired them onward against the Argives. Athena now looked down on a battlefield deep in carnage. Shouts and war cries roared above the clash of shields and weapons.

As she reflected on the next step in her strategy for achieving Greek victory, Athena listened to the music of war, watched the thrilling drama of men reaching for immortality as heroes. She listened to the warriors shouting: Courage! Take heart! Be men! She watched champions on both sides fall, ripped apart, life torn from them, as the war shouts mingled with death cries. The Trojans, supported by Ares and Apollo, felt close to victory as they rampaged through the Argive lines, killing, collecting booty, and taking prisoners to be sold as slaves.

White-armed Hera also watched; she saw the mauled Argives desperate in the bloody press of the Trojans, and sent a message flying to Athena to come at once. Do something, she begged Athena. Disaster is falling on our heroes. Daughter of mighty Zeus, you who are tireless and fiery-eyed, Hera implored Athena, stop the murderous Ares. Hera reminded Athena that they had promised Menelaus that victory would be his, that he would sack the mighty Trojan walls before he sailed home in his long boats.

Athena had already assessed the damage being done to the Greeks and needed no encouragement from Hera to return to the battle; this time she would do more than move invisibly among the men and inspire them with her immortal words. Now Athena would enter the battle herself; she would be the bravest among the brave, the most glorious among heroes. And so she placed the golden harness on her team and called for the glorious wheels to be brought to her—wheels with eight bronze spokes each, golden fellies, and silver hubs to cover the iron axle. The chariot body was of gold and silver lashings woven tightly into deep curves, with a strong gleaming-silver yoke pole. Queen Hera led Athena's deathless racers forward to be hitched to the glorious chariot. The horses, like Athena, blazed for war and the ringing shouts of battle.

Athena dropped her richly woven robe, a fine pliant garment that she had made with her skillful hands, on Zeus's threshold. She pulled on her battle shirt, buckled her breastplate, and slung her aegis over her shoulder; the terrible shield was tasseled sometimes with gold and sometimes with writhing snakes, the Gorgon's monstrous face leered from the surface, so frightening in aspect, it was said, as to stop whole armies and to strike men dead.

Round the warrior-goddess stood like flickering flames the forces of war: Panic, Hate, Assault, Defense, all panting eagerly to go into battle with Athena, to do her bidding.

The warrior-goddess lifted onto her head her horned and knobbed golden helmet, a massive and crested helmet engraved with figures of fighting men. Then, splendid and terrible to behold in her soldier's gear, Athena stepped into her chariot, hefted her massive spear. And Hera stepped into the chariot beside her, cracked a whip, and Athena's team thundered through the gates of heaven, roared past the Seasons, heaven's gatekeepers. Through the vaulting skies, down from the heights of Olympus, piercing the massing clouds, the bright-hoofed horses forged toward earth, and toward glorious battle on the Trojan plain.

Meanwhile Zeus sat apart and watched, troubled and indecisive, hating all mortals, and deploring the behavior of the gods. Then Hera appeared before him. Are you not incensed, she asked, that Ares goes about his brutal work, killing Achaeans to spite me? Father Zeus, she mewed to her husband and brother god, you know that Ares has no sense of justice. Let me, she wheedled, hurl a stunning blow at Ares. And Zeus, master of storm clouds, consented. Very well, he told his nagging wife, go ahead; send Athena against Ares. She is his match and will defeat him in pain.

And so Hera returned in a flash to Athena's chariot and again lashed the blazing horses of the warrior-goddess, and again the great thundering stallions flew, arching over the wine-dark sea in a single stride, and bringing the immortal Hera and Athena, cloaked in mist, to the shuddering plains of Troy.

As Hera stepped into the fray, shouting shame! disgrace! cowardly Argives!, blazing-eyed Athena slid close to Diomedes and chided him so that only he could hear. So, she said, Diomedes is smaller than his father, and less of a fighter. What a hero your father was! A power, a champion at Thebes, a man of courage who single-handedly defeated hordes. She herself, Athena reminded Diomedes, had stood by his father, had urged him on, had kept courage afire in his breast, and given him immortality as a hero. And you, Diomedes, she said, also know my presence, know that I stand with you and guard you. Here, she said, I will lift your fatigue, pour new energy and strength into your limbs; now, go and fight the Trojans.

ARES

Diomedes knew the voice of Athena, and answered the cunning goddess, the daughter of thunder-throwing Zeus. I am not a coward, he told her, and am not gripped by fear. I have obeyed you, have stabbed Aphrodite as you urged, and have withdrawn from fighting the immortals as you commanded. Now I wait, knowing that Ares himself will charge at me.

Athena's eyes blazed with delight. There is nothing to fear, she told Diomedes, from Ares or any other god. I will fill you with winning spirit, so go now. Charge Ares first, strike him hard at close range. He is a maniac, a lying and cheating god. And so Athena stepped into the chariot with Diomedes, and took the reins and whip.

Like the feral dogs who slavered over corpses on the battlefield as darkness closed the day's fighting, blood-covered Ares was zestfully stripping the dead. Athena made herself invisible, behind the dark armor of Death, so that Ares saw only Diomedes bearing down on him. He dropped the corpse he was plundering, and charged, hurling a bronze spear at Athena's warrior. But Athena grabbed the hurtling spear out of the air and threw it away.

Then Diomedes gave his great war yell, and lunged with his spear: Athena, still invisible, drove it home, deep into Ares' stomach, gouging him and wrenching the spear out of his bowels. Ares shrieked, a thundering bellow as loud as that of ten thousand men crying out in unison, a scream so furious that terror struck the men on both sides.

And a black cloud descended, wrapped Ares, and took him to the throne of Zeus. Oozing ichor, clutching his wound, and pitying himself, Ares stood before his father. Are you not incensed, he asked, to see how gods suffer at the hands of gods? Angry and humiliated, Ares accused Zeus of bringing a senseless and murderous Athena into the world. Why, he demanded, must every other god on Olympus bow down to our father god, each overpowered by the god of thunder and clouds? And why, Ares demanded of Zeus, do you never chide or chasten Athena, never by word or action turn her from her will? Why do you spur her on to devastation? Look, Ares pointed to the plains of Troy, at Diomedes: Athena caused him to stab Aphrodite, to charge me with supernatural strength.

Then Zeus spoke. Be quiet, he told Ares. He glared at the war god. I hate you most of all the gods, he said, you who are lying and double-faced. Yes, Zeus admitted, war and strife filled him with pleasure, and he never tired of the bloody press of battle. But Ares, he said, was driven by rage as incorrigible as that of his mother, Hera. If you were not my child, Zeus said, if you had been born to another god, I would long ago have shut you in Tartarus and let you rot in that dark pit. Then Zeus turned away from Ares, and ordered the healing god to tend his wounds.

Athena and Hera returned to Olympus knowing that they had stopped the brutal Ares and turned the tide of battle in favor of the Argives. Athena knew, too, that Zeus had taken her side against Ares, that the thunder thrower had recognized that she was a greater warrior than Ares, and that barbarity had been checked by intelligence—strategy! cunning! courage! She would have her way, her will would be done.

THE TROJANS APPEAL TO ATHENA

And so Athena watched the battle rage on: helmets split beneath mighty blows and bloodied brains spilled on the earth; blood drenched the soil and covered the warriors. Cowards begged for their lives, but the heroes of both sides laughed at them, hacked them down into dark death, and stripped their bodies. The cheers and war cries of the living drowned out the moans and prayers of the dying.

The Achaeans knew that Athena was everywhere among them, and their strength and resolve swelled with her confidence. Anticipating sweet victory, Agamemnon swore that all Trojans would be killed, that not even unborn baby boys in their mothers' bellies would be spared; and the dead Trojans would not be honored with fitting burials or gravemarkers. Nestor called out to the younger men: do not waste time now in plunder; this is the time to kill!

The Trojans, advised by a seer who read the flights of birds, fell back to a defensive position. Then Hector went inside the citadel and found his mother, Hecuba and spoke to her in earnest tones: Convene the noble women of our city, he told her, in Athena's temple. There, in the goddess's divine precinct, he instructed, enter the most sacred inner chamber and present to Athena the most beautiful robe in the city. Spread it on the knees of the sculpture of Athena, promise her that twelve heifers will be sacrificed to her, and beg her to show mercy to Troy, to save the women and children, to hold Diomedes away from the city.

It was known that Athena defended cities, and that she had long been honored as Troy's special protector. It had been prophesied that Troy could not be taken so long as Athena's palladium stood in her temple. So Hector knew by the presence of the sacred image that the goddess defended Troy and would hear his mother.

After Hecuba watched battle-bloodied Hector leave her, she obeyed his instructions. She chose the largest, most beautiful gown in Troy, a garment richly worked and shimmering as a star. Then she led the noble women of Troy in holy procession to Athena's shrine on the city's Acropolis. The women stretched their arms to Athena and cried to her for help; they prayed to the daughter of mighty Zeus and promised her sacrifices. But the Trojans did not know the truth: the great grim goddess Athena hated all Trojans. She turned away and refused to hear their prayers.

But trusting Hector believed that Athena had heard the women and accepted their offering; he could not imagine that the goddess whose image lived among them would abandon Troy. In his faith, and accompanied by Paris, Hector led the energized Trojans in a fresh onslaught against the Achaeans.

Because Athena hated Troy, she rushed down from Olympus to bring about the defeat of Hector and his men.

ATHENA AND APOLLO; AJAX AND HECTOR

As Hector led the rampaging Trojans, Athena flew onto the battlefield and into conflict with the god Apollo. She knew he was as set on victory for the Trojans as she was for the Greeks. But she also knew that clear-thinking Apollo was a more fitting adversary than bloodthirsty Ares or sluttish Aphrodite. He would not succumb to flattery or be easily beaten in physical contest. No, she thought, overpowering Apollo would require cunning, strategy, and courage.

As Athena flew onto the battlefield, Apollo stopped her beside a great oak tree and, face to face, demanded to know what next? What now did she blaze after? What heroics stirred her to action? She would, Apollo granted, now no doubt turn the tide of battle and give victory to the Achaeans. But, he asked, had she no mercy for mangled and dying Trojans? He pleaded with her: could they not halt the battle for the day, put off until the next day the certain doom of Troy?

Athena's eyes lit at Apollo's implicit recognition of her greater power, and of the certain victory of the Achaeans under her inspiration. She agreed to Apollo's suggestion. But, she asked the Archer, how can the battle be stopped? Apollo laid his plan before her: Let us contrive to persuade the noble Hector to challenge one of the Argives face-to-face in a duel to the death.

Graciously accepting Apollo's deal and promising to effect it immediately, Athena quickly disguised herself as Hector's brother Helenus, and approached Hector, calling him brother. Let me advise you, she said in a voice sweet and familiar to Hector's ears, even though you are a mastermind at war. Hector listened as Athena, executing the plan she and Apollo had hatched, told him to ask for a temporary truce between the armies. When all men, Trojans and Argives alike, are seated, Athena told him, challenge the Achaeans to send their bravest man to duel with you to the death.

Hector rejoiced at the prospect of ending the war and went forth to follow Athena's advice.

As the armies on both sides sat to hear Hector's proposal, Athena and Apollo turned themselves into vultures, settled into the high branches of an oak tree sacred to Zeus, and watched their plan take shape. The gods listened to leaders from both sides make bragging speeches glorifying war until, at last, Great Ajax[*], was chosen to fight Hector and, as was the custom, lots were drawn to see which hero would hurl the first spear.

The immortals disguised as vultures hunched in Zeus's tree and watched Great Ajax's lot leap forth, and heard that soldier pray to Zeus. Let me have victory, he petitioned, but let us have equal glory in battle. Then Ajax buckled on his shining armor, covered his legs and chest in bronze, and walked like a god out to battle. He smiled, and tremors of fear shook his enemies. Giant Ajax, challenger lusting for battle, held his heavy body shield before him easily. He called out to Hector: What kind of heroes are you Trojans? Now, man to man, lead off. Do battle.

Hector shook his head and replied: Ajax, don't toy with me like a woman unsuited for war, or like a runty boy. I know war and butchery, know the drills of battle, know all about fighting. Big and boastful as you are, let us fight. With that, Hector hurled his spear, but it struck Ajax's shield and stopped. Then Ajax hurled his bronze shaft with such force that it penetrated Hector's shield. But

---

[*]There are two Ajaxes—Great Ajax, son of Telemon of Salamis, and half-brother of Teucer, so called because of his gigantic stature; and a smaller warrior, Little Ajax, son of the Locrain king Oileus.

Hector dodged death, and the two men drew their spears from the shields and went for each other with swords. Lunging and thrusting, they battled like hungry lions. Ajax wounded Hector on the neck, but the bleeding Hector continued to battle. He lifted a heavy rock from the ground—some say it weighed a ton—and flung it at Ajax, striking the Achaean's giant shield. Then Ajax hefted an even larger boulder and, swinging around to put his full weight behind it, hurled it straight at Hector. The stone hit the Trojan's shield, buckling his knees and knocking him to the ground, where he lay pinned by his great shield.

As Athena watched, Apollo intervened, pulled his man to his feet, and stepped back.

The two warriors drew swords and again prepared to hack one another to bits. But men from both sides rushed in, put their spears between the dueling heroes, and called the fight off. Night is coming, they said. Yield to darkness now.

And so the heroes parted, each giving the other rich gifts, as was the custom among aristocratic warriors. As Hector and Great Ajax promised to fight again, soldiers from both sides departed to their camps, and the gift of sleep came to them.

ZEUS DECREES

The next morning at dawn, Zeus was fully aware that his two most intelligent children—the most splendid of all the gods—opposed each other over the outcome of the mortals' war. He would not prevent Athena from humiliating Aphrodite or beating down Ares, but he would not allow open conflict to erupt between Apollo and Athena. Zeus summoned all of the gods. From the crown of Mount Olympus he addressed them: Hear, he told them, how powerful I am. Pay attention to my words, and do not dare disobey me. Neither lovely goddess nor god will escape the wrath of lightning and exile to Tartarus if my strict decrees are violated. Remember, the lightning hurler told them, I am the god of gods, with power to bring any of you to punishment. Now, he said, stay away from those battling mortals and let them fight to the end of their fates.

The immortals sat silent before their raging father until clear-eyed Athena rose gracefully, demurely. She spoke quietly to her father, son of Cronus, acknowledging his great power. No one, she told him, can stand against you; you are indeed all powerful. We pity these suffering mortals, these Argive fighters who die in blood, she said. But, yes, she continued in her reasoned tone, we shall obey your command; immortals will keep our distance from the affairs of mortals.

Then Athena spoke to her father again, saying that she desired only to give counsel to the Argives, to advise them on tactics merely. She would not gear up as a warrior again and fight alongside them, she promised. She only wanted to advise her heroes, she said, in order to prevent them from offending Zeus.

Zeus smiled at Athena and addressed her, calling her third-born of the gods, calling her his dear child. Athena, he said, trust me. You have my goodwill.

With that Zeus left the assembled immortals. Athena watched her father god, knowing that he expected her to obey him, to trust him, and to remain aloof from the war. She watched Zeus harness his horses to his chariot, strap on his golden armor, and fly down from heaven to earth. He sat atop a mountain and, looking out over the plains of Troy, he watched the Achaeans and the Trojans take their morning meals and prepare for another day of battle. He watched them march onto the plain, heard their shields clash, heard their death cries. As the sun grew stronger, shadows of spears criss-crossed the blood-soaked earth. Then Zeus held out his golden scales and placed measures of fate and death on either side. When the scales dipped, the Greek fate fell, a bitter prediction for Athena's heroes.

She watched still, as Zeus hurled a thunderbolt at them on the battlefield below. The warrior-goddess saw that the white terror of Zeus's message sent most of the heroes into retreat.

But Diomedes and Nestor refused to honor the sign, and whipped their crested stallions forward, still aiming to conquer Troy. Then Zeus threw another thunderbolt directly at the flashing feet of the powerful horses, and wise Nestor cried out to Diomedes that their fate had been sealed. Victory, he said, cannot be made by mortals; it is a gift from Zeus, and Zeus is handing triumph to Hector. And then Diomedes and Nestor, too, retreated.

The Trojans, fired up by Zeus, pursued the Greeks. Arrows and spears flew from side to side and found flesh, until the earth could absorb no more blood. Warriors stood shield to shield, cried out as they thrust their swords into their enemies. The Achaeans, pinned against their ships on the beach, faced slaughter, as Hector led his soldiers into their midst.

Athena brooded deeply. Despite fate's sign to Zeus, she could not tolerate the thought of a Trojan victory. She needed cunning, strategy, courage. The Achaeans had fate as well as Zeus against them; Athena considered how she might reverse fate and win Zeus to her cause.

HERA AND ATHENA AGAINST ZEUS

Hera, too, had been watching Zeus; she, too, saw the rout, and called to Athena. Look, she said to the daughter of Zeus, look what is happening to the Argives. They are dying under the hacking sword of Hector, that slaughterer.

Athena's eyes blazed in anger. Let Hector die, she answered; let him be destroyed on his own soil by the Argives. Dark-hearted Zeus rages, Athena said, and ignores my wishes. He forgets how I saved his beloved son Heracles, and he shows no thanks.

Zeus hates me, Athena grumbled to Hera, and foolishly honors the word he gave to Thetis to give glory to her son Achilles. But he will call me his darling girl again, Athena said. So now I will have my way.

Athena, throwing aside her promise to Zeus that she would not enter the war again, commanded Hera to harness her splendid racing team. Then, buckling on her fighting gear, Athena prepared to fly down to earth. Now, she boasted to Hera, we'll handle Hector. His body will soon fill the bellies of wild dogs and vultures.

As Athena and Hera thundered through the gates of heaven and through the clouds toward earth, Zeus saw them and knew immediately that they intended to disobey his orders to leave the mortals to their own battles; he knew they aimed to aid the Argives. He flew into a dark rage and sent Iris, the messenger of the gods, to warn them.

As Zeus thundered, Iris raced the wind and intercepted Athena and Hera. Do not battle the father god, she pleaded, for the sake of mere mortals. Let them die or live; it does not matter which survives, which perishes. It is for Zeus to decide the fates of the men of Troy and the men of Argos.

Athena knew wisdom when she heard it and, bowing to Zeus's greater power, she and Hera turned back, their hearts heavy with frustration, and returned to the Olympian hall of the gods. Zeus, shaking thunder with his rage, entered the great room and sat upon his golden throne. But Athena and Hera pouted and turned their faces away from him; they would not sit near him, nor would they speak to him. He mocked them, asking if they were tired from their efforts to save the Argives. You two like war too much, he said. Consider yourselves fortunate that I did not strike you with lightning and remove you, once and for all, from Olympus.

Athena and Hera refused to look at Zeus, but drew closer together and grumbled to each other; they were now more determined than ever to bring about Troy's destruction. Zeus continued to mock and thunder at them until Hera rose before him in anger. Son of Cronus, she said to Zeus, we know your power, and know that you overwhelm all who contest it. Although we pity the Greeks, we'll stay away from them, we'll merely offer them inspiration on tactical matters that may save them from your awful wrath.

Zeus answered Hera, calling her his ox-eyed queen, and telling her that on the next day he would kill still more Argive soldiers. Fate cannot be overturned, Zeus said: Hector will continue fighting until Achilles quits sulking beside his ship and goes forth to battle over the body of Patroclus. That, the god of gods said, is the ancient prophecy and it will come to pass.

Now, Zeus said to Hera, rage on.

On earth, beneath the angry gods, the day ended and the armies parted. Athena, unwilling to accept Zeus's edict, watched a thousand campfires burn on the plains of Troy. Tired men and horses rested; they would fight again at dawn, the Trojans as certain of victory as the Argives were of death and defeat.

GREEK STRATEGY

In the night, Zeus sent panic to roam the Greek camp and to seize the men with grief, to curdle their blood with fear. At dawn after that dark night Agamemnon addressed the mustered troops. Zeus, he told them, is a cruel and treacherous god. He will cut us down if we stay here to fight. I am already doomed by Zeus's will, Agamemnon told his men, but we must take to our ships and flee for home. It is our only chance.

The panic-wearied men dumbly listened. Then Diomedes, Athena's courage still warming his heart, rose to oppose Agamemnon. We Argives are not cowards, he contended; we do not run. And the soldiers shouted their assent, stirred by Diomedes' ringing words. Then wise Nestor rose and proposed that Agamemnon lay a feast before his generals and that they devise a strategy to save themselves.

When the men sat down to the hospitable feast offered them by Agamemnon, they discussed the causes of the war, their losses, the future they faced; they sought a means for survival if not for glory. How, they asked one another, could mortals alter fate; how could they influence the gods, win their favor? At last, fully aware of the ancient prophecy, the Greek heroes decided that Achilles— half man and half god—must be persuaded to enter the war: only he could defeat Hector.

Achilles must have splendid gifts, diplomatic Nestor insisted, and an apology from Agamemnon who kept the girl Briseis, the girl Achilles desired. Agamemnon consented, and told his field marshals that he had behaved insanely, and would apologize to Achilles that very night. He would return the girl and swear that he had never made love to her. He would lay rich gifts before Achilles, and promise him a large share of plunder.

Athena hovered near, knowing that her cause was not yet defeated. The Argive leaders washed their hands and offered libations to the gods, and Odysseus and Great Ajax were chosen as emissaries to Achilles.

And so Odysseus and Ajax, prayers filling their hearts, approached the camp on the shore, and drew near the fire where Achilles played his lyre and sang to his beloved friend Patroclus.

Seeing the emissaries, Achilles rose to greet them warmly, called them dear friends, and offered them hospitality. Achilles placed full wine cups in his friends' hands, and salted and roasted for them the choice cuts of a sheep, a goat, and a pig. They sat together as host and guests, not as adversaries from different sides of a disagreement.

Odysseus toasted Achilles and thanked him for the bountiful feast. Then Odysseus spoke earnestly to Achilles. We are afraid, he said, that we will lose the battle, that we will be slaughtered. All of us will die in defeat unless you enter the fray and defeat the slaughtering Hector. Odysseus begged Achilles not to fail his friends, but to accept Agamemnon's apology and gifts, and to rejoin the Achaean forces. Put away your pride, he implored, and rid yourself of your heart-corrupting anger. Athena and Hera may still be persuaded to help us; we might yet triumph and raze the Trojan citadel.

Achilles responded: Let me be clear, he told Odysseus and Ajax, I hate Agamemnon as I hate the Gate of Death. He will not win me over. We all face the same end: both cowards and heroes go down to death. Why are we battling these Trojans? he asked. For Helen and her deathless beauty, her long and shining hair? Why, he asked, are we risking our lives for the wife of Menelaus? Is he the only one who has loved a woman? No, Achilles said, reminding them that he had loved Briseis and that she had been stolen from him no less than Paris had stolen Helen from Menelaus. No, he continued, he would not fight for Agamemnon and Menelaus. Return to Agamemnon, Achilles ordered, and tell the dog that I will not fight.

Achilles reminded his visitors of the ancient prophecy, of his two fates that his goddess mother, Thetis, had revealed to him. If he fought at Troy, he would be killed but would be remembered as a hero; if he returned to his home, he would not be honored and glorified, but would not be a hero.

Now look, Achilles, told his friends, Zeus has spread protection over Troy. It is a lost cause. Take my advice. Sail for home immediately.

Athena watched Odysseus and Ajax return to camp and lay the disappointing news before the silent Argives. The comrades thought for a long time, and then discussed their situation at length. At last they agreed with Diomedes. Let Achilles sail for home, Athena's favored Diomedes said, but let us unite, and rekindle our courage. Let us attack at dawn. Lead us into battle, he pleaded.

Athena was well pleased with Diomedes, and also with the Greek decision to attack the Trojans at dawn. She watched as her heroes drank wine before they took the gift of sleep.

ATHENA, QUEEN OF PLUNDER

While all the other Achaeans lay in gentle sleep through the night, Agamemnon and Menelaus agonized together over the fate of their men and sought a strategy to save the Greeks from Zeus's cruel hatred of them and their cause. They conferred with Nestor, the wise old cavalryman, and decided to send spies into the Trojan camp. Then Diomedes joined the council and volunteered to undertake the mission; he chose Odysseus to accompany him because, he said, everyone knew that Athena loved and protected Odysseus. Diomedes himself knew from experience the value of the warrior-goddess's beneficence.

Athena had been watching and listening and, as the two men drove forth in their chariot, she sent a sign to them to assure them of her presence: a heron veered close to them in the night and pierced the darkness with its cry. Odysseus, knowing the goddess was nearby, prayed to Athena: hear me, he asked of the deity who always stood by him, and be my comrade. Give me support. Grant us victory and glory.

Then Diomedes, too, prayed to Athena. Hear me, daughter of Zeus and tireless warrior, he said aloud. Be with me, and help me as you helped my father to victory at Thebes. You stood by him, goddess, in the grisly work of war. Stand by me, protect me. I will, he promised Athena, make a sacrifice to you: I'll wrap a young heifer's horns in gold and offer her to you.

Athena heard the prayers of Odysseus and Diomedes, and watched them as they made their way as stealthily as two marauding lions across the battlefield, through the sprawled corpses, piled armor, and pools of blood.

On the other side of the bloodied battlefield the Trojans, too, were awake, kept alert by Hector. His chiefs sat before him in war council, listening to his plan for victory. He, too, proposed to send a spy into the enemy camp to determine the morale and physical condition of the Argives. When Dolon, known equally for the riches of his father and his own fleet-footedness, boasted that he alone was suited to undertake the mission, Hector sent him forth, promising, Glory will be yours and fine rewards as well.

But Odysseus, moving in quietly and swiftly in the shadows with Diomedes, saw Dolon coming. Let him pass us, he told Diomedes, then we'll turn back and take care of him. Diomedes and Odysseus fell face down on the earth, and watched Dolon speed past them. Then the two Argives, cutting off Dolon's means for escape, ran after him like hounds after a hare. True to his boast, speedy Dolon began to pull ahead of his pursuers and might have evaded them, but Athena drew close to Diomedes and poured great strength into him. With that additional energy, the powerful Diomedes gained on Dolon and threw a warning spear to stop him in his tracks.

Dolon's bragging heart failed him before the Achaeans, and he begged them to take him alive, promised to ransom himself for great riches from his father. But Odysseus, full of Athena's cunning, spoke to the prisoner in gentling tones, telling him to have courage. Be at ease, he smoothly urged, and tell us why you are prowling among the ships in the dead of night. Did you come to loot the corpses, or to seek glory for yourself? Or, he asked, are you Hector's spy?

Dolon blathered his innocence, claiming that he had been hoodwinked by Hector who had promised him Achilles' great stallions and chariots in exchange for intelligence about the Greeks' plans and their condition. He told his captors that the Thracian soldiers, among Troy's best, lay sleeping, confident of their safety and of tomorrow's triumph.

Odysseus coolly laughed at the quaking Trojan spy, and pried him with wily words to gush out still more information about Hector's plans. More, Odysseus demanded, more information and more precise details. When Dolon had emptied himself of information, he again begged that his life be spared.

No, Diomedes answered, you are in my hands; and then Diomedes drew his sword and beheaded Dolon. The amputated head, still screaming, rolled across the earth while Diomedes and Odysseus stripped the corpse and pledged the trophies to Athena in gratitude for her assistance.

Here, Odysseus called out to the goddess, rejoice! Queen of plunder, he addressed Athena, these trophies are yours. You are first among the gods. Now, Athena, the Achaean hero prayed, guide us as we take the Thracian camp. And so the goddess of war, who was well pleased with her heroes and by the plunder they promised her, did just that.

First, Odysseus and Diomedes left the trophies offered to Athena on a tamarisk bush; then they made their way once again through the soggy carnage of the battlefield until they spotted the Thracian camp where, as Dolon had said, the soldiers lay sleeping. Athena was with Odysseus and Diomedes, as close as the night air; her immortal heart soaring, she filled Diomedes with bloodlust and superhuman strength. He waded swiftly into the flock of soldiers sleeping in the enemy camp, hacking left and right with his great sword, cutting and slashing the enemy until blood ran across the earth. He stood above his prey, twelve men in all, and hacked them to pieces. Then Odysseus dragged their bodies out of the way, making a path for the horses and chariot they intended to steal.

When Diomedes found the Thracian king, the thirteenth victim, he killed him, too. Meanwhile Odysseus loosed the king's horses from their tethers, hitched them together, and called Diomedes. But Diomedes, exhilarated by his butchery, wanted to kill more Trojans. Athena cleared the mists from his mind, however, and cautioned Diomedes, telling him to forgo the elation of butchery and remember the purpose of his mission. Go back now, she told him. Think only of returning to your ships. Some other god, she cautioned, may wake the Trojans.

Diomedes knew Athena's voice, and he obeyed her command and joined Odysseus in the splendid chariot pulled by the great horses of the Thracian king. And they sped into the night, returning to their camp, victorious and laden with plunder.

Of course, Athena was right. The great archer-god Apollo was prowling the area. Always unfriendly toward the Argives, he was now outraged by their slaughter of the sleeping Trojans. Apollo had been tricked: Athena had guided and strengthened Odysseus and Diomedes in their hideous work while Apollo was guarding the Trojans. Now more furious than ever with Athena, the archer-god raged into the Thracian camp and roused the soldiers. They woke to find comrades gasping and dying, dead and mutilated. Horrified by the bloodbath before them, the remaining Thracians cried out in frustration, grief, and anger.

Meanwhile, Odysseus and Diomedes sped across the dark battlefield toward their camp, stopping only to gather their offering to Athena. Then they raced the shining silver horses into the gathering of comrade warlords. Nestor was the first to greet them. Dazzled by the stolen horses, the old cavalry soldier rejoiced and proclaimed that Zeus must love the two heroes, and that Athena must have looked with blazing eyes on them.

Athena watched as Odysseus and Diomedes waded into the sea, washed the carnage from their bodies, purified themselves with ritual baths in polished tubs, and rubbed themselves with oil. Then, remembering the source of their triumph, the cleansed heroes poured honeyed wine to the great goddess Athena before they restored themselves with food.

ATHENA FAVORS ODYSSEUS

When the battle resumed, the heroes clashed hand to hand and tore one another apart. Corpses littered the field, and blood and gore spattered men, horses, and chariots.

Athena's favored Odysseus, cut off from his comrades, pumped up his courage by reminding himself that a coward in his situation would cut and run, and that he was not such a man. Instead he drove himself back into battle with the knowledge that the man who wants to be a hero must stand and fight, and no matter to a hero that he may suffer wounds or be killed. Athena knew his thoughts and watched Odysseus stand his ground although ringed by Trojans.

As his enemies moved in on Odysseus, Athena's warrior lunged and lunged again at the Trojans, hacking and stabbing and killing. Woe to the charioteer who jumped down from his car to fight Odysseus: Athena's protégé split him from crotch to navel, leaving him gutted, clawing at the earth and dying.

But Odysseus was outnumbered. Trojans moved in from all sides, and one—Socus, famous breaker of horses and son of a noble family—stabbed at Odysseus, cut through his shield and breastplate, and sliced the skin from his ribs. Even though bleeding profusely, Odysseus knew that his end had not come: Athena, he knew, had prevented the sword from piercing his vital organs. With the warrior-goddess as his shield, Odysseus turned on his attacker and addressed him. You poor man, he said, death is about to claim you. You may have stopped me from fighting the Trojans, but your bloody doom is upon you. My spear will gouge you. While I live in glory, you will be death's trophy.

The Trojan turned to run, but Odysseus speared him in the back between the shoulders, driving the spear straight through his chest. Odysseus stood over him. Poor Socus, he said, rampaging death outraced you. Your parents will never close your eyes in death now, but shrieking vultures will claw them out of your head, their wings will beat your corpse.

Then, as another group of Trojans closed in on Odysseus, he called out to his comrades for help; and Menelaus and Ajax raced to his side, killing Trojans left and right on their way. They swept Odysseus, favorite of Athena, into their chariot and took him to camp for attention from a healer.

Athena stood near the Greeks, their bravery whetting her appetite for the glory and gore of war. Yes! They would win. It was her will.

ZEUS FAVORS THE TROJANS

The Trojans still fought under Zeus's protection, and they pushed the Greeks back to the beach. There the Argives dug a huge trench and built ramparts to protect themselves, their ships, and their high-piled plunder; but they neglected in their frenzy to offer sacrifice to the gods to ensure immortal protection of the fast ships and rich booty heaped within them. The gods, thus slighted, let the Trojans move toward victory.

While Trojans stripped gleaming armor from dead Greeks, Hector prepared to breach the fortification on the beach. But a sign flashed before his eyes—a fatal bird-sign. An eagle—everyone knew that it was Zeus's own bird—appeared high on Hector's left and flew in front of him; the wide-winged bird clutched in its talons a huge bloody serpent, writhing but still alive, struggling to bend back and strike the fierce bird on the neck and chest. Stung by the serpent's bites, the eagle hurled the serpent into the midst of Hector's army. Then the great bird shrieked, caught a gust of wind, and veered off. The Trojans—seers and common soldiers alike—understood the portent, and pleaded to Hector to heed the sign from Zeus, to turn back.

But Hector rejected the sign. No, he told his companions, that is not a sign from Zeus. Keep your trust in Zeus and fight for your country. Why, he asked, are you afraid of the butchery of war? Are you cowards?

Then Hector shouted and led his men in another charge against the Greeks. Bloodcurdling war cries clouded the air. And Zeus, from his seat on Mount Ida, responded with a howling gale and a blinding dust storm to pin the Greeks against their ships while the Trojans attacked the trench and fortification, pulled down towers and battlements, and peeled away the Argives' protection. The Trojans wanted nothing more than to rip into the Greek armies and batter them into oblivion.

But Athena's Argives fought valiantly. They propped up the fortifications with their shields and pitched rocks at their attackers. Then from the Trojan side the Lycian prince Sarpedon, son of Zeus and Laodamia, stormed the Greek wall, his handsome beaten shield before him, his mighty sword held high. His comrades followed the godlike warrior. Hector cried out and urged them on. Drive through, he shouted, drive through, my stallion-breaking heroes! Set fire to the Achaean rampart.

Hector was convinced that Zeus, despite the bird sign, was with him and his armies, and that, surely, the great god of gods gave protection and strength to his own fighting son Sarpedon, who, although wounded, did not cry out, but tore at the wall with his hands, opening a way for the Trojans to pour through.

Hector could not know Zeus's mind, however, could not know that even though Zeus loved Sarpedon, he hated the war and he hated the mortals on both sides. When he had allowed Hector's forces through the fortifications and to the Argive ships, Zeus turned away and left both armies to their war. It was, as he had insisted to the Olympians, a matter to be solved between mortals; it was no affair for gods. Zeus was resting on Mount Ida; he was not watching the warring mortals.

HERA HELPS POSEIDON

In withdrawing from the plain of Ilium to rest on Mount Ida, Zeus made a grave error. He believed that the other immortals would stay away from the war, too, as he had commanded them, but Athena was not alone in challenging the thunder thrower's authority. With Zeus's attention diverted from the war, both Hera and Poseidon moved to exert power and capture strength among the gods.

Poseidon, in his usual blustering manner, rose from the sea in a great storm, charged ashore, and, knowing that Zeus preferred the Trojans, sided with the Greeks. The Argives were quick to realize that they had the benefit of the god, gathered their courage, and told each other that Poseidon's presence surely meant further assistance from Athena, driver of armies.

Hera saw Poseidon whipping the Greeks to a frenzy, and heard the roars of the furious battle reverberating against the skies. It was, she knew, a time of crisis for mortals and immortals alike, and a time for her to keep Zeus's attention away from the warring armies. She sat on her golden throne in heaven and looked down on the mounting din of war. The Trojans, believing bloodthirsty Ares to be near them, charged the white-armed goddess's favored Achaeans, attempting to pin them to their ships on the beach. But Hera's heart quickened with hope when she heard Poseidon's powerful voice shake the earth as he exhorted each of the Achaeans to stand firm, to fight to the death.

Fearing that Zeus might stem Poseidon's campaign for the Greeks, Hera looked about surreptitiously for her husband. She saw Zeus resting beside the tranquil springs of Mount Ida, confident that the other immortals were obeying his command to remain aloof from the war between the detestable mortals. Hera was filled with loathing for her husband-brother. How, she wondered, could she outmaneuver Zeus and bring death to the Trojans she hated?

But Hera knew all of Zeus's weaknesses as well as his strengths, and soon hatched a plan. She did not operate like Athena, the warrior-goddess who was able to cajole the thunder thrower with sweet reason or dazzle him with wise strategies that would be the envy of any male, mortal or immortal. Hera used what she considered the best weapon women had against men: sex. Tricking Aphrodite into helping her, Hera made herself as alluring as the goddess of love, went to Zeus, aroused great desire in him, and made love with him on a carpet of flowers.

Then Zeus slept while Poseidon went unchallenged in his fight on the side of the Greeks. When the sounds of the clashing armies woke the cloud gatherer, he looked down and saw his treacherous brother Poseidon working his mischief among mortals. Zeus saw the Trojans in retreat and the heroic Hector lying wounded on the battlefield. He knew in an instant that Hera had tricked him. He turned on her. You, Hera, he growled with a dark look, are treacherous and uncontrollable. You have sown a whirlwind, and you shall reap it. I'll whip you yet. You seduced me and you betrayed me.

Hera shook before her husband's thunder and, lying, swore her innocence. It's all Poseidon's doing, she insisted; he has disobeyed you. He is driven by his great rage against you. He pitied the Argives. Blame him, not me.

But Zeus was not fooled by Hera. And, bound by his promise to Thetis that her sulking son Achilles would have glory, Zeus roared in fury and blazed down to earth to do war with his brother, another deathless son of Cronus.

ZEUS AND THE WILL OF ATHENA

Zeus, still raging, commanded Poseidon to return to the sea, and Apollo to restore Hector to battle fitness. Zeus spoke to the gods and decreed that the war would come to an end according to his dictates. Hector, he proclaimed, would be allowed to whip the Argives once again into retreat. Then Achilles, seeing the sorry state of the Achaeans, would send his lover and friend Patroclus into battle. Attired in Achilles' armor, brave Patroclus would win eternal glory by slaughtering whole battalions of Trojans, Zeus determined. As an appeasement to the other gods, Zeus traded the death of his own son Sarpedon for that of Patroclus, who would be slain by the noble Hector. Then, Zeus told the other gods, Achilles will enter the war to revenge his friend, and he will be allowed to cut Prince Hector down. With Hector's death, said Zeus, the tide of war will be finally turned. The Achaeans will take victory.

He bowed his head; Athena's grand design, he admitted, would be realized. But savage Ares raged against Zeus's decree, and defiantly prepared to enter the battle again. Her cause now protected by Zeus, Athena leaped from her throne, pursued the god of war through the gates of heaven, tore the helmet off his head, and ripped the shield from his back and his spears from his hand. Maniac, she called him. You're crazy. Have you not heard Zeus's will? Are your ears dead? Or can you not recognize the truth? Defy Zeus, Athena threatened Ares, and he will ignore the mortals to turn his wrath on the deathless gods.

Athena stood next to Zeus, unchallenged, and prepared to see the war to the conclusion she desired and her father god now dictated.

GODS AND MORTALS

Now all the gods knew what would happen; and they knew their roles. Obediently the gods directed mortals through the great tragic script prepared for them. Apollo, knowing what awaited Hector, did not flinch from his part in Zeus's plan; he swooped down from heaven like a hawk and roused his favorite hero. Courage, Prince Hector, he said, I am Apollo, come from Zeus to take your side and protect you. I am lord of the golden sword. Rise, Hector, and command your troops. I'll clear the way and you bend the Argives to retreat.

Tricked by Apollo into believing the gods were on his side, Hector quickly assembled his fighters and drove them against the Achaeans. The Greeks, too, saw the will of Zeus behind the revived prince, and trembled in fear. As he had promised, Zeus defended his champion Hector, giving him glory, for soon his life would be cut short.

Athena was preparing Hector's fate even as he shone in battle against the Achaeans and pushed them back to their beached black ships. The warrior-goddess called down upon the battlefield a bright light, and the Greeks could see proud Hector and all his troops ready to slaughter them on the beach beside their ships.

Athena knew that Zeus's will—her will!—moved inexorably among the doomed mortals, and that the war would end with the slaughter of the Trojans and the sacking of their city on the hill. And so, patience adhering wisdom to strategy, she watched.

ACHILLES AND PATROCLUS

As Zeus had decreed, Patroclus, great friend and lover of Achilles, saw the Argives suffer at the hands of the Trojans and begged his beloved, Achilles, to let him go into the battle. Although Achilles' heart throbbed with outrage and dark hate for Agamemnon, he agreed, and said to his dear friend, Here, take my armor. Go fight these wretched Trojans. I pray Father Zeus, Athena, and lord Apollo that not one Trojan will escape his death, not one; and I pray equally that not one Argive will survive either. Only you and I, Patroclus, should walk from the field of slaughter. And we together and alone should bring down Troy's towers—you and I alone!

Then, unknowingly enacting Zeus's will, Patroclus strapped on Achilles' gleaming bronze armor and covered his legs in well-made greaves. He took Achilles' bronze-bladed and silver-hilted sword, and he set the heavy helmet with its horse-hair crest over his strong head. But not even Patroclus could heft Achilles' great spear: only Achilles, among all the Achaeans, could lift and toss the deadly shaft, the same spear that had been given by the gods as a wedding gift to his father.

Achilles' immortal warhorses, Balius and Xanthus, wedding gifts from Poseidon to Peleus and Thetis, were brought forth, yoked together, and hitched to the radiant chariot. Then Achilles, half man and half god, ordered his troops into formation behind Patroclus.

Sending his beloved Patroclus into battle, Achilles then returned to his tent and took a splendid wine cup from the trunk his mother, Thetis, had prepared for him. He purified the vessel, washed his hands, and poured wine into the cup. Standing before his tent, Achilles lifted the cup and poured wine onto the earth, praying to Zeus, confident that the father god's promise to Thetis held good. If you heard my prayer and so punished the Greeks, hear me again, Achilles prayed, and bring to pass my plea. My comrade has gone forth with my troops. Launch them in glory, Zeus, lord of thunder. Fill Patroclus with courage. Let him fight well and win victory. Then, so prayed Achilles, let Patroclus return to me unharmed, protected in all my armor.

Zeus heard Achilles' prayer, and silently granted part and denied part. Patroclus, in accordance with Zeus's plan, fought gloriously and saved the beached Argive ships. His glory around him like a nimbus, Patroclus did the gods' work. Unaware that black death was the price of his glory, Achilles' friend fought everywhere and everyone at once, stabbing and cutting his way through the Trojan ranks. As hero killed hero, Patroclus fought his enemies toe to toe until the earth was littered with amputated limbs and heads, with mangled corpses and streams of blood. Black death engulfed men of both sides, dropped them into the dark underworld, and waited to claim Patroclus.

As Zeus had planned, his son, Sarpedon, fought Patroclus; the two magnificent heroes leaped from their chariots and with battle cries rushed each other. Zeus watched sadly. It is my own cruel fate, he said to Hera, that my beloved Sarpedon, the man I love most, my own son, is doomed to die at Patroclus's hand. My heart breaks. Should I save him? Should I reach down and snatch him from death, send him home to the sweet land of Lycia?

Hera widened her eyes, affronted and incredulous. Powerful Zeus, she said in an innocent wheedling voice, what are you proposing? That a mere mortal, a man with his fate sealed long ago, might be set free? If you interfere in his fate, save him from pain, you will lose the respect of all the other immortal gods. There are many sons of gods slaughtering and being slaughtered around King Priam's city. If you save your son, you will endanger the others. You must let Sarpedon die his own brutal death, according to fate, according to your own decree.

So Hera argued to Zeus. And Zeus bowed his head and sacrificed his son—after all, a mortal—to keep his credibility, his authority, among the gods. He watched Patroclus launch his spear and strike Sarpedon in the heart, and saw his beloved son go down to death on the plains of Troy.

But now death approached Patroclus. Zeus, as he promised, first give him glory in battle, causing even the brave Hector to turn coward and retreat. When Patroclus pursued Hector, cutting down Trojans all the way, and then assaulted the Trojan citadel, even Apollo could not break his determination. Three times Apollo fought the splendid hero back; but when Patroclus attacked again, the archer-god spoke to him. Back, said Apollo, it is not fated, Prince Patroclus, that Troy fall before your spear.

Then Apollo, guided by Zeus, inspired Hector to charge Patroclus with renewed strength. As Hector approached Patroclus, Apollo stripped the armor from Achilles' friend and shattered his weapons. A Trojan speared Patroclus from the rear. But even stripped and defenseless, the wounded Patroclus still turned to fight and, brave-hearted, he staggered toward Hector. The Trojan prince rammed his spearshaft through Patroclus's body, piercing his bowels and breaking through his back, tearing the life from his body.

Hector gloated to the dying Patroclus: The vultures will eat you raw!

Patroclus struggled for breath. Hector, he tried to shout, you have glory and victory now—a gift from Zeus, and from Apollo. They—not you—brought me down. They tore the armor from my back.

As death closed around Patrocolus, he saw plainly the plan of the gods and knew that great royal Achilles, too, would soon die.

ATHENA AMONG HER WARRIORS

Athena, who relished the unfolding fate that would end the war
with the total destruction of the Trojans, watched the gushing blood
and flashing armor of the doomed heroes, and thrilled to the ruck
of war. She watched Menelaus spring forward to protect Patroclus's
body. Challenged by Hector, Menelaus called for help from Great
Ajax. But Apollo put courage in Hector's heart, and the son of
Priam retrieved the splendid armor of the dead Patroclus, strapped
it on himself, and returned, intending to hack the body and toss its
parts to the feral dogs who lurked around the battlefield.

Zeus looked down on the awful bloodbath, saw Hector in
the armor of Achilles. Poor mortal Hector, Zeus thought in his
deep heart, you are unaware of the price you must pay for glory,
for the death that is even now at your side. Hector, you may don
the gear of a great hero, but you have killed that man's gentle,
strong friend; you have violated Patroclus's corpse. Zeus decreed
then that Hector might savor the glory of the moment, but that
he would not return from battle and that his wife, Andromache,
would not receive Achilles' armor as booty.

Then Zeus unleashed bloodthirsty, savage Ares to go among
the Trojans, fill them again with zest for battle and the anticipation
of victory within their reach. Driven by Ares, the Trojans rushed
forth like pounding surf against the Argives, Hector in the lead.
But Ajax, great in build and second only to Achilles in war, stood
before the Trojans to allow his comrades to remove Patroclus's
corpse and deliver his dead body to Achilles.

Then the Greeks regrouped and became the aggressors,
driving the Trojans back to their city walls. Hector's army would
have retreated inside, but Apollo appeared to Aeneas and assured
him that Zeus still protected the Trojans. Aeneas, known for his
piety and his ability to read signs from the gods, shouted the message to Hector. And so the Trojans remained outside their fortifications and continued to fight, still hoping to drag Patroclus's
body inside their city.

Athena gave her war cries first here and then there among
the Greek lines, firing the blood of her heroes and driving them

to attack and attack again. She cut the blinding dust of battle with light to give them advantage; she moved close to powerful Menelaus, urging him to protect the body of Patroclus.

Menelaus heard the goddess and in turn prayed to Athena to give him strength, to lift his grieving heart. Hector, he told the bright-eyed goddess, blazes in terrible fury, his bronze spear stabbing everywhere. Zeus gives him glory.

Athena, thrilled that the hero she admired had prayed to her before all other gods, put new strength in Menelaus's limbs, filled his heart with brash daring; she clouded his mind with the desire to spill warm human blood. Backed by Athena, Menelaus stood over Patroclus and fought to save the body from the attacking Trojans.

But Zeus still allowed Apollo to protect Hector, and to lead him into day of glory before he was sent down to the House of Death.

Fate, known by the gods and hidden from mortals, unwound inexorably, twisting and knotting its way through the hearts and minds of heroes on both sides, weaving mortal and immortal beings into the fabric Zeus had mapped. Doomed Achilles, hearing of the death of his beloved Patroclus, gave his heart into black grief. His loud cries reached Thetis, the immortal sea nymph, deep within the salt green depths, and she left the silver shimmering cave of her father and went to her wailing son. Thetis stepped onto the shore beside the long black boats and found Achilles. My child, she asked him, why are you crying?

Achilles answered his immortal mother. Patroclus—my beloved, the man I loved more than I love myself—I've lost him. Hector has killed him. I must fight Hector, batter him down with my spear until he gasps out his life; he must pay the blood price for Patroclus.

Thetis knew that Achilles' doom was then upon him, and spoke to him through her tears, repeating the old prophecy. Oh my son, she said, hard on the heels of Hector's death your death must come.

With Patroclus dead, Achilles put aside his spite and anger toward Agamemnon. Since he could not save Patroclus from death, he told Thetis, he would avenge his death and, in so doing, would help the Greeks destroy Troy. Thetis accepted her son's decision, even applauded his bravery. Then she went to Olympus to engage Hephaestus, the lame blacksmith, to make new armor for Achilles.

Zeus, without waiting for Achilles to get his new armor, sent Iris to tell him to show himself to the exhausted Greeks, to let them know that he was entering the war and would turn the tide in their favor. But, Achilles protested, how could he present himself as a warrior? His magnificent armor had been stolen from the body of his dearest friend.

Then Athena, never far from her beloved Greeks, swept in, slung a tasseled shield over Achilles' shoulder, crowned his head with a golden cloud, and surrounded him with blazing light. She lifted Achilles up, and as the Trojans saw him, Athena gave her unearthly war cry, driving panic deep into the hearts of Hector's men.

Achilles then echoed Athena's war cry, screamed his own famous call to war three times, and each time the Trojans dropped back in fear, giving the Greeks opportunity to seize Patroclus's body and drag it away from the fray.

And Hera caused the sun to set, bringing blackness to the battlefield.

ATHENA AGAINST THE TROJANS

But Athena's work was not done for the day. She moved invisibly among Hector's disheartened troops and heard them talk of retreat, and of their longing to retreat to their fortified city. To prevent her enemies from taking refuge in their impenetrable citadel, and to keep them vulnerable to Greek attack, Athena moved close to Hector and poured false hope for victory into his mind so that he rejected the suggestions of his captains to retreat. Then Athena moved among Hector's men, loosened them from their senses, drove away their cowardice, and fired them up to assault again the Argives and their beached ships. She made them crazy for war, and caused them to go forth to meet the doom the gods had planned for them.

As Athena maneuvered the Trojans toward black death, Achilles received Patroclus's corpse, washed it and closed the wounds, and laid the body on its bier; then, with his men, Achilles mourned the death of Patroclus all night long. Thetis stood by as her heroic son prepared to meet his relentless fate. She watched him put on the wonderful armor made by Hephaestus, and promised to protect the body of Patroclus, to keep the carrion flies from invading his wounds, to stay the ravages of putrefaction.

But Odysseus, Athena's great tactician, stepped in. Let us not go to war now, he said. Rather, feed the men and see that they are rested. Only then, when the men are properly prepared, and when they are not caught between gods still clashing on opposite sides, will victory come to the Greeks.

And so the Achaeans sacrificed to the gods, and Agamemnon handed the girl Briseis over to Achilles and swore that he had never laid a hand on her, never forced her to slake his lust, never taken her into his bed. Then Achilles prayed to Zeus: You deal out terrible blinding frenzies to men. If not for you, my fury would never have been roused against Agamemnon—that undying rage that consumed me. The girl Briseis would not have been taken from me. But Zeus decreed the death of Greeks, and the slaughter came to pass. Now, let us feast; then let us go to war!

While the men feasted, Achilles, still mourning for his companion, refused to eat. Zeus heard Achilles proclaim his love for Patroclus and, taking pity on the doomed hero, called Athena forward and spoke to her: Have you abandoned Achilles forever? Is he not your favorite man of war? Is there no more feeling in your heart for this hero? Go to him. He refuses to eat. Put the strength of the gods' food, nectar and ambrosia, deep within him, and stave off his starvation.

Athena was already prepared for action, she told Zeus, and swooped down from the sky shrieking like a sharp-winged hawk. As the men were buckling on their armor and preparing to battle the Trojans again, Athena went among them, filling their hearts with the joy of battle. Then she pressed the gods' food deep into Achilles, and with that gave him the strength he needed for the battle he faced and for his fateful role in bringing about her will.

As the troops moved into position, Athena flew back to Zeus's throne. Below her, on Ilium's plain, the blaze of shining armor lit the skies, and the whole earth shook under the trampling feet of massing armies.

GODS AND MORTALS AT WAR

Achilles ground his teeth, his eyes flashing and rage burning within him; he donned his battle gear and lifted the lance that only he could handle. Then one of his great immortal horses, given voice by Hera, spoke to him: You have been sentenced by a great god and the strong force of fate. Patroclus was killed by Apollo, who handed Hector the glory of the slaughter. We are the strongest, swiftest horses on earth. But we cannot save you, Achilles. You are doomed to die, cut down by a god and mortal man.

And Achilles answered, Why prophesy my doom? You waste your breath. I know well that I am destined to die, but I will never stop till I drive the Trojans to their bloody end.

And so the furious Achilles shrieked his high war cry and lashed his stallions forward. He was hungry not for food but for war.

And the gods, too, were hungry for war. Mortals fought to avenge wrongs—the sacred laws of hospitality had been violated, a man's property, his wife, had been taken from him. But gods fought for the power of attribute and identity, for status in the hierarchy of deities, for everlasting power in the universe.

As the mortals prepared for the fateful clash, Zeus assembled all the immortals, from the most humble nymph and nature spirit to the most exalted who lived on Olympus, and told them that he feared that Achilles, bent on revenging his friend's death, might be such an indomitable hero that he could twist fate, that he might go against the ancient prophecies and single-handedly raze the walls of Troy. The immortals, as Zeus knew all too well, had been meddling in the war between the Greeks and the Trojans from its inception. Now, however, he blessed their participation and told them to go fight. Choose your sides, he said, and spur these mortals to even greater bloodshed.

Zeus knew that gods split between the two forces, with Athena, Hera, Poseidon, Hermes, and Hephaestus rushing to help the Greeks, and with Ares, Apollo, Artemis, and Aphrodite to aid the Trojans. During the time the gods had been on Olympus and aloof from the fighting, the Greeks had gained glory. Now, fully intending to seal their victory, the great Achilles blazed across the fields, slaughtering Trojans at every step.

With Zeus's blessing fresh in her ears, Athena stood on the edge of the trench the Greeks had dug to protect their ships, and she bellowed her war cry across the plains and against the cliffs. Ares, from across the lines, answered with his war cry. Poseidon shook the earth mightily, and Zeus threw down thunderbolts. And so both armies were roused to new passion for war as the world reeled and shook beneath their feet, and as the gods used men in their civil war for immortal power.

But it was no longer a war merely among mortals, no longer a war in which the gods used humans as puppets. Now the gods openly fought one another. Apollo launched arrows at Poseidon; Artemis fought Hera; and Athena fought the god she hated most, Ares. When the dust settled and the blood sank into the Trojan plain, the gods would reckon their victories as carefully as the Greeks would hoard their plunder. Athena intended to be the victor among gods and mortals.

Even as god went against god, the red barbarity of war consumed both sides of mortals. Achilles sought Hector, yearning to glut the earth with his warm blood, and roared through the Argive lines urging his men to fight. But Apollo appeared to Hector, stood by his side, and counseled him not to fight Achilles in front of his lines. Rather, he urged, withdraw to your massed army and pull Achilles toward you.

Achilles ripped his way toward Hector, stabbing and hacking the Trojans who stood in his way. When Polydorus—Hector's youngest brother who had been forbidden by their father to fight—appeared on the edge of the battle, Achilles swirled on him and pierced him straight through with a spear. The boy fell to the earth, trying to hold his bowels in his body, screamed with pain, hunched and died.

Hector held back no longer, but pushed forward to meet Achilles. Here comes the man who has most hurt my heart, Achilles exulted, the man who killed my cherished Patroclus. There can be no more dodging each other now.

He taunted Hector. Come. Rush me. The sooner you come, the sooner you meet your death.

Hector replied, You can't frighten me with words, Achilles. I know you're brave, and far stronger than I. True. But we both know that the outcome of our battle lies in the laps of the gods. With that, Hector drew back his spear and hurled it toward Achilles. But Athena stepped forward and blew it back, and it fell at the feet of tall Prince Hector.

Achilles raged and charged, eager to cut Hector to death. But Apollo snatched Priam's son from death, wrapped him in mist, and made him invisible.

Apollo may save you now, dog Hector, shouted Achilles, but I'll finish you next time. Now I will kill anyone I can touch. And so Achilles whirled into battle, stabbing a Trojan warrior in the neck; ripping the life from another with his great sword. He pulled a charioteer from his car, crashed him onto the ground, and stood over him and butchered him. When a young Trojan nobleman fell at his knees and pleaded with Achilles for his life, the swift runner answered by cutting out his liver. Achilles was like fire, inhuman and unstoppable, spreading his hot rage across the earth. He sped across the battlefield, grinding the dead beneath the wheels of his chariot, his mighty stallions' hoofs splashing blood. And so Achilles fought, spilling gore upon the earth, causing the river to foam with human blood, and sent Trojan heroes down to the house of death.

Both Poseidon and Athena stood by Achilles, urging him on, even making themselves visible to him. Poseidon spoke to him, saying: Have courage, Achilles! Have no fear. Athena and I are with you—gods-in-arms. We bring Zeus's blessing. It is not your fate to be killed here and now.

ATHENA FIGHTS ARES AND APHRODITE

Zeus watched the gods fighting for their heroes, fighting one another, and laughed to himself. They were as feckless as mortals. He saw Ares charge Athena, and rail at her: Flea! What are you doing, driving the gods to fight to satisfy the cravings of your barbarous heart? You helped a mortal wound me once before, he shouted at the goddess, and now I shall pay you back for that outrage!

Ares stabbed at Athena's shield, but to no avail. Not even Zeus's thunderbolts could break that snake-tasseled guard. Athena stepped back and lifted a great boulder from the earth, a wicked black and jagged rock weighing a ton or more, a stone that had been set in the earth long ago by a race of gigantic men who marked off plowland with such boulders. Athena hefted the stone easily and hurled it with great strength and precision. It struck Ares' neck and knocked him senseless. The savage war god fell to the earth, sprawled over seven acres; his hair sank into the dust and his armor crashed around him.

Athena laughed loudly. Look at you, she taunted, big fool! You never can match my strength. I am greater than you by far. Your own mother, Hera, laughs at you now, groveling as you are in the dust. You, who ran to help the Trojans against your mother's will!

Aphrodite ran forward to lift and comfort her lover Ares. Athena smiled, her owl eyes blazing, and walked serenely away. But Hera was not content. Look at them! she winged words at Athena. You are the daughter of Zeus whose shield is thunder and storm; you are tireless, Athena, and have great wisdom. Are you going to let Aphrodite get by with this? She'll set Ares—that man killer—on another rampage unless you stop her. After her, Athena!

Athena needed little encouragement from Hera, for she had no use for Aphrodite or Ares. Her heart filled with the joy of battle, and she charged after Aphrodite, caught her, whirled her about and beat the love goddesses breasts with her fists. Aphrodite, no match for Athena, fell to the earth with Ares. Athena stood over them and the reckless ways they represented, trumpeting her victory: Down! And may all the gods who favor the Trojans fall. May they all have the same hollow courage of Aphrodite and Ares, the same puny fury against my power!

Hera smiled, and listened happily to Athena's boasting.

So it is told that the red barbarity of war engulfed mortals and immortals alike, and the Trojans retreated in disorder.

DOOMED TROY

That night the dog star Orion, a fatal sign, hung over Troy. Hector's distraught father, Priam, tore his hair in grief for the sons and daughters he had lost, and wailed in the face of doom. Even the tame dogs I have fed at my table, he told Prince Hector, will eat me raw, will lap my blood. The death of an old man, the dogs' mutilation of his genitals, this, moaned Priam, is the saddest sight in the wretched lives of mortals. And Hector and Priam wept together, knowing that death was near and unavoidable.

But it is better, Hector told his father, to go out and face one's fate than to take shelter and cringe like a girl.

Zeus looked down on Hector and Achilles, his heart torn for the Trojan prince. Hector had been faithful and reverent, had sacrificed many oxen in Zeus's honor. And now the great god saw the dashing Achilles closing on Hector and Priam's city. Knowing what fate held for the noble Hector, reconsidering his decree, Zeus spoke aloud: I must decide now. Either I save Hector or, here and now, plunge him into death at Achilles' hands.

Athena overheard her father, and came close to him and looked at him with wide gray eyes. Father, she said in soft tones, you are lord of thunder and lightning. You are king of clouds. What is this vacillation over a mere mortal? Hector's doom has been sealed. If you set him free from fate, from the pains of death, you will lose your power over all of the gods. They will mock you and disobey you.

Zeus heard Athena's words and understood; he responded to his wise daughter. Athena, third-born of all the gods, my dear child. I am not serious. Go down to earth and do your will. You need no longer hold back.

Athena, confident that she would prevent Zeus from interceding, was already poised for action; she swept down from Olympus, her war spirit launched by Father Zeus.

She saw Achilles hound Hector, as the two circled the walls of Troy, each shouting war cries and threats, each looking for the opportune moment to strike the other down. Zeus looked down, and took up his scales with the two fates of death, and saw that Hector's fate dropped down to death. Knowing the sign and accepting the ancient prophecy, Apollo abandoned Hector.

This was the moment Athena had awaited; she rushed to Achilles, her eyes shining, and stood beside his shoulder. My brilliant swift runner, Achilles, she said to the Greek hero, Father Zeus loves you, and will grant you great glory. We'll kill this Hector. He may be mad for battle, but he cannot escape his death now. Not even Apollo will protect him against his fate. You, Achilles, she said, must now hold your ground, catch your breath, muster your forces and courage. I will go to Hector and trick him into fighting you face to face.

Achilles gladly obeyed Athena.

ATHENA TRICKS THE TROJANS

Then Athena again tricked the Trojans, mortals who worshiped her, who kept a temple sacred to her, who sacrificed and prayed to her, and who honored her image, the palladium that fell from heaven. But Athena had long ago abandoned the Trojans. Now she disguised herself as Deiphobus, son of Priam and Hecuba, brother of Hector, and approached the Trojan prince.

Hector, dear brother, she said in Deiphobus's familiar voice, let us stand together, shoulder to shoulder, and fight this Achilles. No more chasing round and round the citadel. Let's beat him back!

Hector's helmet flashed in the sun as he turned to face Deiphobus. I honor you for coming to my side, while others stay inside the city gates and cleave to safety.

Our dear father and mother sent me, Hector, the treacherous warrior-goddess answered in the voice of Deiphobus. Comrades begged me to stay in safety, true, but my heart filled with grief for you. Now, let us fight headlong. Spare no weapon. Achilles will have to kill us both and drag our bloody armor back to the Greek ships, or we together will send him down to dark death.

Thus lured by the cunning Athena, Hector stood his ground, called out to Achilles, and taunted him. Come on, Achilles. I am not running in fear from you. Three times I let you chase me round the city, but no more! Now it is kill or be killed! Come and swear to the gods this pact: the survivor will not mutilate the one who dies in this battle. I promise to give your body to your comrades, undamaged. Promise, Achilles, that you will do the same.

But Achilles answered with a dark look and fierce words. Unforgivable Hector, don't talk about pacts! There can be no binding oaths between men and beasts. And there can be no pact between us. We will hate each other to the death. You'll pay now for killing Patroclus!

With that, Achilles hurled his spear. Hector ducked, but did not see Athena retrieve the spear and pass it quickly back to Achilles. You missed, taunted Hector. So much for your bluffing. And now I shall kill you with my long spear! So Hector hurled and the shadow of his spear flew across the earth as the point struck Achilles' shield dead center, glanced off, and fell to the earth. Hector fumed at his wasted shot, and shouted to Deiphobus for help. But Deiphobus was nowhere near him, was not to be seen at all, and Hector knew the awful truth: My time has come, he thought, and Athena has tricked me. The gods are calling me down to death. Grim death looms beside me. I cannot escape now. This was the gods' pleasure, my fate sealed long ago. Well, then, let me die, but not without struggle and not without glory! Men in years to come will hear of my death!

With that resolve, Hector drew his sharp sword and, like a high-wheeling eagle, swooped toward Achilles. The Achaean had drawn his sword, too, and also charged against the man who had killed Patroclus, and who wore the armor—Achilles' great armor—that he had looted from the body. The gleaming bronze armor seemed to encase all of Hector; only one spot lay exposed. And so Achilles drove his spear into the soft flesh where the neck rises from the collarbone, and Hector fell to the ground.

Achilles spoke to the dying prince: You thought when you stole Patroclus's armor that you would be safe! You failed to fear me, you fool! I have smashed you, Hector, and sent you down to the house of death. The dogs and birds will maul your corpse, will shame you while we Achaeans bury my beloved friend in glory!

But Hector used his last breath to beg Achilles to return his body to his parents: Don't let the dogs devour me, he implored, but give my body to the men and women of Troy so they can honor me with the rites of fire.

Achilles stared grimly at Hector. I only wish, he said, that my rage could now drive me to hack you to bits and eat you raw. No, Prince Hector, there will be no returning your body, not even for ransom. Blood and bone, you belong now to the dogs, Achilles said to Hector as the Trojan warrior's soul went winging to the house of death.

As blackness fell on Hector's eyes, Achilles pulled his spear from the corpse, retrieved his famous armor, and shouted for mortals and immortals to hear: Hector, for your death I will gladly now face my own!

But Achilles had not had his fill of atrocity. Promising his troops that the pleasures of rape, pillage, and victory over Troy would soon be theirs, the doomed warrior strung thongs through holes he punched in the ankle tendons of Hector's corpse, and attached the body to his chariot, the head of the valiant Trojan dragging in the dust, and whipped his horses to breakneck speed. Circling Troy, defiling Hector's corpse, Achilles howled in rage and triumph, as the mother and father of slain Hector watched and wept.

FUNERAL RITES AND GAMES

As the Trojans grieved the loss of Hector, the Greeks withdrew to the beach to honor the memory of Patroclus. Chanting sorrow, their tears drenching the beach, the Achaeans gathered great timbers for a bier, and Achilles prepared to offer sacrifices to the gods and to set a proper funeral feast before his men. Achilles cut the throats of twelve captured Trojans and sacrificed them on Patroclus's bier, and also sacrificed many pale oxen, sheep, goats, and swine.

He gathered blood from the victims to pour on the funeral fire, and cut his own hair and tossed it onto the body of his friend.

Athena stood nearby as Achilles was visited by the ghost of Patroclus, as the two friends swore eternal loyalty, and as Achilles lit the pyre. The doomed son of Thetis poured generous libations of wine on the pyre, and all night long the funeral fires burned, and he kept watch and lamented.

Then Achilles ordered the Greeks to compete in funeral games for great prizes, and to honor Patroclus. Athena, who loved games as she loved war, helped her favorite warrior-athletes. She filled Diomedes' horses with speed and stamina so that they might claim the prize for chariot racing. As Odysseus and Little Ajax ran toward the finish line in the footraces, Athena remembered Ajax's arrogance and his insulting ways before the gods. She had never liked him anyway. Deftly Athena put out her foot and tripped Ajax as he raced and sent him sprawling in cattle dung. He called out, Foul! The goddess fouled my finish! She favors Odysseus as always, he whined.

Then rising from the dung, Little Ajax continued his tirade against Athena. She is like his mother, always helping Odysseus, always pushing his rivals down into the dust! But the Achaeans roared with laughter, adding injury to the already soiled pride of the braggart warrior.

Athena watched with satisfaction as the games continued and rich prizes were given to the winners.

But twelve days after Hector's death, the Olympians determined that the body should be returned to Priam. Zeus called Thetis to him, and Athena invited the sea nymph to sit on her throne while she listened to the father god's words.

I will grant Achilles glory, Zeus told Thetis, and so claim your loyalty and love for me for all the future. But you must go now to Achilles and tell him that the gods are angry with him. Tell him that I am sending Iris to Priam and commanding him to ransom his dear son Hector. Tell Achilles that he is to dissolve his rage and accept Priam's gifts. He is to return Hector's body to Priam.

Thetis returned to earth and recounted Zeus's command to Achilles. So be it, responded the swift runner. Priam will bring a ransom and will take away the body if that is the will of Olympian Zeus.

Priam also received Zeus's message, and took gifts to Achilles, who received him courteously. The two men made peace with one another, and Achilles promised to hold back the assaulting Greeks until Priam's people could provide a regal funeral for their prince.

Thus the *Iliad* ended as the Trojans buried Hector, warrior and horseman, Priam's son who died in glory. But Athena had yet to achieve her goal—the complete destruction of Troy.

Throughout the *Iliad,* Athena shows herself to be a fierce and bloodthirsty warrior, an easy companion to the heroes she admired and supported; she demonstrates her wiliness, cunning, and trickery—as well as her wisdom and resolution—in her association with her favored Greeks, as well as in her treatment of the Trojans she hates; and she nudges and reasons with Zeus, sulks and speaks to him in soft words, until she turns him from his preference for the Trojans. Athena, sharply defined as a warrior-goddess by the Trojan War, ascended to a more prominent position among the gods as a result of the Olympians near-civil war that raged as a parallel to the mortal combat on earth.

*Athena, a favorite subject of Athenian vase painters, is depicted
typically with helmet, snake-tasselled aegis, shield, and is often
accompanied by her owls.*

part six

ATHENA'S WILL IS DONE

DEATH AND GLORY

At the end of Homer's great epic, the way was clear for Athena's heroes to punish Troy. Zeus's promise to Thetis was resolved; Achilles, having won great glory, was fated to die a hero's death and to be remembered eternally for his splendid bravery. Although Zeus had initially favored the Trojans, and had held Hector in high esteem, in the end he was persuaded to bow his head to Athena's goal: Troy was doomed to annihilation. But, perhaps more to the point, Zeus cared only vaguely what happened to mortals, while Athena desired that mortal affairs be resolved in accordance with her will. Zeus did care, however, about his position as overlord of the gods, and he wanted peace among the Olympians. While he commanded all the immortals to work in unison to bring about the sequence of events he decreed, he allowed them to fight among mortals and thus against each other in a contest for power among themselves.

So, while the earth and rivers of the Trojan plain choked on the spilled blood and flesh of the heroes, Athena concentrated on the outcome she willed—the complete destruction of Troy and its people. The gray-eyed goddess had successfully coaxed and manipulated Zeus, had flattered and fought the other Olympians, and had exploited, tricked, and spent human beings to get her way. Now the fate that awaited Troy would also assure Athena of a second-only-to-Zeus authority among the other gods and among mortals. She would have vengeance.

Knowing then that her power was unassailable, Athena turned her attention to the utter degradation and destruction of Troy. As the war ended, Athena's bloodlust was tempered by neither pity nor remorse; she directed her cunning strategies to enabling her beloved Greeks to sack and plunder the citadel of Hector and Priam, a pleasure that motivated them across the butchering field of Ilium. For herself, Athena looked forward to the exquisite pleasure of rewarding and punishing the heroes according to her preferences, to ridding herself and the world of those who had displeased her, and of letting all mortals and immortals know that she lifted up, blessed, those who had pleased her.

Athena watched Achilles drive the Trojans against the wall of their city, and waited for the gods to send him down to dark death. She saw Apollo, obedient to Zeus's will, confront Achilles and order him to retreat and let fate unfold in accordance with the will of the gods. When Achilles refused to submit to the god's demand, it is told that Apollo himself shot him in the heel with an arrow, thus striking Thetis's son's one vulnerable spot and killing him. Achilles' fate was realized: he had been given a short life and great glory as a hero rather than a long, mundane existence among ordinary men, and his glory was all the more celebrated because godlike Achilles was killed not by another mortal but by a god.

The Trojans closed in on the dead Achilles to mutilate the corpse and strip it of its glorious armor, but Athena's favored warriors, Great Ajax and Odysseus, stood over the remains and fought with the same fervor that had marked the protection of Patroclus's corpse. Only a blinding storm from Zeus ended the battle that day, and allowed the two Greek warriors to return the body of their comrade to camp.

Thetis and the Muses called for a funeral celebration; and Athena anointed the body of the beautiful slain hero with ambrosia to preserve it from decay. After a period of mourning and games to honor Achilles, his body was burned on a pyre. His ashes, mixed with those of Patroclus as both friends had wished, were secured in the wedding gift from Dionysus to Thetis—a marvelous golden urn made by Hephaestus.

ATHENA PUNISHES GREAT AJAX

Although Thetis had known that Achilles would die on Troy's fields, she grieved for her lost son and, after the funeral, declared that she would give Achilles' armor to the most courageous and best of the Greek warriors. She left the selection of the champion to Agamemnon. But only Odysseus and Great Ajax—both of whom had fought bravely throughout the war and had defended Achilles' body against plunder and mutilation—stepped forward and claimed the prize.

Once companions in arms, Great Ajax and Odysseus now competed for the same treasure. Each man boasted of his prowess in battle, and each claimed to have inflicted the greater injury to the Trojans. It is said that Agamemnon went among the Trojan prisoners and asked who of the Greek soldiers they most feared. Whether from spite or sincerity, they answered Odysseus, and Agamemnon duly handed Achilles' armor to the Ithacan prince.

Great Ajax was offended. He had brought twelve ships to the siege of Troy, and had fought fearlessly for the Greek cause and his own glory. From behind his thick oxhide and bronze shield, he had struck down countless Trojans and had engaged Hector in a series of ferocious battles. He considered himself a far superior warrior to Odysseus, a man he thought boastful and untruthful. But, it should be remembered, Athena loved Odysseus and Great Ajax had offended the goddess of war.

It was a well-known story. As Great Ajax set sail for the campaign against Troy, his father, Telamon, counseled him to use his spear well, but always to seek the help of the gods. Arrogantly, Great Ajax sneered: Any coward can win if the gods help. In further flout he tore the picture of Athena from his shield.

But at the time he was denied the armor of Achilles, Great Ajax was not thinking about his earlier impudence; rather, he was outraged that he had been denied what he considered rightful honor and booty. He was so infuriated by the decision that he planned to right what he considered a wrong, to punish Odysseus and his companions that night. Athena, however, hovered nearby and read his thoughts; she stepped in, struck Great Ajax mad, and turned the maniac loose among the sheep and cattle that had been rustled from Troy, and corralled as food for the Greeks. Great Ajax swung and thrust his sword, killing great numbers of the dumb beasts. Athena stood watching the maddened Achaean hero in his tent, surrounded by blood and fragments of slaughtered animals. Even after the terrible butchery of war on the Trojan plain, the scene was awful—a hero absolutely disgraced by uncontrolled violence, totally degraded by insane violation of dumb innocents. This was not the savagery and butchery of war, which were necessary in the defense of honor and the pursuit of glory; this was a mortal debased by bloodletting against the blameless, a hero defiled by madness. Athena had seen Great Ajax rise to heights of immortal glory; now she used his uncontrolled jealousy and hate to hurl him into dark punishment, to turn his ferocity from bravery to evidence that he was more base than the animals he murdered.

When Athena saw Odysseus approach Great Ajax's tent, she knew that Odysseus had been stalking the depraved warrior, and she spoke to Odysseus, saying: I have always known you to hunt and destroy your enemies. And so like a hound you have followed Ajax. What is your grievance with Ajax? Tell me. I am on your side, Odysseus.

Odysseus recognized the goddess's voice and answered: Athena, your voice is the dearest of all the gods to me. Although I cannot see you, I know you are speaking to me. I am stalking a man I hate, the shield-bearing Great Ajax. He has done a hideous thing, and it was intended for his comrades. He has murdered our livestock. Athena, you have come, as always, when I need you. You shall be my guide. Tell me what to do.

And so Athena invited Odysseus to draw closer to Great Ajax's tent. Yes, she said, this is the man who thought he was murdering you when he cut the throats of the livestock. And Athena told Odysseus that she had seen Great Ajax preparing his revenge, had stepped close to him and clouded his mind with madness, to prevent him from moving stealthily upon his comrades. I filled him with obsessions, Athena explained, and set him in the mingled droves of livestock. There he hewed and hacked, thinking he was killing Greeks. His diseased delusions suffused his mind, but I drove and pressed him into the fatal net of madness.

Now, Athena urged Odysseus, look upon the maddened Great Ajax. Why do you shy away from the sight? What are you afraid of? she asked. Do you not want to laugh at your enemy? Are you afraid of facing a madman?

With that, Athena summoned Great Ajax from his tent, to mock him and to demonstrate the extent of his delusion to Odysseus. Is this, the goddess inquired of the stricken warrior, how you treat an old comrade?

Great Ajax responded by flicking the bloodied whip he carried and hailing Athena, daughter of Zeus. Welcome, Athena, he said jovially. You have stood by me and now I shall make great golden sacrifices to you in thanksgiving for allowing me to destroy my enemies. Then Great Ajax told Athena: I have killed many Greeks, and lying Odysseus is a captive in my tent. He will be tortured before he dies; he will be bound to a pole and beaten until his back is crimson with blood. Do not try to dissuade me of this, goddess, but stand by me in this endeavor as you have in the past.

So you see, Odysseus, Athena said with near-fiendish delight, how great is the power of a god. But Odysseus expressed sympathy for Great Ajax, only to be hushed impatiently by Athena. Consider him an example, Athena instructed Odysseus, and do not vaunt yourself up before the gods, nor be vain and falsely proud because of your wealth or strength. Mortals swing in the balance of one short day, and may sink or rise as the gods decree. But know, Odysseus, that the gods honor men of reason and probity.

Then Athena lifted the madness from Great Ajax and revealed to him what he had done. Showing no compassion, the vengeful goddess flooded Great Ajax's mind with unbearable guilt and shame. He fell upon the ground and prayed to call forth the Furies, the Eryines, to persecute his enemies; then he went to the seashore to purify himself before he planted the sword given to him by Hector in the ground. With all the force of his giant body, Great Ajax fell upon the sword, committing suicide. It is said that hyacinths sprang from the earth where his blood splattered.

Athena used Great Ajax to demonstrate the folly of mortal pride and arrogance, and to show that human beings are allowed to claim separation from—superiority to—other creatures only through the grace of the gods. Madness and savagery await the mortal who lacks piety. War, madness, and savagery on the one side and piety and . . . what? . . . on the other: Athena, wise goddess, has yet to explore the equation.

ATHENA AND THE PALLADIUM

With Great Ajax punished for his insolence, Athena again looked upon the waning war between the Trojans and Argives. Now the goddess would savor the conclusion she desired for the war. Now she would stand beside the Achaeans as they utterly destroyed Troy, that well-built city with its sacred temple of Athena. The goddess did not need to remind the Greeks that the palladium—the ancient image of Athena that had fallen from the sky—would have to be removed from her temple inside the city walls before the city could be taken. It was known by all that so long as the image of Athena stood in her temple, Troy was protected.

Athena sent Odysseus and Diomedes, two of her favorite heroes, to steal the palladium. The two men crept by night into the city, killed the sentries on duty, removed the sculpture from its plinth, seized the sacred image from its sanctuary, and set out across the plain with Diomedes carrying it. But Odysseus wanted all of the credit for the rescue of the sacred image, and fell behind Diomedes. When the low-hanging full moon cast Odysseus's shadow, however, Diomedes saw his companion drawing his sword and moving toward him. Diomedes whirled and confronted Odysseus, then forced him to walk ahead of him on the remainder of the trip.

So, with the help of the goddess herself, the image of Athena left Troy; nothing could now prevent the Greeks from taking the city.

THE WOODEN HORSE

But Odysseus was incorrigible, it would turn out, and claim credit, too, for the building of the wooden horse used to defeat Troy. In fact, however, it was Athena's idea, and she chose others to carry out her strategy for entering Troy. First she selected Pyrlis, a son of Hermes, to put the idea forth; then when Parnassus, a skilled carpenter, volunteered to build the horse, she gave him added strength to carry out the task.

And so he worked to build the enormous hollow horse. He placed a trap door in one flank, and consecrated the fir-plank horse to Athena with the words, "In thankful anticipation of a safe return to their homes, the Greeks dedicate this offering to the Goddess."

Odysseus took command of the expedition and selected the bravest of the heroes to climb into the horse. In addition to Odysseus, the horse soon held Menelaus, Diomedes, Acmas, Thoas, Sthenelus, and Neoptolemus—all fully armed.

With Athena nearby, Odysseus then instructed Agamemnon to lead the remaining Greeks in a mock withdrawal. They burned their camp, boarded their ships, and put out to sea. The Trojan sentinels saw the departure of the ships, but did not see them go into hiding on the far side of offshore islands. Quietly, the Greeks awaited a signal to return and to destroy Troy.

The next morning the Trojans sent scouts to the Greek camp. Yes, they reported, the Greeks had withdrawn, leaving ashes where they had once camped. But they had left a huge horse on the seashore, a mysterious wooden construction dedicated to Athena. The Trojans, puzzled by the horse, argued about its significance. Some wanted to burn it immediately, believing that any relic of the Greeks would bring injury to the Trojans. But others—Priam among them—argued that the horse was dedicated to Athena and therefore sacred.

Cassandra, gifted with prophecy but under a curse that no one would ever believe her, warned that the belly of the horse contained armed men. Still, Priam and his supporters insisted that the horse be pulled inside the walls of Troy.

Athena had prepared the Greeks well, however, and they had left behind a fake escaped fugitive, Sinon, who now appeared and allowed himself to be captured by the Trojans. When questioned by the Trojans, Sinon explained that he had been persecuted by Odysseus, and left on shore as a sacrifice to ensure good winds for the departing fleet. Sinon vehemently expressed hatred for Odysseus, and for all of the Greeks who had wronged him.

Priam believed Sinon, and asked him about the wooden horse: What is its significance? Why did the Greeks leave it upon the shore? What has it to do with the goddess Athena? Sinon was well prepared for the interrogation. He explained that the Greeks had lost Athena's support when Odysseus and Diomedes stole the palladium from her Trojan temple.

The ancient image of the goddess, Sinon told his Trojan captors, surrounded itself by flames three times to show the goddess's fury at the Greeks. Following that sign, Sinon continued, the seer Calchas persuaded Agamemnon to sail for home and leave the horse as a gift to Athena, a token of the Greeks' sorrow for offending the goddess.

But why, asked Priam, did they build such a large horse? Sinon repeated the answer he had been coached to give: It is large to prevent you Trojans from confiscating it and taking it into your city. Calchas has prophesied that it would give you power to gather new armies and strength and to invade and conquer Greece.

Although several Trojans—including the priest Laocoon— tried to dissuade Priam from taking the horse, the Trojan king was determined that it should be moved inside the city's walls. He ordered the walls breached and the horse taken into the citadel.

Inside the horse, meanwhile, the Greeks were terrified that they might be discovered. Odysseus silently signaled to the men to remain quiet, to control their fear, and to wait for the right moment to spring free from the horse. But when Helen strolled by the horse, caressed its flanks, and spoke in the voice of each man's wife in turn, Odysseus struggled to keep order among his heroes.

While the Greeks crouched in fear with the enormous wooden horse, the Trojans rested peacefully in their beds, too deeply asleep to realize that Helen held a bright torch in her chamber window, indicating her location to the watching Greeks.

Moreover, at the darkest moment of the night, Sinon stole from the Trojan citadel and lit a beacon fire on the tomb of Achilles. Agamemnon, waiting for the signals from Troy, responded by lighting a fire in a metal dish on board his ship.

Then, as Odysseus commanded his men to move from the horse, Agamemnon led the Greek fleet back to the Trojan beach.

MENELAUS RETRIEVES HELEN

As the heroes tumbled from the wooden horse, some ran to open gates and others to slaughter sentries; but Menelaus ran toward the house of Deiphobus, who, after the death of his brother Paris, had married Helen.

The Greeks poured through the streets of Troy, crashed into houses, and slit the throats of Trojans as they lay in their beds. Priam, Hecuba, and their daughters clung to one another beneath a laurel tree at Zeus's altar. Hecuba held Priam back from the fighting, telling him that he was too old and weak to defend his city. Then their son Polites ran toward them and, as they watched, was overtaken and slain by the Greek Neoptolemeus.

Priam quickly threw his spear at Neoptolemeus, but missed. The Greek warrior grabbed the old man and butchered him on the steps of the altar, mixing the blood of father and son on the sacred ground, a sacrilege for which Zeus later punished Neoptolemeus.

Meanwhile, Menelaus and Odysseus raced toward Deiphobus's house, intent upon killing him and Helen. Fighting their way with Athena's help, they broke into the chamber where Deiphobus stood ready to fight them. Some say that Helen emerged from the shadows where she had been hiding and plunged a dagger into Deiphobus. But, however Deiphobus met his end, Menelaus immediately thereafter turned his attention to Helen, shouting to Odysseus that she must die. Helen, it is said, stood unafraid and proud before Menelaus and dropped her robe to expose her beautiful breasts, and that her wronged husband went weak in the knees at the sight of her divine splendor, threw away his sword, and embraced her.

THE HOLOCAUST OF TROY

Cassandra had taken refuge at Athena's temple and clung to the new image that had been put on the plinth to replace the stolen palladium. Little Ajax found her there and tried to pull her away from the image, but she clung tightly to its feet, praying to Athena. Little Ajax knocked over the image of Athena and, while the image fixed its eyes on the heavens, the Greek warrior raped Cassandra, Athena's priestess.

The seer Calchas soon warned Agamemnon that Athena had been offended and that she required placating for the violation of her priestess in her temple. Odysseus urged his companions to join him in stoning Little Ajax to death, but the wily warrior took sanctuary at Athena's altar himself and swore his innocence.

Athena's wrath should not have been ignored.

But the Greeks were fully occupied with the holocaust they inflicted on the Trojans. When the city had been thoroughly destroyed—and the Greek heroes were sated with rape, slaughter, and pillage, the victor's rewards—they razed the great walls of Priam's citadel and burned the dead. When the Greeks realized that Hector's infant son Astyanax still lived and that it had been prophesied that he would avenge his parents and his city if allowed to live, Odysseus grabbed the infant by the foot and hurled him against rocks to spill his brains and kill him.

The Greeks divided the women among them: Agamemnon took Cassandra; Odysseus received Hecuba, but it is said that she cursed him and the Greeks so savagely that they put her to death, and that she became a frightening black bitch fated to roam restlessly throughout eternity.

Their bloody victory accomplished, the Greeks prepared to sail home. Menelaus ordered ships to prepare to cast off at once in order to take advantage of a fine breeze. No, insisted Agamemnon, we must first sacrifice to Athena and give the goddess our thanks for our victory. But Menelaus scoffed at the idea. Athena, he said, had let the Trojans win far too many battles and she protected the citadel when she should have let it fall to the Greeks. Athena, of course, was with them although invisible, and heard Menelaus brandish his ingratitude.

PEACE AND PUNISHMENT

As the Greeks prepared to sail away from the Trojan shore, Athena and Poseidon stood on a clearing before the still-smoldering city of Priam and Hector. They had helped the Greeks kill all the Trojan men, take the women into slavery and concubinage, and either kill or take the children into slavery. Poseidon looked at the ruins and praised Athena for the wooden horse, a device of war that will be remembered and lauded forever. But he also said to Athena: Look at the blood-spattered altar where Priam was murdered. And look at the Achaeans loading their spoils into their ships. Pallas Athena, he said, child of Zeus, you willed this ruin to Troy, these riches and glory to the Greeks.

Great divinity, Athena addressed Poseidon, you are my closest kin save for my father, Zeus. We have quarreled in the past, it is true, but let us make peace now.

Poseidon agreed, assuring Athena that the bonds of kinship among the gods were stronger than tricks of magic and enchantment. What, he asked, could he do to serve Athena's wishes?

The goddess looked with her bright eyes at her uncle, god of the seas. Let us give favor to Troy now.

But, Poseidon objected, it was you, Athena, who hated the Trojans most, who worked most assiduously to bring them to this devastation and utter ruin.

True enough, the goddess responded, but I hate the Achaeans more now. They show me no gratitude, and they ignore the rituals of sacrifice. They are filled with pride, and believe that they won victory and spoils with their own strength and cunning. They must be brought down from their pride, must be returned to fear and respect for the gods.

Athena, Poseidon answered, this is a stunning change in your sympathies. Why, he asked, must you hate so hard, love so hard?

They, said Athena, pointing to the Achaeans swarming around their ships, defiled my temple and insulted me. Ajax violated Cassandra in my temple, in the presence of my image; and the Achaeans did nothing to punish him.

A true outrage, Poseidon agreed, for Troy was taken by your strength alone, Athena. I am ready to do what you ask. What evil shall we do the Greeks?

And so Athena laid out her plan. When the Greeks sail for home, she said, Zeus has agreed to batter them with rain and storm, to shove them about with roaring winds that threatened their long boats. And he has given me the use of his thunderbolt so that I may dash and threaten with fire the Greek ships. But yours is a special domain, Poseidon, and I ask you to make the sea thunder, to raise the waves higher than men have seen them before, to spin the vessels round on swirling pools, to strike fear into the hearts of the Greeks.

Poseidon agreed to help Athena. The mortal who goes to war, who sacks cities and who does not honor the sacred places, the hallowed sanctuaries, is a fool. His turn will come.

And so as Athena and Poseidon plotted, Agamemnon, Diomedes, and Nestor turned away from Menelaus and gave thanks to the goddess of war; then they sailed home safely, protected all the way by Zeus, Poseidon, and Athena. But Menelaus, with Helen beside him, set sail immediately, making no offerings or sacrifices to Athena, pouring no libations on the earth in her name, not even uttering a single word of thanksgiving for her help. And Athena, as she had told Poseidon she would, sent a great storm to destroy all but five of the vessels in his fleet, to drive him first to Crete and then to Egypt, and to keep him away from his home for eight more years.

ATHENA AND LITTLE AJAX

Athena's wrath took a particularly sharp edge when it fell on Little Ajax. With Poseidon's help she tortured him at sea, tossed his ships on wicked waves and before bawling winds until all were destroyed. Little Ajax swam to refuge on a great rock, climbed upon it, and smirked: he had survived the wrath of the gods he told himself. But Athena lifted the thunderbolt she had borrowed from Zeus, threw it at Little Ajax and split the rock to which he clung; she stirred the seas with Poseidon's help, and drowned the strutting little warrior who had violated her temple and her priestess.

But she had not spent her rage against Little Ajax, and so blanketed her wrath over his family and country, over the land of Optunian Locris. Plagues took the people into sickness and death; crops failed; and animals and people alike were barren. Sick, starving, and suffering miserably, the Locrains sought advice from the Delphic Oracle. The Pythoness told the cursed Locrains that they would have no relief from their agony unless they sent two young girls to Troy every year for a thousand years. The girls, to be chosen by lot, must be taken ashore in the dark of night, and must be conveyed stealthily to the sanctuary of Athena. If caught, the girls would be stoned to death by the Trojans. If, however, they reached Athena's precinct, they would be safe. As the goddess's servants, they would have their hair cut; they would wear the rags of slaves; and they would live as servants in Athena's temple. It is told that after many years, and many pairs of young girls given to Athena's temple in Troy, the Locrains decided that they had fulfilled the conditions of their penance, and stopped sending maidens to Athena. But the pestilence, famine, and agonies returned to the Locrains, and they quickly resumed the annual gift of two maidens to Athena's temple in Troy.

*Athena (center) helped Perseus decapitate the Gorgon. She holds
the hideous head, indicating that it can be viewed by mortals
only in a reflection. To enable Perseus to decapitate Medusa,
Athena gave the hero a mirror, and guided his hand.*

part seven

ATHENA AND THE ODYSSEY

ATHENA, ZEUS, AND ODYSSEUS

After the Trojan War ended and all the heroes save Odysseus had met their fate and been accounted for, the immortal gods met in assembly. Only Poseidon was absent; he had gone to Ethiopia to accept a sacrifice. From his throne Zeus addressed the immortals: It is regrettable that men should blame the gods for their troubles, he said. They get what they deserve; their own transgressions drag them into suffering. Look at Aegisthus. He stole Agamemnon's wife, then he and that faithless wife, Clytemnestra, murdered Agamemnon when he returned home. Aegisthus knew the result would be his own disaster. We gods sent Hermes to warn him that Agamemnon's son Orestes was duty bound to avenge his father's death. And so Aegisthus has met his end at Orestes' hand.

Flashing-eyed Athena, sensing that Zeus was prepared to preach at length on the nastiness and stupidity of the mortals he hated, interrupted her father and rose to speak: My father, she said respectfully, mightiest of the gods, son of Cronus, it is true that Aegisthus met his deserved end. But my heart is wrung for Odysseus. He has been away from his family too long, and he pines on a lonely island in the middle of the sea. It is a beautiful island, well wooded, the home of the goddess Calypso*. She, too, is beautiful, and every day she offers new pleasures to Odysseus, seeking always to banish Ithaca from his memory. She uses soft persuasive words, and offers the hero gifts and eternal life if he will marry her. But Odysseus desires only to see the smoke rising from his own hearth. He grows despondent, weeps beside the sea, and yearns for death.

Athena continued: Why is your Olympian heart unmoved by the suffering of Odysseus, Father? He is not like other mortals. Have you forgotten the sacrifices he has made to you to win your favor? Why are you [and the goddess of war made a pun] so at *odds* with *Odysseus*?

In putting Odysseus's cause before the Olympians, pleading for him before Zeus, Athena assumed that there is an unwritten agreement—a covenant—between gods and mortals, and that the gods are beholden to protect those who show respect and piety, for those are worthy. And, Athena argued, Odysseus is worthy of the gods' protection.

Zeus responded kindly to his daughter: Nonsense. I haven't forgotten Odysseus, one of the wisest and most admirable men alive, and most generous in his offerings to the gods who live here in Olympus. No, it is not I who cause him trouble, but Poseidon, the shaker of the earth, who hates him. But, Zeus mused aloud, if all the rest of the gods are against Poseidon in his campaign against Odysseus, he will relent. He cannot sustain his grudge against all of us!

Athena, in anticipation of again having her father side with her, looked upon the great Zeus with her bright eyes. King of the gods, she said, if it is now the desire of the gods to return Odysseus to Ithaca, send Hermes, messenger and giant-killer, to tell Calypso that Odysseus must be set on his way home.

---

*Sometimes identified as a goddess, sometimes as a nymph, Calypso was the daughter of the Titan Atlas.

Athena continued: Now I will go myself to Ithaca and put courage in Odysseus's son. He must stand up to the suitors who pursue his mother, disreputable men who squander his inheritance, who slaughter his sheep and cattle. I shall have him speak his mind to them, and then I shall send him to Sparta and to Pylos to seek news of his father from Menelaus and Nestor.

ATHENA VISITS TELEMACHUS

Athena took her sword with its sharpened bronze point, then put her untarnishable gold sandals on her feet and flew with the speed of the wind over water and unending land. The daughter of Zeus, dauntless warrior and second in power only to her father, flew down to Odysseus's house. At the threshold to his courtyard, she disguised herself and appeared as the family friend Mentor, but with Athena's bronze spear in hand.

The goddess embarked on this mission with the same zeal that had characterized her pursuit of Hellenic victory on the Trojan plain, and began her transition from goddess of war to goddess of wisdom. She knew everything that either deity or mortal could know about war; and she flaunted before both gods and humans her delight in the savagery and heroism of the battlefield. But perhaps she was satisfied with the vengeance against the Trojans that she had engineered; or perhaps, having disposed of her enemies, she envisioned a new—and peaceful—organization for human life. Perhaps Odysseus—proven hero with characteristics much like her own—provided the mortal means for effecting her new goal for the species she had helped create.

Athena, the best of all gods and mortals in strategy, pondered the work before her; she took the measure of the suitors in front of Odysseus's house. A sorry sight they were, too. Some of the idlers lolled about on the skins of oxen they had slaughtered for their continual feasting, joking, gambling; they drank the wine and water mixed by their servants. Others roasted enormous slabs of meat in preparation for another evening of banqueting in Odysseus's house and at the expense of his son's inheritance.

Near the dissolute suitors, Athena saw Telemachus, a godlike youth, and entered his mind to know his dreams for the return of Odysseus and the banishment of the suitors from his vaulted house. Telemachus looked up, caught sight of Athena, and went immediately to greet the disguised goddess. The well-brought-up Telemachus had been instructed in the sacred law of hospitality: a stranger is a guest and must not be left unwelcomed or without food, drink, and companionship.

Friend, Telemachus called out, welcome. When you have eaten, you can tell us how you came here. And he led Athena into the great banqueting hall, took her spear and put it against a sturdy pillar, and seated her in a beautifully carved chair with a comfortable stool for her feet.

As Telemachus sat before his guest and provided food, the swaggering suitors came into the banqueting hall for their evening carouse. Disguised Athena watched the boisterous assembly. Then Telemachus bent his head close to hers and spoke quietly: Friend, I must say something. It is easy for that gang to indulge in music and songs. They are sponging off another man—my father whose bleached bones rot in some unknown land. If he appeared here in Ithaca, those louts would pray for speed in their legs rather than gold and fancy clothes! But I see no hope. I fear that my father will never return.

Athena sat quietly, and Telemachus, the considerate host, shifted his mood and spoke again to her: But tell me about yourself? Where do you come from, and who are your parents? You cannot have come on foot, so you must have sailed in a vessel? Why are you in Ithaca? Is this your first visit here? Or have you come in the past, a friend to my father, and been entertained before in this house?

My name is Mentor, said Athena, looking with her bright eyes on Telemachus. My father was the prince Anchialus, and I am chief of the seafaring Taphians. I came across the wine-dark sea with my own ship and crew, now beached some distance from here. We carry a cargo of iron to trade for bronze.

As Telemachus listened to Mentor, Athena continued her ruse: Our families have long-standing ties, as your grandfather would attest if he were here. I understand that Laertes, king of Ithaca and father of Odysseus, no longer comes here but lives in poverty on a distant farm, with only an old servant woman to give him food after his work in the vineyards.

With these and other words, Athena caused Telemachus to trust the family friend who sat with him at his table. As Mentor, Athena moved ahead with her plan. I came here because I heard that your father had come home, she said. The gods must be slowing his return, because I know for a fact that Odysseus is not dead. He must be on some distant island in the sea, or held by enemies, maybe savages, who will not release him. Of course, I am not a seer or soothsayer, but let me venture a prophecy that comes to my mind from the gods. Your father will soon come home. He loves this land, and not even iron chains can prevent his return. He is clever and brave.

Telemachus attended Athena's words politely, hopefully. But are you really the son of Odysseus? she asked. Your resemblance to him is startling, but you have grown up. I have not seen him since he sailed for Troy.

Friend, Telemachus answered, no man can be certain of his parents, but my mother, Penelope, tells me that I am Odysseus's son. Would that he were here, among his riches, master of his land. But, I will tell you, the man who is said to be my father is the most unfortunate man on earth.

With Penelope as your mother, Athena answered, your house cannot be doomed.

The goddess continued her conversation with Telemachus, testing him: But tell me what this banqueting is about? Who are these men? And who are they to *you*? Is this a wedding feast? These loutish men—surely they have brought their own food— seem to me to be insolent and bullying. Their behavior is altogether disgraceful.

Telemachus courteously answered: This house was once rich and respected. But that has changed since the gods have made sinister plans for Odysseus and have made him vanish. If my father had died among comrades at Troy or at home as an old man, I would not be distressed. His people could have built him a funeral mound, and I would have inherited his great name. But Odysseus has been snatched away from his proper end. He cannot be seen or found, and I am left in sorrow and tears. And I grieve not just for Odysseus, but for myself and the sorrows the gods have piled upon me. These wretched suitors! They come from every corner of the land, each wanting to marry my mother. And although she hates the idea of marrying, she knows she must if my father is dead. Still, she cannot bring herself to accept or reject these boors. And meanwhile they are eating and drinking away our resources. I have no doubt that they will destroy me.

Damnit, Athena cried. You miss your father! You need him to throw these wretches out of his house! If only he could appear right now at these gates, his helmet and shield shining, his two long spears held ready. When I saw him here last he was a happy man, strong and optimistic. He had just returned from a trip to procure a deadly poison to put on the tips of his arrows. Ilus, the god-fearing man he had visited, had refused to give him the poison. But my own father, who loved Odysseus, gave it to him. Odysseus was fearless then. If he returned now, he could confront these suitors, put them to quick death—the sorry wedding they deserve.

Athena added: Of course such matters are in the laps of the gods. The immortals will decide if Odysseus is to return and thrash these ghastly suitors.

ATHENA INSTRUCTS TELEMACHUS

And so Athena continued to talk with Telemachus, and to draw him into her plan and the will of the gods. Listen, she said to the aristocratic young man, I hope you will find some way of ridding the house of Odysseus of these dreadful suitors. Here's what I suggest. Call all of the Achaeans to assembly tomorrow morning and, asking the gods to be your witness, tell them your plans. Tell them that if your mother must marry, she must return to her father's house and let him arrange a marriage and offer a dowry—the only right thing for him to do for his beloved daughter.

As for yourself, Athena continued, I hope you will accept my sound advice. Take your best ship and twenty oarsmen. Go in search of your father. Someone will have heard news or may have heard rumors as to Zeus's will. Go to Pylos and sit with the wise and excellent Nestor. Then go to Sparta and seek information from the red-haired Menelaus, the last of the Achaean heroes to reach his home.

Telemachus listened, and Athena continued: If you hear that your father is indeed on his way home, you should adjust to another year with these terrible suitors. But if you learn that he is dead, you must return to your home, build a funeral mound, and oversee the proper rites. Then you must do the proper thing and give your mother in marriage to a new husband.

Then, Athena instructed, having settled your parents' affairs, you must by cunning or fighting destroy this gang that has invaded your house. You are not a child, and you must now act as a man.

Telemachus heard her words and knew that the advice was sound. Then Athena added further encouragement: You must have heard of Orestes and of the fame he has gained in the world by avenging the murderer of his noble father? You, my young friend—tall and splendid son of Odysseus—must be as courageous Orestes. Future generations will know your name and sing your praises.

Athena rose to take her leave. My crew must grow restless waiting for me, she said. I leave these matters we have discussed in your hands. Think about what I have said to you.

Telemachus promised to follow the fatherly advice given by Mentor, and thanked him for speaking from his heart. Stay longer, he suggested, and bathe and refresh yourself. I should like to give you a fine gift—the sort of thing a host gives a guest who has become a friend.

No, answered the glowing-eyed Athena, pleased by Telemachus's good manners, I must be on my way. As for the gift you offer, I hope you will let me fetch it on my return trip and take it home with me. Make it a good gift, and it will bring you good fortune.

The next moment Athena was gone. Telemachus's heart beat rapidly with the courage she had given him, and his imagination filled with the vivid images of his father that she had called forth. In his near euphoric state, the young man realized that he had been in the presence of a god, and put that knowledge deep in the secrets of his heart. Then, godlike himself, he joined the suitors who were listening to a bard entertaining them with verse about the disasters Athena had visited upon the Achaeans on their journeys home from Troy.

The bard's song rose in the vaulted house and went to Penelope in her room in the women's quarters. Pierced by longing for Odysseus and sadness, Penelope, accompanied by two waiting-women, left her quarters by a steep staircase and entered the banqueting hall. She drew a veil across her face and stood by a pillar, a maid on either side, and listened to the minstrel. She could stand it no longer and, weeping bitter tears, begged the singer to entertain the suitors with another song.

But Telemachus moved to his mother's side and gently urged her to return to her quarters, and leave the singing and decision making to men. With the courage Athena had placed in his heart, Telemachus told Penelope: I am master of this house, now. And so Penelope withdrew to her bedroom, and there she wept for Odysseus until Athena came softly near her and closed her eyes in sleep.

When the suitors asked about Telemachus's guest, the young prince answered with the same cunning that had made his father famous. An old family friend, he said. But he knew that he had been visited by Athena. That night, Telemachus lay awake and planned the journey Athena had recommended.

TELEMACHUS OBEYS THE GODDESS

The next morning Telemachus instructed heralds to call the Achaeans to assembly. As the men gathered, Athena endowed Telemachus with glowing beauty and godlike grace. He entered the assembly, his bronze spear in his hand, and only his two favorite hunting dogs walking at his side. All eyes turned in admiration toward him; the elders cleared a path and watched Odysseus's son take his father's seat. A suitor immediately rose before the assembly to condemn Penelope's trickery. She had promised to marry one of the suitors, he said, as soon as she finished weaving a shroud for Laertes. But, faithful to Odysseus and hopeful that he might still be alive, Penelope had deceived the suitors; she had spent the days weaving and the nights undoing her day's work. This she had done for three years, and was caught in her trickery only because one of her servants reported Penelope's practices to the suitors.

She must take care, warned the suitor, not to test the patience of the suitors and not to count too heavily on Athena's gift, her great skill in weaving. She is an admirable woman, he said, intelligent and beautiful, accustomed to having her way. But she has abused us. And we will not go away, Telemachus, but will continue to eat you out of house and home until Penelope chooses one of us to marry.

Telemachus responded thoughtfully: I cannot force my mother to marry against her will. My father may be alive. If I should send my mother back to her father, Icarius, against her will, surely the Avenging Furies, who watch over women, would descend on me; the gods themselves would heap disasters on my head, and my countrymen would be furious with me. If this makes you angry, Telemachus advised the suitors, then leave my house. Go feast and revel somewhere else. But if you remain in my house, squandering my inheritance, I pray that Zeus will bring you to justice and let me destroy you.

Zeus heard the young man's prayer and sent two eagles as a sign. The glistening birds careened down from the mountain tops, hovered with outstretched pinions over the assembly; they hung still in the high air, their wing tips touching, until they caught the attention of the men. Then they clawed at each other, and cast foreboding of death into the hearts of the assembled men.

A prophet among them watched the birds of Zeus, then solemnly addressed the suitors: A great reckoning is on its way to you. Odysseus will return soon. He is at this very moment nearby, and plotting doom for you suitors.

But the suitors did not respect the sign from Zeus. The assembly argued back and forth until they adjourned and returned to their homes or, in the case of the suitors, to King Odysseus's palace to continue abusing the absent nobleman's hospitality.

Telemachus went alone to wash his hands in the gray sea, to purify his thoughts and to lift a prayer to Athena: Hear me as you did yesterday when you visited my house. I seek to follow your command, to sail the sea in search of news of my father. But my countrymen and those terrible suitors beseige my mother and thwart my plans.

Athena heard the prayer of Odysseus's son; she drew near Telemachus and spoke to him: Telemachus, you are neither fool nor coward, but the son of Odysseus and in possession of his manly vigor. And what a hero he was—a man strong in action and debate! Your journey will not be in vain, Telemachus. Only a few sons are like their fathers; most are worse. But you are indeed the son of your father, with his resourcefulness. Forget the suitors for now, and brush aside their plots and threats as the blather of fools. Dark fate is stalking them and in due time they will all be struck down in a single day.

Athena continued: Now, Telemachus, you must prepare for your journey. I am your father's friend, and I will find you a fast ship and accompany you myself. Go home. Let the suitors see you. Do not arouse their suspicion; go about your daily routine but unobtrusively prepare provisions: stow wine in jars and barley—the grain that gives men strength—in skins.

While you are attending to provisions, Athena promised, I will muster a crew and from all the fast ships of Ithaca I will select the best for you. She'll be rigged and ready for the open sea.

Telemachus heard Athena's words and did not linger. Although his heart was anxious, he set about obeying her.

ATHENA AND TELEMACHUS AGAINST THE SUITORS

When he returned to his palace, Telemachus found the suitors skinning his goats and barbecuing his fat hogs. They taunted him for his speech to the assembly, joked about his promise to search for news of his father, and brazenly invited him to join them in a feast. Telemachus refused to join the rowdy band of men, and renewed his vow to bring them to a reckoning for their treatment of him, his mother, and the hospitality of his home.

Then he shrugged off the insults and derision from the suitors, walked calmly away, and sought the housekeeper Eurycleia, a faithful servant who had been his nurse when he was a child. Swearing her to secrecy, he implored her to prepare provisions for his journey. The nurse-housekeeper begged him not to go away, but to remain and take care of his mother and his father's house.

Dear nurse, he said gently, do not be afraid for me. I am following the gods' wishes. So promise me that you will not tell my mother until she asks my whereabouts.

And so the nurse-housekeeper promised Telemachus to keep his secret, and she began to prepare the provisions he had requested.

Meanwhile Athena, goddess with great skill in strategy, had another idea. She disguised herself as Telemachus and went through town selecting a crew for the ship. Then she procured a strong ship, as she had promised Telemachus. As darkness covered the harbor, Athena moved the ship into the water, filled it with all the necessary gear, and moored it in a remote cove. Still disguised as Telemachus, Athena then moved among the gathering crew, speaking encouraging words to each man, showing the mastery of persuasion and leadership that Odysseus might have imparted to his son.

Seeing that the ship and crew were ready, Athena returned quietly and invisibly to the banqueting hall of Odysseus's palace, and cast a spell of fatigue and half-drunken stupor over the suitors, causing them to go home to their beds. The bright-eyed goddess then again assumed the form of Mentor and in his voice called to Telemachus. Come, she said to the son of the godlike Odysseus, your well-armed companions are at their oars. They await word from you to begin the journey. Do not delay.

And so Athena led Telemachus swiftly to the ship and he took command of the crew. Athena brought the West Wind to Telemachus and his men in the black ship. They poured libations to the gods, cast off from the mooring in the safe harbor, and Athena sent them over the wine-dark sea.

ATHENA LEADS TELEMACHUS TO NESTOR

As the sun rose out of the east, bringing light to the immortals and to mortals on the generous earth, Athena led the way for Telemachus to moor his ship at Pylos, in sight of the brave old cavalryman Nestor's stately citadel. Nine companies of five hundred men each were sacrificing black bulls to Poseidon on the shore; as the thigh bones burned to the god, the men tasted the entrails.

Athena, still in the guise of Mentor, urged Telemachus to overcome his reticence. Go straight up to Nestor, tamer of horses, she admonished, and appeal to him to tell you the truth. He is a wise man.

But, Telemachus protested, how shall I greet him? I am inexperienced in these formalities and am embarrassed. I am a young man with little experience, and I am in awe of the older and wiser Nestor.

Bright-eyed Athena did not desert her young charge, but was pleased by his modesty and advised him thoughtfully. Telemachus, where your good sense fails, a god will inspire you. I believe the gods have blessed you in your birth and again in your path toward manhood.

Then Athena led Telemachus toward the assembled people of Pylos.

When Nestor and his sons saw the strangers coming toward them, they stopped skewering and roasting the meat in preparation for a fine banquet, and went to meet their guests, and to offer them choice pieces of the ritual meal. Politely they gave a gold cup of wine to Athena, who still appeared as the elder, Mentor. The daughter of Zeus, pleased by the good manners of Nestor and his family, responded by offering a prayer to Poseidon. Hear me, Poseidon, she implored in Mentor's voice, and grant us our wishes. We make offerings to you for your honor. We ask you to grant glory to Nestor and his sons, and to give them fortune in exchange for the honor they pay you. Grant, too, that Telemachus and I may accomplish our task, and that we may return safely home in our fast black ship.

As these petitions rose from Athena's lips toward Poseidon, she winged messages of her own to Poseidon to ensure that they would be granted. She then passed the ritual cup to Telemachus, and he repeated her prayers. The feast continued until all had satisfied their hunger and thirst. Then, in the custom of the land, Nestor respectfully asked his guests to identify themselves and to tell him why they had come to his shore. Athena inspired Telemachus to respond in a spirited manner and to gain respect for himself.

Nestor, son of Neleus, great glory to the Greeks, Telemachus addressed his host, We come from Ithaca, at the foot of Mount Neion. I am here in search of news of my noble father, the heroic and long-absent Odysseus. It is said that he fought by your side some years ago at Troy. We know the fates of all the other Achaean heroes, where each met his pitiful end, or how each returned safely to his home. But Zeus has wrapped mystery around Odysseus, and no one can tell us if he is dead or alive. So I have come here to seek your wisdom. Did you witness his unhappy end? I know my father was born to suffer, so I beg you not to soften the news on account of my feelings.

Nestor, as famous for his lengthy speeches as for his bravery as a horse soldier, spoke to Telemachus of the long war at Troy, of the miseries endured by the brave Achaeans, of the deaths of noble warriors. No one, Nestor said, could unfold for you all that happened, all that we endured in our strategy to bring down Priam's city. Zeus made it difficult for us. But through it all, Odysseus proved himself our best strategist.

And now, Nestor continued, you stand before me and I look at you in awe for you talk exactly as your father did.

Then Nestor resumed his summary of the war with Troy, telling Odysseus's son that Zeus decreed disaster for the heroes on their homeward journey because they had failed to behave sensibly. The Achaeans, he said, had brought down Athena's wrath when they failed to make ceremonial offerings to her. Nestor said that he, along with half of the group, left in his ship stowed with booty and captive women, while the other half—under Agamemnon's command—remained.

Then Nestor told of Agamemnon's return and his murder by his wife, Clytemnestra, and her lover Aegisthus; and he told Telemachus that Agamemnon's son, Orestes, had avenged his father's death. Telemachus replied that it was only proper that Orestes' fame should travel throughout the world. If the gods would give me strength like his, Telemachus declared, I'd exact revenge for the suitors' crimes against my family, their thuggish disregard of what is right, and their humiliation of me.

Nestor nodded sympathetically and told Telemachus that he had heard that a crowd of suitors made havoc in his house. I wish, Nestor offered, that Athena could give you the care she lovingly gave your father at Troy. I have never in my life seen a god display such open support and affection as Athena showed toward Odysseus. If she helped you as she helped your father, you could knock ideas of courtship out of the heads of your uninvited guests!

But Telemachus responded dejectedly that he had no hope of bringing justice down on the suitors. Who knows, he mused, whether Odysseus may come back, alone or with followers, to do violence to these suitors. Athena stood beside him as Mentor, and spoke to him in Mentor's voice: Telemachus, she asked, what is this? A god can cause anything to happen, can bring anyone safely home no matter how far away he might be. For myself, I would rather live through hardship and be able to live on my own hearth than to come easily home and die as Agamemnon did. But it is the common lot of mortals to die, and the gods cannot prevent it when death takes a man down to darkness.

Telemachus begged Mentor not to discuss painful subjects further. The gods who are themselves immortal, he said, have already set my father on his path toward death.

Nestor then told of Agamemnon's return, Clytemnestra's treachery, and Orestes' vengeance. He came to the end of his story as the sun went down after a full day of sacrificing, feasting, and storytelling. Athena, still as Mentor, spoke to Nestor, complimenting him on his well-told story. But come, she urged, cut up the sacrificial victims' tongues and mix them with wine, so we can make our final offerings to Poseidon and the other immortals before we sleep. It is not right to remain feasting and honoring the gods after nightfall.

Athena's words were heard, and when all had made their last offerings of the day and drunk their fill of wine, Athena and Telemachus rose to go to their ships. Nestor stopped them, and offered beds and comfort for the night. No son of Odysseus, he told them, shall sleep on a ship's deck so long as I or my sons live and can offer hospitality.

You are right, my Lord, said Athena, and Telemachus will accept your invitation to sleep in your palace. I shall return to the black ship and be with the men. I am an old man and must give courage to Telemachus's companions who are no older than he. Tomorrow I must go to visit the Cauconians, but since Telemachus is your guest, you should send him on in a chariot drawn by fast and strong horses, the best in your stable.

Then Athena turned herself into a vulture and flew off. Old King Nestor and all of the others marveled at the sight. Telemachus, Nestor said, you have the gods on your side. Athena has been among us, the daughter of Zeus who honored your father among the Argives. With that, Nestor prayed to Athena: Goddess, be good to me and my sons and my honored wife. Give us fame and in return we shall sacrifice to you a yearling heifer, broad-browed and unbroken. We will gild her horns and honor you.

Athena heard his prayer and watched as Nestor led the way to his palace where he mixed wine, poured libations, and prayed again to Athena, daughter of Zeus, who holds the aegis.

When dawn came Nestor made good his promise to Athena, and sent his sons to select a fine heifer to be brought to him for sacrifice to the goddess. And he sent for the goldsmith to gild its horns. It was Athena, he said, who came to me in person last night at the sumptuous feast for the gods.

Athena returned and watched over the sacrifice. The heifer's horns were worked in gold, and then she was led forward. Nestor's son met her with a flowered bowl of lustral water in one hand and a basket of barley meal in the other. Nestor prayed to Athena, throwing a tuft of the heifer's hair onto the roaring fire that had been prepared. Then the victim was struck down with a sharp axe, and a dish was held to catch the sacrificial blood. As the heifer collapsed, the women of Nestor's house raised their voices in celebratory cries. The sacrifice to the goddess was accompanied by prayers, and the thigh bones and fat burned to honor Athena. Nestor sprinkled wine over the fire, and then the meat was carved and roasted and the feast began.

After Athena had been honored in this way, Nestor ordered a chariot and horses for Telemachus, and commanded his son Peisistratus to travel with Odysseus's son. After courteous leave-taking, the pair left the high city of Pylos behind them and traveled until the sun went down and the earth grew dark. They spent the night with a generous host, but set out at dawn and traveled a full day.

ATHENA WATCHES TELEMACHUS VISIT MENELAUS AND HELEN

Athena saw Menelaus, red-haired husband of Helen, receive Telemachus and Peisistratus gladly and offer them the hospitality of his rich palace. As was the custom, the host asked no questions of the strangers until he had seen to their comfort. Menelaus turned

the two travel-weary young men into the hands of maids who
bathed them in warm water, rubbed them with rich oils, and
dressed them in fine clean cloaks. When the young princes
appeared before Menelaus, the host put before them food and
wine, a ritual of generosity and hospitality by which strangers
were turned to friends.

Soon the divinely beautiful Helen, richly robed and splendid
in gold jewelry, joined the men, and greeted them, her eyes lingering on Telemachus. Surely, she said, this must be the heroic
Odysseus's son, Telemachus. He was only a baby when his father
set out for Troy and war for my sake.

Menelaus agreed with his wife's observation, pointed out
resemblances between the father and son—similar hands and feet,
hair growing identically—and recalled fondly the bravery and
comradeship of Odysseus. Telemachus, moved by Menelaus's
description of his father, tried to cover his tears by drawing his
cloak over his face.

Menelaus, favorite of Helen, leader of your people, son of
Atreus, Peisistratus explained to his host, this is indeed Telemachus,
Odysseus's son. He is modest and holds you in such esteem that
he hesitates to speak to you. I am Nestor's son and sent by my
father to accompany Telemachus on his search for news of his
noble father. Odysseus's son, who has no father at home, is made
to suffer many injustices and has no protection.

And so Athena saw the host and guests exchange stories, and
make themselves fast friends. Menelaus, seething with indignation
at Telemachus's humiliation by the suitors, exclaimed, Cowards!
So they want to crawl into a hero's bed, do they? Odysseus will
return like a lion, I promise you, and the suitors will meet a grisly
fate.

Menelaus then told Telemachus that he did indeed have
news of Odysseus. While on his journey home, he said, he had
learned that Calypso held Odysseus captive on her island. It was
told that Odysseus, stranded without a ship, stood on the shore
looking toward home and crying.

ATHENA AND PENELOPE

Meanwhile the suitors, learning that Telemachus had sailed off in search of news of his father, plotted to lay in wait for him on hidden ships, and to murder him. But a loyal servant, Medon, overheard the plans and reported to Penelope: My Queen, your suitors are planning a shocking crime. Pray Zeus will not let them succeed! They are set on murdering Telemachus.

Penelope, faint at the news, found speaking difficult. Tell me, she at last asked, why has Telemachus gone? When she heard that her son had gone to seek information about his father, Penelope was racked with anguish, and paced her room and wept. She sent for Eurycleia, the nurse-housekeeper who had assisted Telemachus in preparations for his journey, and insisted on hearing the details of his departure.

Kill me with a cruel knife if you must, Eurycleia answered, but I knew the whole plan. And I prepared bread and wine and all else that he requested. He made me promise not to tell you, dear lady, not wanting tears to spoil your cheeks.

Penelope washed and changed her clothes, filled a basket with sacrificial grains, and prayed to Athena, saying: Daughter of Zeus, unwearied goddess who bears the aegis, hear me. Remember the heifers and sheep Odysseus has sacrificed in your honor, and save my dear son and guard him against the evil of these ruthless suitors.

Athena heard Penelope crying out and praying, and heard also the suitors bragging and shouting among themselves. As Penelope prayed to Athena, the suitors boasted that Telemachus would soon die, and that Penelope would be forced to marry one of them.

Athena's eyes flashed, and she took hold of another idea. She sent to Penelope the image of her sister Iphthime. The phantom stood by the weeping queen, and spoke quietly. Are you asleep, Penelope? Are you exhausted from grief? I have come from the gods to tell you that, although they themselves live easy lives, they pity you. Your son has done no wrong in their eyes, and he will return home.

Penelope, who lingered in sweet sleep at the Gate of Dreams, answered: I am not accustomed to seeing you, Iphthime, you who live so far away. How can I forget my sorrows? I married and then lost the best and bravest man of our race. And now my beloved son is in terrible danger. He is a mere child, and he has cruel enemies plotting against him and thirsting for his blood.

Be brave, the phantom Iphthime said soothingly. Telemachus has the best escort a man can have. Athena in all her power accompanies him, and it is she who sent me to you with this message.

If you come from Athena and have heard her voice, Penelope implored, tell me then about Odysseus, too.

No, answered the dream image, I will not give you news of your husband. You will know in proper time.

Then Iphthime disappeared.

While Athena sent the message to Penelope, the suitors sailed forth intent upon murdering Telemachus. They set their ambush in a strait between Ithaca and the coast of Samos, near the rocky island of Asteris.

ATHENA APPEALS TO THE OLYMPIANS

Odysseus, by all measures, was fortunate. He, favored by Athena, would reach home safely, his story recalled by Homer in the *Odyssey*. But other heroes of the Trojan War did not fare so well and, by the time Homer began his story of Odysseus's return to Ithaca, Athena had already dispatched those warriors who had earned her animosity. Those who had insulted the goddess by not offering thanks to her for victory were not allowed to reach home at all, but were subjected to bitter endings engineered by the enraged and vengeful goddess. To inflict maximum torture with maximum efficiency upon her enemies, Athena formed an unusual alliance with Poseidon, a god she never liked but whose power she respected, in order to annihilate the disrespectful warriors with raging sea storms, monstrous waves, treacherous shores, and shipwrecks.

Those heroes who acknowledged Athena's role in their victory, however, were allowed to return home. Thus, after a long and difficult journey, Menelaus reached Sparta with Helen and resumed his pleasant life in the midst of his great riches. His brother Agamemnon reached home, too, but was murdered by his wife and her lover.

But Athena's attention was fixed on Odysseus. He was, she believed, being treated cruelly and unjustly by the gods. So, as dawn gave light to immortals and mortals, Athena rose to speak to her fellow Olympians about the injustice of Odysseus's plight. Gods did not—either by nature or proclivity—represent mortals and their causes in the court of the immortals; no contract in the form of holy writ or common understanding existed to give human beings reason to hope that particular forms of behavior would extract benevolence from the gods. But Athena, growing away from her celebrated preeminence as a warrior and toward support of civility and justice among humankind, spoke in reasoned tones: Father Zeus and you other blessed gods who, unlike Odysseus, live forever, hear me. No longer should any mortal who rules, who has authority over other mortals, be obliged to exercise kindness, generosity or justice. He might as well be a tyrant or an outlaw. Look, she said, at what has happened to Odysseus. That admirable man and king! But today not one of his people gives him a thought. He is the nymph Calypso's captive, and languishes in misery in her home on her island. He is unable to reach Ithaca, for he has neither fitted ship nor crew with oars.

Athena continued: Meanwhile, Odysseus's beloved son has traveled to Nestor's high citadel in Pylos and Menelaus's rich palace in Lacedaemon to seek news of his father. And as Telemachus begs news of his noble father, the brutal suitors who compete for his mother mean to assassinate him on his return to his home.

Zeus heard Athena's words, and answered: My child, what are you saying? You planned this yourself. You arranged it all so that Odysseus could return home and take revenge on the suitors. As for Telemachus, you have the power to bring him home to Ithaca and to keep him safe from the suitors. Use your skill, your power.

Then Zeus called Hermes and sent him to Calypso with a message. Tell the nymph of the plaited tresses, Zeus instructed, to release the long-suffering Odysseus. She is to furnish materials so that he may build a raft and set out on his own. He will be helped by neither god nor mortal, and on the twentieth day, after great hardship, he will reach the rich country of the Phaecians, who are favored by the gods. They will give him hospitality, will love him and treat him like a god. They will give him many rich gifts of bronze, gold, and woven materials—far greater gifts than he could have taken as plunder from Troy—and they will take him by ship to his home. That is how it is fated that Odysseus shall return to his high-vaulted house and see again his friends.

And so, prodded by Athena, Zeus set the fate of Odysseus before the gods.

ATHENA WATCHES OVER ODYSSEUS

Then Hermes, messenger of the gods and giant-killer, flew like a gull over the wide sea to Calypso's cavern and island home. The nymph sat singing and weaving with a golden shuttle before a fragrant fire on her hearth. Her cave, sheltered by graceful trees and bountiful vines, was watched over by wide-winged sea birds. The sound of crystal water ran from four different springs, its song mingling with that of the nymph. Even a god gazed with wonder and delight on Calypso's island home.

When Hermes delivered Zeus's message, Calypso promised to comply immediately. But why is it, she asked, that you gods may make love with any mortal you seduce or rape, but you are outraged if any goddess sleeps with a mortal? You envy me for living with a mortal man. I rescued this man from certain death. I dragged him from the sea and tended him. I offered to make him immortal and ageless, but he thinks only of returning to his home.

And so Calypso went to Odysseus, who sat weeping beside the shore. It was true that he had shared her bed at night, had been a cold lover and she an ardent lady. But all through the days he sat and groaned with heartache, stared out over the sea and cried out in despair.

Athena saw Calypso sweetly tell Odysseus of Zeus's command, and give him tools to cut timber and make a raft. When

Calpyso had stored provisions for Athena's warrior, she then bathed him and dressed him in sweet-smelling clothes, and she saw him off onto the wine-dark sea. For seventeen days he stayed on course, and on the eighteenth spotted the mountains of the Phaecians' country.

But before Odysseus could make land, the god who hated him most, Poseidon, happened to see the hero heading toward safety. Poseidon flew into a rage: The other gods have no doubt decided to spare this hateful fellow, he said to himself, but I shall see that he has a bellyful of trouble before he sees his home again.

With that, the roaring sea god summoned winds and stirred the sea; he roused stormy blasts and brought down dark clouds. Odysseus shook with fear as wave after great wave rolled over him, and he expected to be pulled down into ignoble death at any moment. He was thrown and thrust this way and that by the angry sea, and only barely managed to hang onto his damaged raft. But Ino, once a mortal and now a sea nymph, took pity on him and gave him her divine veil, which she promised would enable him to reach the shore. The veil, she told him, would prevent him from drowning, no matter how fiercely the sea tried to take him down to black death.

But Athena pitied her favorite, Odysseus, and intervened at this point, halting the winds in their rampage and ordering them to calm down and go to sleep. Then she commanded the North Wind to flatten the waves and make a path for Odysseus so that he could swim ashore and be rescued by the seafaring Phaecians. Poseidon, however, still raged against Odysseus, who had blinded his son, a Cyclopes and even with Athena's help Odysseus was driven for two days and two nights by the sea god's angry waves and tides. Finally, on the morning of the third day, dawn opened the world to a calm sea, and Odysseus made for shore where thundering surf and riptides again and again drove him back into the depths of the sea.

Again Athena helped him, this time leading him to a rock where he could cling and get his bearings; she moved close and gave him the cunning to find a way through the sea and safely onto shore. Naked, cold, and exhausted, Odysseus found shelter under bushes. As he covered himself over with leaves, as a farmer might bury a glowing log to preserve his fire, Athena came to Odysseus and filled his eyes with sleep to soothe his pain and vanquish his weariness.

ATHENA, ODYSSEUS, AND NAUSICAA

While Odysseus slept beneath bushes in the land of the Phaecians, Athena moved like a welcome breeze into the palace of the ruler, King Alcinous, and rested softly beside the bed of princess Nausicaa. The bright-eyed goddess took the form of Dymas, the princess's best friend, and spoke. Nausicaa, how is it that your mother has such a lazy daughter? Your clothes are everywhere, and dirty. Is this any way for you to gain a good reputation and get a fine husband?

With this, Athena had Nausicaa's full attention. The goddess then instructed the princess to ask her father for a wagon and mules the next morning, and to take her maidservants and go to the washing pool near the shore.

Satisfied that Nausicaa would do as she wished, Athena withdrew to Olympus. There, it is said, the gods make their eternal home in a cloudless high region untroubled by wind, rain, or snow; and there the immortals enjoy their days of pleasure.

From Olympus Athena watched Nausicaa and her companions doing laundry and spreading freshly washed clothes on the ground to dry. Their chores done, the young girls played games and sang; they bathed and rubbed themselves with sweet oils; and they took their meal in the warm sunshine. The girls gathered the sun-dried clothes and prepared to return to the palace, but a few lingered and frolicked with a ball. Athena, moving to work her way among mortals, caused one girl to miss the ball tossed to her. Just as the ball fell into the water and the girls gave a loud shriek, Athena prodded Odysseus awake. Hearing the shriek, the naked hero wondered where he was—among savages or gods or humans who might speak as he did.

Dirty and naked, caked with salt and clutching a leafy bough to cover his genitals, Odysseus crept from his hiding place and stood before the princess and her friends. Nausicaa was the only one who did not run away from the naked stranger, but stood firm, filled with courage from Athena. Odysseus asked for her help, and the princess realized from his speech and manner that he was a nobleman. Identifying herself as the daughter of King Alcinous, Nausicaa called her maidservants to have no fear because, she told them confidently, the gods would not let evil people set foot on the soil of the Phaecians.

Invisible but attentive, Athena watched over Odysseus as he bathed the dirt and salt from his body, and rubbed himself with olive oil that Nausicaa gave him. Then Zeus's daughter caused Odysseus to seem taller and more muscular, and thickened his hair and tossed it round his head like a hyacinth in bloom, making him the handsomest of men; she mixed in him equal measures of nobility and virility, and made him radiant as a god. Athena enjoyed practicing her artistry and, like Hephaestus giving a lovely finish to a fine piece of shaped metal, the goddess endowed Odysseus's head and shoulders with glowing beauty.

When the king of Ithaca, touched by Athena's magic, stepped forth, Nausicaa looked on him with admiration. For so Athena had planned it to be.

Wise in her understanding of the people of her kingdom, however, and wishing to avoid unpleasant gossip, Nausicaa instructed Odysseus in how best to approach King Alcinous for help. Go, she told Odysseus, to a fine poplar wood around a spring sacred to Athena. Sit there and wait until we have time to get into town. Then come to the palace, and go first to my mother. Fall at her knees and ask her help. If she is sympathetic, you may be sure that you will have my father's help.

Following her directions, Odysseus found the sacred place of Athena, and there he prayed to the daughter of Zeus: Hear me, Athena, you who ignored me when I was shipwrecked and Poseidon battered my raft. Grant now that the Phaecians may look on me with compassion and offer me kindness.

Athena heard Odysseus's prayer, but held back from him out of respect for her father's brother Poseidon. The heart of the sea god, she knew, still boiled with rage at Odysseus.

Out of concern for Odysseus, however, Athena enveloped him in a supernatural mist that made him invisible as he rose from her sacred grove and walked into town. She wanted him to arrive safely at the palace without interference from a villager who might question the intentions of a stranger.

Then Athena went ahead of Odysseus and turned back to meet him, disguised as a young girl carrying a water jug. He stopped her: I wonder, my child, Odysseus said to Athena in the form of a young girl, if you could show me the way to the palace of King Alcinous. I am a stranger and have endured great hardship. I know no one here or hereabouts.

Athena replied courteously: Sir, I will gladly show you King Alcinous's house. It is close to my father's house. But you must follow me, she cautioned, and neither look at nor speak to anyone we might meet. Ask no questions. People here are not fond of strangers and do not welcome uninvited visitors. These are seafaring people who honor Poseidon, and who fly fast as birds across the sea in their ships.

So Athena led the way and Odysseus followed obediently and, safely enveloped in the goddess's mist that made him invisible, unnoticed. When they arrived at the palace, Athena, still in the form of the young girl with the water jug, spoke: Sir, here is the palace. Princes favored by Zeus feast here. Be bold. The first person you see will be Queen Arete. Athena then recited the genealogy of the royal family, and as was the custom among the nobility, she assigned a divine origin to both king and queen.

Then, while Odysseus made his way into the palace of Alcinous, Athena left the pleasant land of the Phaecians, crossed the great sea, and came to Marathon and then the broad streets of Athens, her favorite city. There on the Acropolis she entered the great palace of Erechtheus.

Athena returned to Phaecia the next day, however, to further her plan for Odysseus. When he was to appear before the Phaecian assembly, Athena disguised herself as a herald and, in summoning members of the assembly, said to each: You will hear about a stranger who has come to our king's palace after much hardship on the seas. He looks like a god!

Knowing that she had made certain that many eyes would fix on Odysseus, Athena again granted divine beauty to the hero she had favored above all others.

It is told that the Phaecians listened courteously to Odysseus and found him worthy of their help. Then they promised to escort Odysseus home in their large black ships, but first invited him to join them in ritual sacrifices and in games. Odysseus gladly entered into the festive mood of his hosts. But he held back from competition until, insulted by a Phaecian's derisive remarks about his athletic prowess, Athena's much-blessed hero angrily tossed the largest discus in the kingdom. As it flew through the air, Athena again disguised herself in order to help her favorite hero. Joining the watching Phaecians, and speaking as one of them, she exclaimed: What a toss! No one among us could outdistance that throw.

And so the Phaecians cheered Odysseus, and he was invited to tell his story at the great feast that followed the games. He told of his long and ill-fated journey from the battlefields of Troy to the splendid house of Alcinous.

When Odysseus finished his tale, Alcinous, proud to be the good and proper host to such a distinguished warrior, sealed their friendship with many wonderful gifts to his guest. At dawn the next day, the gifts were stored in the ship that was to take Odysseus to Ithaca. To ensure a safe journey for Odysseus, an ox was sacrificed to Zeus of the black cloud and lord of all, and Alcinous presided over a lavish feast. But Odysseus was impatient to be on his way home, and watched the sun cross the heavens and sink into night. He appealed to Alcinous to let his oarsmen take their places and to let the journey begin with his blessing. But Alcinous was not prepared to halt the festivities, and offered yet another round of libations and prayers. Odysseus's impatience turned toward despair when Alcinous at last gave orders to his men, and the last segment of Odysseus's journey home began.[*]

ATHENA AND ODYSSEUS IN ITHACA

Later Odysseus awoke on land; he was alone and confused. He was on his native soil, but Athena, who was there when he arrived, had enveloped Ithaca in a mist that distorted its contours. Before he raced headlong to his home and into the gang of suitors, Athena wanted to prepare him and to assure his triumph. She planned to make Odysseus invisible or unrecognizable, so that he could reconnoiter and make plans without being identified by family, friends, or enemies.

Athena let King Odysseus look around and lament as he saw only an unfamiliar landscape. He wondered if he had been the victim of a foul trick, if he had been beached on an unfriendly shore and his rich hoard of gifts stolen. But even though his Phaecian escorts had disappeared, he found that all of his rich gifts were safely stored near the seashore.

Athena now came to Odysseus. She wore a handsome cloak and fine sandals and carried a javelin, and appeared to be a young nobleman, a delicately beautiful prince attending sheep. Odysseus, delighted to see one of such aristocratic bearing, called out: Friend, you are the first person I have seen on this shore. Help me save these treasures and myself, I pray. I kneel at your feet as I would at those of a god, and I ask for your help. Tell me where I am. What is this country? Who lives here? Am I on an island or have I found my way to a fertile sunny slope of the mainland?

Athena's eyes glistened: Sir, she answered, How can you not know the name of this glorious place? It is known to thousands, known by all who live between dawn in the east and twilight in the

[*]O XIII.1-186; *Od.* XIII: After an argument with Zeus, Poseidon punished the Phaecians for their courtesy to Odysseus by turning one of their returning ships into stone. It is said that a great rock in the harbor of Corcyra (Corfu) is that ship, and proof that Odysseus's Phaecia was Corcyra.

west. It is rugged, perhaps unfit for horses; it is not large but it is a rich land. Wine and corn grow abundantly here, for rain and dew are never lacking. Goats and cattle thrive in its lush pastures and near its enduring watering places. Timber grows strong and tall.

After teasing Odysseus with these words, Athena added: Sir, this place is called Ithaca, and its name has traveled even as far as Troy. I am told that Troy is far indeed from Achaea.

Odysseus, his heart leaping for joy, held back his true feelings and lied to the noble shepherd-boy Athena: Yes, of course, he said, I heard of Ithaca even in my home on Crete. Sly Odysseus went on to identify himself as an exile, banned from his home because he had murdered a man who had tried to cheat him out of booty he had won in the Trojan War.

As Athena listened, she became playful; she changed herself from an aristocratic shepherd boy to a tall, beautiful, sophisticated woman. She smiled alluringly at Odysseus, and caressed him with her hand. She spoke to him, saying: Even a god who met you would have difficulty in surpassing you as a trickster, sir. You have always been stubborn, a wily intriguer and a subtle liar. Now that you are on your home soil, it appears that you do not intend to drop your lying tales. Enough, Odysseus!

You may have no rival among men in wisdom and cunning, the goddess continued, but I am preeminent among the gods in my ability to get what I want, in wisdom and ingenuity.

And you did not recognize me, she scolded. I am Pallas Athena, daughter of Zeus. I have been by your side and have guarded you through your long adventures. It was I who ensured the hospitality of the Phaecians.

And here I am again to help you, this time to contrive a scheme with you, to protect your treasures from the Phaecians— also prompted by me, Athena boasted.

She continued: I am here to warn you of the trials you must yet undergo in your own home. You must bear these tests with patience. Meanwhile, not a single person must know that you have returned from your journey, and you must endure all insult, derision, and irritation in silence. You must submit first in order to triumph finally.

Odysseus heard Athena's words, and knew that she spoke truly; he answered Zeus's daughter: Goddess, it is difficult for a mortal to recognize you. You are wiser and wilier than all of us, and you change your disguises at will. But, he continued, I appreciated your help in the past, and know that we Achaeans would have been lost at Troy had it not been for your wisdom and support. But, Goddess, after we sacked Priam's citadel and took to our long ships, I did not notice you among us then, nor see you on my ship to protect me from the dangers I have endured. Far from it. I was abandoned, Odysseus complained, and I wandered through the world with a broken heart, until you comforted me with words and took me at last to the land of the Phaecians.

Now, Athena, Odysseus spoke boldly, I beg you in the name of your father—no more tricks! Tell me, please, am I truly home? I cannot believe it. Is this my beloved Ithaca?

Athena, goddess of the flashing eyes, answered: That shows the subtlety of your mind. And that is why I protect you above all others, and will not abandon you in your misfortunes. You are persuasive, quick-witted, and self-assured. Any other man who had survived your adventures would have rushed home to the arms of his wife and children. But you, contrarily, are diffident and cunning. You do not ask news of your wife, or question me about your home.

But, Athena added, Penelope has done nothing but sit at home and weep for you as slow nights and long days have passed in sorrow. I was never in doubt that you would return home. I knew you would lose all of your men, but I was not prepared—you must understand this—to oppose my uncle Poseidon. He cannot forgive you for blinding his son, and nurses a grudge against you.

Then Athena set about convincing Odysseus that he was indeed on the soil of Ithaca: Look, she said, here is the harbor of Phorcys, the Old Man of the Sea. Look over there, at the head of the harbor, and see the long-leaved olive tree. There is the hazy cave, pleasant and cool, sacred to the nymphs whom some men call Naiads. In that high-vaulted cavern you made many sacrifices to the nymphs. And surely you remember the forested slopes of Mount Neriton, there, behind you.

As she pointed out the landmarks familiar to Odysseus, Athena lifted the mist from each one, revealing Ithaca shining beneath the sun. Odysseus, overcome with joy, knelt and kissed the land, then lifted his hands and voice in praise of the nymphs of the hazy cavern: I have never forgotten you, nymphs of the spring, daughters of Zeus, and have prayed to set eyes on you again. Hear my loving prayers, acknowledge my greetings! If Athena allows me to live and see my son grow to manhood, I will give you gifts in the days to come.

ATHENA AND ODYSSEUS PLOT AGAINST THE SUITORS

Odysseus asked Athena's help, and the goddess heard her favorite hero and commanded: Have courage, and rid yourself of worries, clear your heart of anxiety. All will be well. But first we must hide your gifts from the Phaecians in the sacred cave. And then we must plot a course for the future.

Athena swooped into the sacred cave and effortlessly cleared a place for Odysseus's gifts of gold, bronze, and fine fabrics. She showed him where to stow them securely and sealed the entrance to the cave with a giant boulder. Then Athena sat with Odysseus on the trunk of a sacred olive tree, and together like old companions—which, of course, they were—they schemed vengeance on the thuggish suitors.

Athena spoke first: Odysseus, favored by Zeus, son of Laertes, master of wiles, think now how best to treat these shameless suitors. For three whole years they have been swaggering about your home, trying to seduce your wife, and sponging off your resources and your son's inheritance. All this time Penelope has grieved for you and longed for your homecoming. Although she has held the suitors at bay with manipulative ways, her heart has never veered from love and loyalty to you.

Odysseus answered solemnly: Goddess, had you not told me this, I would have entered my home and misunderstood. I would have come to the same end as King Agamemnon without your counsel.

Athena nodded.

Odysseus continued: Yes, now let us devise a plot to bring these suitors to justice. Stand by me, I pray, and fill me with courage as you did on the day we pulled down Troy. Lady of the Bright Eyes, he implored, if you will be as generous in your aid to me now as you were then, I will slaughter three hundred. With your support, gracious goddess, anything is possible.

Athena answered Odysseus: I will be there by your side. When the time comes to bring the suitors to justice, I will not forget you.

Athena, although looking forward to guiding Odysseus through a successful fight for justice, was still the war goddess, and ever eager to see her enemies savaged. She placed her vision before Odysseus: I can already imagine the blood of the suitors staining your broad floors, their brains splattered underfoot.

The fate of the suitors settled in her mind, Athena turned her attention to the business at hand. To work! she commanded. I am going to disguise you so that you will not be recognized. I shall put wrinkles all over your smooth skin, and remove your dark thick locks from your head. I shall wrap you in rags, dim your eyes, and make you look repulsive. The suitors—yes, and even your wife and son—will see a wretched beggar, not the hero Odysseus.

Athena instructed her favorite hero Odysseus: Go first to the swineherd who keeps your pigs. He remains loyal to you, and he loves your son and your wife. You will find him at the pastures by the Raven's Crag, near the Spring of Arethusa, where he watches now over the swine as they grow fat and healthy feeding on acorns and drinking clean water from deep springs. Stay there with him, sit in his company, and ask him questions about whatever you want to know.

Meanwhile, Athena continued, I shall go to Sparta, that city of beautiful women, and summon your son, Telemachus. He has traveled to visit Menelaus in the hope of hearing news of you. He does not know if you are alive or dead.

But why, Goddess, Odysseus asked, did you not tell Telemachus that I live? Do you want him lost at sea while the suitors devour his inheritance?

But Athena calmed Odysseus: Do not be worried for Telemachus, she said; I was with him, and ensured that he would gain fame as your noble son. He is seated in pleasure in the palace of Menelaus at this very moment. It is true that some of the suitors plot to kill him before he can reach home. But they will not succeed. No. Those suitors will soon meet their ghastly fate.

Then Athena touched Odysseus, and turned him from king to pauper. His smooth skin withered and his supple limbs stiffened; his bright eyes dimmed, and he lost his dark hair. Then she cloaked him in grimy rags that smelled of smoke, and threw a stag's hide over his back. She gave him a shabby knapsack and a staff, and sent him to find the swineherd.

Athena, satisfied that her plans were working, then went to the land of Lacedaemon to fetch Telemachus home.

ODYSSEUS FOLLOWS ATHENA'S PLAN

When Odysseus, disguised by Athena, approached the swineherd's hut, baying dogs would have attacked him if had not sat immediately and dropped his staff. Eumaeus, the old swineherd, ran to call off the dogs, to welcome the stranger and invite him into his hut. Not recognizing the poor beggar before him as Odysseus, his master, Eumaeus lamented the absence of the Ithacan king: Here I am, he said, fattening my master's hogs for others to eat while Odysseus himself may be starving or lost in an unfriendly land. He may be dead.

Then the loyal Eumaeus, observing the sacred laws of hospitality, invited Odysseus into his hut and put before him wine and bread: I would never turn a stranger away, he explained, even one in worse condition than you. Strangers come in Zeus's name and deserve hospitality, however modest it might be. Some servants stint on hospitality, fearing their masters will fault them for giving gifts to strangers. But this is not so for me! My master trusted me and I prospered under his generous care. But I fear he is dead now, King Odysseus who went to fight the Trojans for Agamemnon.

As Odysseus ate and drank, Eumaeus described the brutish behavior of the suitors, contrasting them with his kind, generous, aristocratic, just master. Odysseus spoke soothingly to his host and promised the swineherd that his master would return shortly.

When asked about himself, Odysseus lied convincingly about the adventures and hardships that had reduced him to a beggar's state and brought him to Ithaca, and told also of hard times that had befallen and detained Odysseus. Although Eumaeus did not believe his guest's stories about Odysseus, he nonetheless took pity on the poor man before him and offered him shelter for the night.

ATHENA BRINGS TELEMACHUS HOME

Meanwhile Athena drew near Telemachus and Peisistratus on Menelaus's portico, and saw instantly that Peisistratus was napping but that Telemachus was fretting about his father. Telemachus, the bright-eyed goddess said, you must not linger abroad any longer and leave your property unprotected. The rabble in your house might eat up all that you stand to inherit.

She continued: Tell Menelaus that you must go immediately to your noble mother. Her father and brothers press her to marry Eurymachus, the suitor who lavishes the richest gifts on her and proposes the largest marriage settlements. Who knows? Should she give in, she might take away some of your rightful possessions.

You know, Athena added slyly, how women are.

It was well known that Athena thought like the warriors she assisted, and saw women as lesser creatures, the property of their fathers, brothers, and husbands; women were necessary to bear children—the seed of men!—but were not capable of straight thinking or consistent behavior. Athena rejected for herself the weaknesses of her gender and took pride in her manly virtues.

A woman, Athena warned Telemachus, likes to take treasures to her bridegroom's house. In marrying again a woman may forget about her dead husband and the children she bore him. So, Telemachus, go home to protect your wealth. Find the woman-servant you trust most and put everything into her keeping.

Telemachus listened to these instructions and took them into his heart, knowing the truth of them.

Then Athena added: Keep this in mind, too. Some of the suit-ors are waiting to ambush you in the Ithacan straits off the rocky coast of Samos. They intend to murder you.

But, the goddess added in a knowing tone, I do not believe they will succeed in preventing you from returning home. No, not at all. Rather, I believe the earth will close over the suitors.

Even so, Athena advised the son of her favorite hero, steer your ship away from the islands. Do not rest, but sail through the night. The gods will escort you and send you a good breeze. Then land on the first point of Ithaca that you reach. After you disem-bark, send the ship and its crew to the harbor. You, however, should go immediately to the swineherd's hut. He is loyal to you. Stay there the night and send him the next day to tell your mother, Penelope, that you are back and safe.

Athena then returned to Olympus, leaving Telemachus to absorb her message and to take courteous leave of his host, Mene-laus. After ritual feasting and gift giving, Menelaus and Helen sent Telemachus on his way home, praying that Zeus would provide the young man with protection. When the feasting and sacrificing ended, Telemachus and Peisistratus parted, and Odysseus's son boarded his ship and set sail, wondering if he would reach his home or be caught by the treacherous suitors.

Meanwhile, Eumaeus had invited Odysseus to remain with him and had promised that Telemachus, on his return, would give the poor beggar new clothes. When Odysseus's son reached the coast of Ithaca, he followed Athena's instructions, ordering the crew to land and allow him to disembark. As Telemachus arrived on the shore of Ithaca, a sign appeared to him—a bird sign, a message from the gods that Telemachus quickly understood.

A hawk flew overhead on his right side, and plucked the feathers from the dove it carried in its talons. The feathers fell between Telemachus and his ship, an omen, the young man knew, that all would be well. The gods' message lightened Telemachus's feet, and he walked swiftly to swineherd's hut.

ATHENA REUNITES FATHER AND SON

Athena watched Odysseus's son arrive at the swineherd's hut, where he was greeted as a friend by the dogs and embraced warmly by Eumaeus. Telemachus joined the two older men in breakfast and, sensitive to his responsibilities as host, whether in welcoming a visiting nobleman or a poor beggar, treated Odysseus with impeccable courtesy, showing himself to be godlike in his good manners and gentle ways. As Athena watched her warrior-hero and his son, the young man offered his disguised father a new cloak, tunic, and two-edged sword.

Telemachus explained that he would like to invite the stranger to his own home, but that the violence of the suitors made it impossible. After describing the situation in his home, Telemachus confided to Odysseus and Eumaeus that he longed to dispatch the suitors, but said: It is impossible for one person to take on that gang.

Odysseus commiserated with Telemachus, saying that he was deeply stirred and troubled by the young man's story and would join him in an instant in ridding his house of the suitors and their outrages against hospitality and civility.

Telemachus asked Eumaeus to go to Penelope and tell her that he had arrived home safely from his journeys. Athena watched and, as the swineherd left, drew near and made herself visible to Odysseus and the farm dogs. She appeared outside the swineherd's hut as a tall and beautiful woman, and stood near the open door and gestured with her eyebrows to Odysseus. When he obeyed her unspoken summons and joined her in the farmyard, Athena spoke to Odysseus: Son of Laertes and favorite of Zeus, quick-witted Odysseus, it is time for you to speak honestly to your son. Hold nothing back. When the pair of you have plotted your revenge on the suitors, you must then make your way into town and begin your work.

Still in the form of a tall and alluring woman, Athena added: I will be with you. I long for the fight.

Then Athena touched Odysseus and restored him to his own form; she gave him a clean tunic and cloak, returned healthy color to his skin, filled out his strong jaw, and invigorated his beard. He stood before her then as himself: virile and handsome, hero and king of Ithaca. Satisfied with her work, Athena disappeared.

When Odysseus returned to the hut, Telemachus looked at him in amazement, then lowered his eyes thinking the handsome man might be a god. You have changed, the young man said quietly. Your clothes, your complexion—surely you are a god. Be kind to us and we will make fine offerings to you.

Odysseus answered his son: I am not a god. I am your father. It is on my account that you have endured so much pain and sorrow, and that you have been humiliated by hoodlums.

But Telemachus could not believe that Odysseus stood before him, that the beggar had changed to king.

I am Odysseus, the father insisted, back from twenty years of wandering. The changes you see were wrought by Athena, the warrior-goddess, who can do anything. She makes me look as she wants, a beggar one moment and a finely dressed young man at the next. Gods have the power to glorify or debase a man at will.

And then Odysseus and Telemachus, tearfully overjoyed at their reunion, began to plot to kill the suitors. I came here at Athena's command, Odysseus said, and she will be with us in our destruction of our enemies.

Confident of Athena's aid, Odysseus and Telemachus devised the scheme by which they would rid their house of the suitors. When Athena gives us the signal, Odysseus said, we will know that she has clouded the suitors' minds and we will act swiftly. Meanwhile, tell no one that I am back in Ithaca.

Father and son set their plan in motion, arranged to get word to Penelope that Telemachus was safe and, simultaneously, to spread false information among the suitors about the young prince's whereabouts and plans. Furious that Telemachus had escaped their ambush and unable to agree upon another scheme for murdering him, the suitors embarked on another round of feasting, drinking, and rowdiness.

ODYSSEUS RETURNS TO HIS PALACE

An idea had come to Penelope, and she confronted the suitors, rebuking them sternly for their arrogance and evil; she castigated them for courting her while plotting to kill her son, and for living free at Odysseus's expense. Penelope then went to her room and wept for Odysseus until Athena came to her and closed her eyes with sweet sleep.

By the time the swineherd returned to the hut, Athena had turned Odysseus back into a poor beggar. And so the three men prepared a suckling pig, and sat down together in the swineherd's hut and enjoyed their supper. Satisfied with food and drink, they lay down on their beds and accepted sleep.

When Odysseus, still disguised as the old beggar, made his way to his palace, Argus, his old hunting dog, recognized him. Now too old to hunt, and sorely neglected, the flea-infested dog was lying in a dungheap. He raised his head slightly, wagged his tail to greet the master he recognized, and died. Although the dog's death cut Odysseus's heart, he gave no sign that he recognized his beloved dog but entered the palace to beg. The suitors insulted him, and violated the code of hospitality that Odysseus, like other aristocratic Greeks, held sacred. As he made his way among the louts who slaughtered his animals, raped his maidservants, and courted his wife, Odysseus took their measure and dreamed of revenge.

Penelope, however, asked Eumaeus to bring the old beggar to her, so that she might hear his claim that he had information about Odysseus.

Meanwhile, Athena brushed Telemachus with supernatural grace as he entered his home carrying two spears. As he strode through the banqueting hall, two dogs at his heels, all of the suitors turned to look at him with admiration. They spoke to Telemachus, their kind words masking the dark evil of their hearts.

As Odysseus moved among the suitors, he incited jealousy from another beggar who regarded him as an invader, and who resented his presence and competition for gifts from the wealthy suitors. The town beggar mocked and insulted Odysseus until, goaded beyond endurance by the town beggar's humiliation of him, Odysseus tucked his ragged clothes around his body and challenged his tormentor to a fight.

Athena had been watching and appreciated the opportunity for fun at the expense of the bullying beggar, and the chance to tease the suitors as well. She came close to Odysseus and enhanced his broad shoulders, muscular thighs, and brawny arms. The suitors remarked among themselves that the wretched beggar, under his rags, was a fine physical specimen; and the beggar-bully from the town quaked with fear. When Odysseus quickly beat his opponent, the suitors laughed, giving no further thought to the lowlife scuffling of mere beggars, and returned to their carousing—to the pleasures they derived from abusing another man's home.

But Athena began to move among them, putting foreboding and shadows of fear into their hearts.

PREPARATIONS FOR BATTLE

Confident of Athena's aid, Odysseus prepared for the coming battle. He instructed the trusted nurse-housekeeper Eurycleia to lock in their chambers all of the women of the palace. Then Odysseus and Telemachus began stowing helmets, shields, and sharp spears in the palace armory. As they moved toward the storeroom, Telemachus noticed a beautiful light that went before them and flooded their way in a golden glow. The stone and wood of the building seemed to be lit from within. Odysseus, knowing that it was light and a sign from Athena, cautioned Telemachus. Hush, he said. Accept the way of the gods who live on Olympus.

Penelope overheard a maidservant abusing Odysseus for his dirty clothes and lowly estate. She chastised the woman and then asked Odysseus to talk with her. Penelope had her disguised husband seated in a fine chair with a soft covering, and asked him about himself. Odysseus lied to Penelope, as he had to others who had shown curiosity about his identity since his return to Ithaca, and said that he was from Crete. There, he said, he had entertained her husband. He described the clothing, bearing, and appearance so accurately that Penelope wept.

When I first saw you, my friend, I pitied you, Penelope told the disguised Odysseus, but now that I know you gave kindness to my husband, you shall be a dear and honored guest in his house.

Penelope ordered servants to prepare a good bed for Odysseus, and she called Eurycleia to bathe him and dress him in fine clothes. In the course of washing Odysseus and rubbing sweet oil into his skin, Eurycleia saw on his thigh an identifying scar—the result of a hunting injury when he was a young man—and recognized her master. Odysseus swore her to secrecy, and Athena distracted Penelope so she would suspect nothing.

Later Penelope lay weeping for Odysseus until Athena closed her eyelids with sweet sleep.

Athena stayed near wise Penelope and gave her an idea that would inspire her to act in a way that would bring great admiration and respect from her husband and son. Penelope dressed beautifully in her finest robe, appeared before the suitors, and made them weak in the knees with desire. She told them that she, now accepting the fact of Odysseus's death, would choose one to be her husband. Therefore, she said, they should honor tradition and compete among themselves for her, each bringing cattle and sheep for banquets, and each offering her—a rich man's daughter!—the valuable gifts she deserved and expected.

Odysseus was delighted by Penelope's cleverness in extorting gifts from the suitors, but knew that her heart was intent on something else altogether.

All the while Athena moved among the suitors, stirring them to continue insulting the disguised Odysseus. She knew that fury was the king's greatest weapon in battle, and she was laying the ground for his battle against the suitors.

That night Odysseus was unable to sleep; his warrior's heart growled like a beast within his breast, and his anger swelled in anticipation of the battle with the suitors. Athena, again in the form of a beautiful woman, descended from heaven and stood at the head of his bed. She spoke soft words to her favorite hero: Odysseus, you are ill fated and sleepless. Why? You are home, your wife is here, and so is your son—a young man who would be an honor to any father.

Odysseus recognized Athena, and answered: Yes, true enough. Still, my heart is troubled. How am I to overpower those shameful suitors? There are many of them, and they are always together. I am one. And there is yet another problem. If it is Zeus's will and yours that I kill them, how shall I escape vengeance? I beg you to guide me in these matters.

Everyone knew that murder had to be avenged, that the relatives of men killed were bound by honor to track down and slay the murderer. It was a cornerstone on which *honor* itself rested. Odysseus, looking beyond the promised victory over the suitors, knew that their relatives would put him and his allies—including Telemachus—to death. But Athena, too, thought about the future; and she willed a conclusion that Odysseus could not imagine.

So Athena chided Odysseus: Oh you are incorrigible. Most men go into battle with mere mortals as allies, but you have my divine cunning on your side. I am a goddess and have never failed to watch over you in all of your trials. Understand what this means: You and I might be surrounded by fifty companies of well-armed men, all eager to spill our blood, but you would still be victor and take away their cows and sheep as spoils.

Now, Odysseus, Athena urged, go to sleep. Tomorrow you will rise above your troubles.

With those words commanding Odysseus to have faith in her powers and cunning, Athena closed the king of Ithaca's eyes in sleep, and she returned to Olympus.

THE SUITORS ARE DOOMED

On the following day, the suitors resumed their feasting and brawling. As they recommenced their plotting to kill Telemachus, a bird omen appeared and frightened them. That unsettling harbinger was quickly followed by Athena, who moved among them, fuddled their senses, and caused them to burst into uncontrolled laughter quickly followed by pangs of dark foreboding. Satisfied that the suitors were thoroughly mired in confusion, Athena then induced the ill-mannered louts to insult Odysseus and Telemachus. In this manner she made certain that both father and son were near bursting with raw anger. And so as the suitors sat down to their bountifully laden banqueting tables, a goddess and a strong man were preparing for them their final fare: the fate that their villainy had won for them.

Now Athena, goddess of the flashing eyes, induced Penelope to produce Odysseus's great bow the next day. It was one of Odysseus's most treasured possessions, and it was said to be an instrument only he could string and shoot. Penelope, full of Athena's well-plotted inspiration, agreed to marry the suitor who was able to string the bow, then shoot an arrow through the rings on a line of axes standing upright.

As each of the suitors struggled and failed to string the bow, Athena stood near Odysseus as he revealed his identity to Eumaeus and to the cowherd Philoetius; then he instructed Eurycleia to lock the doors of the palace. Penelope, unable to bear the tension and the pain of watching the loathsome suitors maul Odysseus's splendid bow, retired to her room, and Athena put her into a deep sleep so that she would not be disturbed by the impending battle.

With the women out of the way, Odysseus, still disguised as a lowly beggar, stepped forward and persuaded the suitors to let him try the bow. He picked it up as a musician might lift his lyre, flexed and tested it; as they watched incredulously, the master of the palace easily strung his bow. Then, just as easily, Odysseus took straight aim, and shot. His arrow flew through the air and missed not a single axe, but drove through the first handle ring and all that followed.

Then, in a display of proper manners, Odysseus offered to help Telemachus prepare a meal for the suitors, and to begin the evening of music and dancing. This was the sign Telemachus had been awaiting: he slung on his sword and gripped his spear, then stood by the chair at his father's side.

SWEET REVENGE WITH THE HELP OF A GODDESS

Odysseus of course was armed with his bow and a quiver full of arrows. He threw aside his ragged clothes and positioned himself on the threshold of the banquet hall. Before the suitors could comprehend the change in the beggar, Odysseus stood before them as himself and, godlike, shot one of the suitors, an especially nasty-mannered fellow, just as he prepared to drink wine. The arrow passed through his throat, the wine cup dropped from his hands, blood spurted from his nostrils, and he fell dead upon the floor. The suitors still thought that Odysseus was a beggar, and assumed he had killed one of them accidentally. But they nonetheless prepared to kill him. The fools!

Their fate was sealed; Athena was there to see that Odysseus won the revenge he deserved.

Dogs! Odysseus yelled: You thought me dead. You abused my family and squandered my goods. You raped my maidservants; you courted my wife—you did all of this with no thought or fear of the gods or of the vengeance you might suffer at my hands. One and all, you are doomed!

The suitors babbled their innocence, each blaming another for his presence, and each quaking with fear. Odysseus, the hero, looked at the mewling cowards. He had seen for himself the sorry state of his home during the invasion of the suitors. Now, assured of Athena's help, he set about taking the revenge he sought. And so Telemachus fetched additional arms, and the battle raged.

Athena appeared again as Mentor, but Odysseus knew that it was the goddess. He watched the suitors abuse Mentor, then promise to give him booty if he turned against Odysseus and helped defeat his lifelong friend. Athena, in Mentor's form, grew furious and called to Odysseus: Where is your thirst for battle, Odysseus? Where is your spirit? Your skill in war? For nine unending years you fought the Trojans, and you killed men time and again. You planned the destruction of Priam's citadel. So now you are in your own home, among the possessions you should protect, and you whine and hesitate in the face of the suitors!

Athena commanded in Mentor's voice: Come, Odysseus, stand beside me and learn how Mentor fights!

But Athena enjoyed the full orchestration of battle too much to give an easy victory to Odysseus and Telemachus. Leaving them to rip their enemies to bloody bits, the goddess turned herself into a swallow and flew into the rafters to watch and to intervene at whim. From her lofty vantage she relished the clangor and bloodshed.

But at last, high in the roof beams, Athena appeared as herself, and raised her deadly aegis and made it visible to the suitors. They knew then that Athena was against them and, like cattle stung by flies, they darted here and there, stampeding and trying to flee.

But Odysseus and his party swooped down on them like great birds of prey, and hacked them down. The suitors could not hide from black death; their screams were ghastly, and—as Athena had promised Odysseus—his wide floors ran with blood, and gore from the suitors stained his walls.

When the killing was finished, Odysseus ordered the slain suitors to be stacked like sacks of grain in the courtyard. The maidservants who had been raped by suitors or taken them as lovers—the circumstances of the sexual congress did not matter—were ordered to clean the banquet hall; then they were hanged. Yet more vengeance was to be done. Melanthius—a flagrantly disloyal goatherd who had insulted Odysseus in his beggarly mein—

was first tortured and then killed, his nose and ears severed, and his genitals hacked off and fed to the dogs as raw meat.

Then Odysseus and Telemachus washed themselves, and saw to it that the house, too, was cleaned and purified.

ATHENA REUNITES ODYSSEUS AND PENELOPE

Athena watched Eurycleia lead Penelope from her chambers to reunite with her husband. But Penelope could not believe Odysseus had returned, or that the beggar was actually her husband. Then Odysseus described their marriage bed with details that only he could have known: he had carved its footboard from an ancient olive tree, still rooted in the earth.

Then Odysseus, his heart as strong as a lion's, was bathed and oiled, and adorned in the most beautiful cloak and tunic in his store. Restored to his home, he went to meet his wife, and Athena smiled on him and enhanced his grandeur from head to foot. Her touch made him appear taller and sturdier, and caused his hair to hang thickly from his head. Athena sent him to meet his wife looking like one of the immortal gods.

Then Athena blessed the reunion by holding the night, and keeping dawn waiting on her golden throne until Odysseus and Penelope had turned from the pleasures of lovemaking to the pleasures of talk.

Only when Athena was satisfied that Odysseus had had his fill of lovemaking and sleep in Penelope's arms did the goddess summon golden-throned dawn to bring daylight to the world.

REVENGE UPON REVENGE

And so morning came and, after taking leave of Penelope, Odysseus called Telemachus and the swineherd and the goatherd and ordered them to arm themselves and—made invisible by Athena—they walked through broad daylight and into the country to visit Laertes, Odysseus's father. Odysseus reminded them of the gravity of the vengeance they had wrought on the suitors, and that their work had not been completed: Remember, he said, the customs of our community. When a man kills someone, he must go into exile, must leave his family and his land. We have killed the young men of the best families in Ithaca.

But Athena saw the vengeance achieved by Odysseus and Telemachus as justified; she watched over the reunion of the Ithacan king and his father, Laertes. Then she restored youth and vigor to Laertes and made him appear godlike to Odysseus.

Meanwhile, the relatives of the suitors had discovered what had befallen the fated lot, and they lusted to revenge the deaths of the young men of Ithaca. It was the honorable thing to do. Blood spilled must be washed away with more blood. With loud war cries, and angry promises to slaughter Odysseus and Telemachus, the suitors' relatives gathered their arms and prepared to slaughter the men who had killed their sons and brothers.

Athena watched the preparations for battle and spoke to Zeus: Father, speak with me and tell me what is in your heart. Is it your will that this strife continue? Or will you bring peace to both sides now?

The cloud gatherer and thunder thrower spoke to his child: Why do you ask me these questions? It was your idea that Odysseus should return and kill the suitors. Now that he has done so, he should be king forever. We must wipe from memory the slaughter of the sons and brothers who were suitors, and both sides must be united in friendship and peace and plenty.

Athena needed no further endorsement from Zeus. She was eager for action, and flashed down from the peaks of Olympus to Ithaca to set forever her code for a higher honor among mortals. Nearing Laertes' farmhouse as the relatives of the suitors closed in for revenge, Athena took again the form of Mentor and went to Odysseus's side.

She spoke to Laertes: Son of Arceisius, dear friend, pray to Athena, the lady of the flashing eyes, then quickly lift your long spear and hurl it.

With these words Athena instilled great strength in Laertes. He hurled his spear, striking the leader of the relatives. And the battle began: Odysseus and his noble son drew their swords and spears, moving forward together to slaughter all before them.

But Athena, bearing her aegis, raised a great war cry and stopped both sides. She commanded: Stop fighting, Ithacans. Separate now and shed no more blood.

Athena's frightening cry and the appearance of the raised aegis chased the color from the cheeks of men on both sides and, in terror, they dropped their weapons. Odysseus raised his own terrifying great war cry and would have swooped like an eagle after them. But Zeus threw a thunderbolt, and Athena spoke to Odysseus: Hold! Stop fighting! So Zeus commands!

Odysseus obeyed, and his heart filled instantly with happiness. Then Athena, disguised as Mentor, negotiated peace between the two sides.

ATHENA AND HONOR

Athena, speaking in one voice with Zeus at the end of the *Odyssey,* demanded a halt to bloodletting, an end to endless chain of honor brandished and honor challenged; she instructed the opposing sides to break the chain of vengeance forged by revenge, and to shun revenge as a weapon hammered from one party's real or imagined trespass on another's territory, home, or vanity. The warrior-goddess's rejection of violence as a means for solving problems among mortals was her last act on Homer's stage, her last utterance before she returned to her beloved Athens, to make her home in the temple her people built for her.

Odysseus was the last of the heroes to reach home, and he had done so with Athena's blessing and assistance. Throughout the Homeric epic, the relationship of Odysseus to Athena reflected the goddess's nature, giving clues to her eventual status as goddess of Athens and symbol of Hellenic civilization. Although Odysseus was as much a liar and braggart as strategist and hero, Athena applauded his propensity to get his way through cunning and trickery as she respected his feats of bravery; he, like herself, possessed practical intelligence. No one knows the sweet words that might have been exchanged between Athena and Hephaestus, but there is no doubt that Athena loved Odysseus; she neared flirtation, or even sexual innuendo, in her open expression of fondness for Odysseus, especially when she appeared to him in the guise of an alluring and accomplished woman.

But despite her love for the hero, Athena withdrew and left him to pay his debts to Poseidon, and to fate; it was only right that he do so, and was but another tax to be paid for the glory he sought among mortals and immortals. Odysseus had insulted the sea god; no matter how much Athena loved him, she could not— would not—cancel an obligation to her father's uncle. And so Odysseus, after ridding his house of the men who in his absence tried to steal his wife and worldly goods, and after strife and vengeance had been put to rest, still had to brave Poseidon's wrath.

Athena watched as Odysseus again left Ithaca, this time carrying an oar inland until the utensil was mistaken for a winnowing fan. At that point, as instructed, Odysseus was to make a sacrifice to Poseidon. He did this, it was told, and then lived into a ripe old age reflecting on his glorious deeds and heroic reputation.

And so the age of heroes ended; Athena was no longer so much a goddess of war as she was goddess of justice, wisdom, and civility.

The Athena Lemnia, by Pheidias (ca. 450 BCE) was dedicated to Greek colonists who went to Lemnos. This head, though a Roman copy in the Museum at Bologna, emphasizes the intelligence and serenity associated with Athena, patron goddess of Athens and symbol of Greek civilization.

part eight

WISE GODDESS OF
LAW AND JUSTICE

ATHENS, HOME OF THE GODDESS

Athena, everyone knows, loved Athens; and it was there in her city that she ascended to her role as goddess of wisdom; in the ancient city-state that cradled civilization, Athena changed from a purely supernatural and mythical being—a warrior-goddess, cunning and vengeful—to a benevolent goddess, mentor to Athens. She became a *historical* being, a recognized presence in the affairs of state and population. No longer a purely mythic being whose stories informed and inspired her people, Athena became a force in real events; she symbolized the basic changes in human consciousness that promoted civilization; and, finally, she moved her residence from a sacred precinct to the secular realm of the human mind.

The changes in Athena's role in human affairs were under way by the end of the *Odyssey,* as she concluded her life as a Homeric deity. The fierce warrior-goddess of the *Iliad,* having disposed of her enemies and protected Odysseus through the perils of both fantasy and reality, denounced vengeance as a means for

righting wrongs or expunging anger. Speaking in one voice with
Zeus, Athena charged mortals to settle their conflicts through
negotiation. Athena, evidently expanding her attributes beyond
those of the goddess who seemed so single-mindedly to relish the
bloody dispatch of the suitors, now commanded men boiling
with rage for blood vengeance: Lay down your weapons!

This is an incalculably important moment: one of the incan-
descent evidences of civilization as a concept. Personal honor is set
aside in favor of civic order; the hero, bristling with honor-to-be-
glorified, has outlived his time. The mortal who lives by code—by
law and social contract—who attains and practices citizenship
becomes the essential unit of civilization. The individual recognizes membership in a group, and is responsible to that group;
conversely, the community counts on the responsible behavior of
the individual, but also protects and supports each of its members.

The scene of Hellenic consciousness shifts away from battlefield and scenes of revenge, away from blood feuds and family
honor. Western culture has appeared; it will mature in Athens,
protected and symbolized by Athena.

ATHENS: HISTORY AND MYTH

Two sets of stories tell how Athens incubated and informed
human consciousness; both involve Athena. They are the stories of
myth and of history, the former occurring in and defining the
Greek mind, the latter occurring in the geographic space of
Attica, an area of approximately one thousand square miles containing a few plains for cultivation and a long coastline with good
harbors. But above all its natural resources and blessings, above its
great beauty and richness, Attica's greatest treasure was Athens.

Athenians have always claimed what twentieth-century
archaeology has confirmed: their place on the earth—the high
ground that would become their city—was always occupied.
Athenians, just as they have always told us, are *autochothonus;* they
are indigenous and of the earth. The site of Athens was home to
Neolithic inhabitants and has been occupied since that time without interruption.

Although Athens does not play a major role in the Homeric epics, it was in Mycenaean times (1600–1200) prosperous and organized enough to build a palace and fortified citadel on the Acropolis. After the Dark Ages, all of Attica was unified under Athens, and by the middle of the eighth century the city was an important center for the production of geometric pottery, a much-prized export commodity. It was during this time, probably around the middle of the eighth century, that Athens began to emerge as an increasingly important cultural and commercial center, with a growing population and an economy based largely on seafaring and trade, and that the city developed a system of government headed by magistrates instead of kings. But democracy as we understand it was a long way from the Athenian mind; power remained in the hands of the aristocratic families, many of them boasting genealogies that included the Homeric heroes, or even gods.

With the spread of literacy and the birth of *history*, however, identifiable men, mortals with names and dates of birth and death, began to grapple with the problems of human beings living in a community. One of the first names to serve as a milestone in the history of civilization is the lawgiver Draco. While history does not reveal details of Draco's laws, it is likely that he sought to put an end to feuds and homicidal vengeance by making murder a crime against the state and, further, punishable by death. In basing government on *written* laws, Draco introduced a revolutionary concept for the ancient Greeks. But he called for punishments so harsh as to win for his work the lasting judgment that it was "a code written in blood, not in ink."[*]

A generation later, in 594, Solon, an aristocrat who understood that the well-being of the state depended on the peasantry, was appointed *archon,* or the highest civic leader. Solon's preserved writings, mostly poetry, reflect his disapproval of the savage and unchecked greed of the rich and the aristocracy. Demosthenes tells us that Solon, addressing people assembled in the Agora, spoke against the rulers, saying, "They grow rich through unrighteous

[*]Plutarch, *Solon* XVII2

deeds, and steal for themselves right and left, respecting neither sacred nor public property."*

Chosen archon of the city in 594, Solon made an effort to address the social tensions caused by increasing population, poverty, and uncertain justice. He brought about the enfranchisement of more people; freed peasants from bondage based on debt; and established a law preventing any future mortgaging of men or women as security against debts. It was Solon, then, who began the slow and often difficult process of building Athenian society on the broad base of a free peasantry, and a written agreement—a constitution—defining the rights and responsibilities of all people. But Solon did not promote *democracy* as we understand it; rather, he created a hierarchy based on wealth instead of birth or political power; and he tied public office to that system of status.

Solon's changes did not prevent conflicts within Athenian society and, after a period of festering tension, an aristocrat who claimed direct descendance from the Homeric Nestor, Pisistratus, gained control of Athens in 546. Under the Pisistratus family, Athens came into its own as the center of Attica and as the precinct of the goddess of wisdom.

Later writers, notably Herodotus and Aristotle, credited Pisistratus with good rule, a judgment somewhat surprising to us since it is known that Pisistratus was brutal to his enemies, eliminating them through murder and exile. But he did not tamper with the constitution implemented by Solon, which may account for Aristotle's opinion that "He governed the city with moderation, as citizen rather than as tyrant."†

Aristotle believed that Pisistratus was supported by aristocrats and peasants alike, and that he ruled with the consent of the majority of the people. The "golden age of Pisistratus" is defined by a number of cultural efforts that, although probably intended to magnify the glory of Pisistratus and his sons as much as to honor the city's patron goddess, resulted in monuments and practices

---

*Demosthenes XIX
†Aristotle, *Constitution of Athens* XVI2.

that established Athens as the artistic and intellectual center of ancient Greece.

During the time of the Pisistratids, a splendid temple to Athena was built on the Acropolis; destroyed in 480 by invading Persians, it was later replaced by the Parthenon. The Panathenaeia, a festival in celebration of Athena's birth, became a grand and city-wide event that brought the people of Athens together in recognition of the grandeur of Athens, as well as to pay tribute to the goddess who blessed the city. And, although it is not certain when coins were first minted in Athens, it seems likely that during the reign of Peisistratus or his son the famous "owls"—Athena's coins—became the international Greek currency.

The classical period, often judged as the high point in Hellenism, is synonymous with the ruler Pericles (ca. 495–429), a man Thucydides judged to be Athen's greatest leader. He came to prominence through his military exploits, entered the political arena of Athens, and initiated an ambitious building program for the city. He is responsible for the great monuments that characterize the city—the Odeon, the Propylea, and the Parthenon. Under Pericles, Athens gained preeminence as a city of culture, intellectual vigor, and democracy, and, above all, as the home of Athena.

But the city state's policy of expansion (perhaps a symptom of her arrogance) and a series of military conflicts weakened Athens, and led to her defeat by Sparta (404). By the end of the fourth century Athens, still the symbolic soul of Greece, fell under Macedonian domination. In the second century Athens remained neutral as Rome established rule over Greece. Although Athens's political, military, and economic power had greatly diminished, she captured the Roman imagination as the center for education; no Roman was fully educated until he had studied literature, rhetoric, history, and philosophy in Athens. Between C.E. 120 and 128, Hadrian spent long periods of time in Athens, added to her architectural monuments, and absorbed and transmitted her learning.

Throughout the period of the third to the sixth century C.E., Athens was raided and sacked by Barbarians, and was subsumed in the Christian movement with its opposition to all things pagan. In 529 Justinian closed the Athenian School of Philosophy. And as Christianity obscured the Olympian deities, Athena's city fell into a long and dark eclipse.

ATHENS AND MYTH

A primary traditional function of myth is to draw people together in shared experience, to reinforce agreement about the meaning of events, and to transmit a sense of identity and group member-ship from generation to generation. In the process of performing these functions, myth has a remarkable mutability, a flexibility in telling that maintains a core of tradition but takes on characteris-tics and emphases that make it contemporary, that make a myth speak directly to the hearts and minds of its immediate hearers. These factors give special importance to the body of mythology associated with Athena and her eponymous city; it scarcely mat-ters in this context whether a myth is fabricated out of whole cloth by artists and writers of the Hellenic period or recast from tradition. In looking at Athenian myth for reflections of Athena in the historic period, it is of no importance to distinguish between a "pure" and a "literary" myth, assuming cavalierly that such a dis-tinction could be established clearly enough to forestall citation of endless exceptions-that-make-the-rule.

As writers of the fourth-century re-created traditional myths in a more rational—one is tempted to say "demythologized"—form, they gave Athenians their history. The writer's style, if not the substance in retelling the old stories, transformed myth to conform to Athenian pride. In this new guise old myths accounted for the past of the great city and its goddess, explained the situations of the day as a result of long-past events and heroes and, overall, promoted the notion that Athens was superior to all other cities, that its citizens were the most favored mortals, and that its aristocratic families indeed could identify a deity in their genealogy.

It is told that Athens was founded by King Cecrops, often depicted as a serpent with a human torso, who was deeply devoted to Athena. In the contest between Poseidon and Athena for jurisdiction over Athens, for example, Cecrops had broken the stalemate among the Olympians and cast his vote in favor of Athena. It was all well and good for the pugnacious Poseidon to offer mortals a salt spring on the Acropolis, and to invent the horse, but Athenians, said Cecrops, preferred a deity who tamed the horse (Athena invented the bridle and earned the epithet *Hippias*), one who gave the olive tree to mortals and who promoted civic harmony.

In further recognition of her importance to his city, it is said that Cecrops inaugurated the cult of the owl among Athenians. But it was Erechtheos, a descendant of Cecrops, who lived at the time in a temple on the site of the later (and still remaining) Erechtheum, and there kept an altar and performed rituals to Athena, thus formalizing the ties between the goddess and the city. The Athenians credit King Theseus with the unification of Attica under the rule of Athens.

The mythic history of Athens that emerged in the Hellenic period is based on a series of stories in no hard-and-fast chronological order in which specific works of art, cults, altars, shrines, as well as literary works promoted the near-deification of the generation of heroes, Mycenaean warriors whose glories were re-created incandescently in the Homeric epics.

And so the history of Athens, by common understanding, soon began with the birth of Athena. The Athena whose personality and attributes saturated her city was not the ancient fertility or household goddess of Crete, or even the bloodthirsty and treacherous warrior-goddess of the *Iliad*. Athena was born miraculously from the head of Zeus, and came to the Athenians as evidence of his special regard for the city. Unencumbered by feminine imperfection, she was her "father's child," known to love the "din of war and battle," and was free of feminine impediments, a masculine female. Athena was so independent that she not only did not grow in the "darkness of the womb," she never suffered the inconvenience or humiliation of helpless infancy, but stepped into the Olympian world as a fully empowered and realized adult deity. In addition to the physical maturity and power she presented at the time of her emergence from her father's head, she brandished weapons, symbols both of power and masculinity. She made it clear to the Athenians that she "sided with the male in every-thing," even though she rejected marriage. Powerful, masculine, and born solely from Zeus, Athena was the confidant of the lord of the universe, and second only to him in cosmic power. She was, in brief, worthy to be the goddess of Athens.

Her denial of femininity, too, corroborated the social struc-ture of Athens, where women were denied citizenship, where they belonged to men and were bartered in marriage by fathers, broth-ers, or uncles. In bearing Athena without female participation, Zeus emphatically denied the importance of women. Without Hera, his consort and legal wife, he could produce Athena—a splendid specimen, an excellent deity; but Hera, without Zeus, could produce only a cripple, Hephaestus, or a monster, Typhon.

The myth of Athena's birth also confirmed the prevailing Greek belief that the father was by far the more important parent, the planter of the determining seed in the inert female earth. Athena's birth, in sustaining that view, also symbolized the rela-tionship between men and women.

Thus, older myths appropriated by writers and artists of the fifth and fourth centuries to chronicle Athens' history were often political in nature, and explicated or promoted ideas important to civilized life in a community. Athena—less a warrior-goddess by Hellenic times and more an emblem of wisdom, justice, citizenly responsibilities—appears in these later treatments of old stories as a divine being, but she consistently applies her powers to further *civitas*. That is to say, the writers and artists of Hellenic Athens invoked Athena for secular purposes and celebrations, for propa-ganda, and for the promotion of civic pride.

And it was through Athens that Athena's attributes—love of beauty, truth, knowledge, and justice—came to be seen as the highest values of human civilization; Athenians saw their goddess as the emblem of their own genius. And so do we.

ATHENA AND THE FURIES

Athena stands at the beginning, middle, and end of the ancient Greek concepts regarding men and women, justice and power, freedom and law. In settling the case of Orestes and dispatching the Furies, Athena signified her city's values and attitudes as well as the problems that denied perfection to the Athenian concept of democracy.

Although allowed to reach his home, Agamemnon met death at the hand of his faithless wife, Clytemnestra, and her lover Aegisthus. Agamemnon expected to be welcomed into his wife's arms and bed; he did not know that Clytemnestra had betrayed him. Not only were they lovers, Clytemnestra and Aegisthus had banished Orestes, Agamemnon's beloved son, from his father's lands and riches; they had forced his daughter Electra into a humiliating marriage to a peasant.

But unaware of Clytemnestra's treachery, Agamemnon began his celebration of his homecoming with a ritual bath. Clytemnestra took the opportunity of her unsuspecting husband's vulnerability to bind him in his robes, however, and to stab him to death. Orestes, now fully grown, heard of the outrage against his father and, half mad with grief and anger, consulted the Delphic Oracle and learned that Apollo commanded him to revenge his father's murder. Orestes returned to Mycenae and, with encouragement if not help from his sister Electra, murdered Clytemnestra and Aegisthus.

But the Eumenides—the Furies, female immortals more ancient than the gods—were outraged by the murder of a mother. They had hovered near mortals and immortals throughout time; unbanishable and untamable, they had refused to cede their power and authority to Zeus and the Olympian gods. They remained frightening cronelike creatures who inflicted terrible penance for murder, and were known to be especially ferocious in punishing matricide. They tortured Orestes, and prevented him from receiving purification for the murder of his mother. They assailed him day and night, torturing him into madness. Unable to escape their persecution and unable to enter voluntary and purifying exile, as was the custom, Orestes returned to Delphi—still followed by the harrowing Furies. Apollo himself took responsibility for the murder, and absolved—or purified—Orestes. Still the Furies persisted, inflicting such extreme madness on Orestes that he gnawed off his finger in anguish. But the Furies continued to howl and wail, to darken the world with their anger and black threats.

Orestes, desperate and under Apollo's guidance, went to Athens and threw himself on Athena's mercy. He fell supplicating before her image, and begged her, the most powerful of the female deities, to intercede on his behalf with the Furies.

But the Furies followed. Their power was older than Athena's; they were female rage and outrage personified; their demands for punishment and justice had been ignored. They were called freakish; some said they had the heads of serpents or dogs, that they were gruesome in appearance and, although feared more for their irrationality than their sense of morality, they were detested. Some even poked fun at them: old crones, old gray ones, silly and mean old women. But they were intent upon punishing Orestes, and establishing once and forever that *matricide* was an unforgivable crime, requiring eternal torture of the murderer.

But Apollo had a different view of justice for Orestes, and so appealed to Athena, the wise one, now residing in Athens. She agreed to assemble the elders, the Areopagia, to conduct a trial of Orestes. In so doing, justice would be defined in terms of a rational and even-handed system, and neither the capricious whim of the gods nor the worldly power of one mortal over another would be allowed to divert *law.* Athena, Apollo, and the Furies negotiated the circumstances to govern a jury trial of Orestes. Apollo argued the case for Orestes, and the eldest of the Furies acted as prosecutor; Athena sat as judge. Apollo argued that motherhood was not important, that a woman is no more than the soil in which men plant their seed. Orestes, he argued, had been justified in killing his mother; she, said the god Apollo, was the lesser parent who had killed the *real* parent, the father. The jury split evenly on the verdict, but Athena cast the deciding vote, saying that she was totally on the side of the father.

The Furies cried out against the verdict, but Athena turned to them, her eyes bright with intelligence and reason, and pleaded with them to "yield" or "comply," to accept the jury's decision over their own fury, emotion. The verdict, she argued, did not dishonor the Furies. Take thought, she urged; do not be angry and emotional.

In gratitude to Athena, Orestes promised to build a temple in her honor on the hill of the Areopagus. Well pleased, the goddess offered a parallel gift to the Furies, saying to them, I will build a seat of worship for you.

But still the Furies howled, and still they railed against the terrible injustice that they insisted had been done to women. Theirs, they shrieked, was the ancient and proper law, and it had been subverted and violated by arrogant *new* gods. They turned away from Athena's reasoning words and threatened to spread their own blood over the land and cause crops to fail, pregnancies to miscarry, and a plague to descend upon Athens and all its people. No one, they warned, would escape their wrath, and the powers of the most ancient laws.

Athena approached the Furies with flattering words, calling them wiser than herself and more comely. She invited them to take up residence on her hill, the Acropolis, and offered to provide for them a special grotto where they could receive crowds of worshipers, and be rightly honored for their attributes. Solemn processions and generous sacrifices would be made for them, Athena said, and they would receive offerings after births; with reverence the first fruits of harvests would be laid before them. She offered them seats in a temple on the Acropolis.

But the Furies rejected Athena's proposal. Her patience running short, the daughter of Zeus spoke sharply to the Furies. I, she said, submit to the will of Zeus. She continued, threat now heard in her voice: I have access to the thunderbolts of Zeus. But yield to me, and there will be no need for force.

The mixture of promises and threats, of potential force and sweet cajolery, however, did not immediately move the Eumenides to cease their raging fury. And so Athena spoke to them again, very soothingly and sweetly, telling them that their compliance with the verdict would be to their advantage. Calm in her approach and respectful to the older goddesses, Athena promised them that she would not weary in arguing for their good. Pious reverence on their part for what is right, she told them, as well as the spell and charm of her own words, should stay their fury and cause them to accept her offer.

And so the Furies, it is told, much charmed and soothed by Athena, conferred among themselves, then joyously accepted the goddess's invitation to live underground, to submerge themselves in a grotto beneath the Acropolis. This is how the Furies were instantaneously transformed to "the Benign Ones."

And so the Furies, led by Athena's priestesses carrying torches and singing their praises, entered the deep cave. There they remained, female rage and outrage submerged in the earth forever, driven beneath the surface on which large and small events occurred, isolated from the daily activities of the people. As ancient female powers melded with the body of Mother Earth, just before they became silent and invisible forever, they sang a hymn to praise and blessed Athens; Athena listened with delight.

I rejoice, she said, and Zeus prevails.

With that the Furies have been forgotten, except, it is said, when they invade the minds of mad women and howl bitterly against the greater madness of the world.

Some say Athena lied to the Furies and tricked them, that she betrayed females by subduing the gods more ancient than herself. But others insist that Athena proved yet again her wisdom, her diplomacy, and, above all, her special love for Athens and its people.

ATHENA, ART AND CIVIC LIFE

By the fifth and fourth centuries the writers and artists of Athens concentrated on their city with such forceful pride and spectacular talent that they may be justly accused of extracting images from myth so forcefully as to create in their work a tradition for their city. The tragedies associated with Orestes, for example, recognized Athens as the center of law and justice, the favorite precinct of Athena.

The artists of Athens made it clear in their vase paintings and sculpture, in their poetry and plays, that their city, from its most ancient inhabitants until their day, had been blessed by special protection from Athena. Their histories—stories, images, heroes, fortunes—were intertwined, each belonging to and existing as a part of the other. It is perhaps owing to the work of Hellenic artists, writers, and philosophers that successive generations have seen Athens as the symbol of Athena and known Athena as the goddess of her city. Moreover, the affinity between goddess and city has been corroborated by relics of the religious festivals of the city, as well as the great civic art projects that link Athens with the goddess.

Athena's birth and character were the subject of works in sculpture and on vases, as well as an accepted fact in the literature of playwrights and poets of the city. In works of art, moreover, Athena was often allied with Hephaestus: he cleaved open Zeus's head and released her; his seed fell on her and then on the earth to produce Erichthonius, an Athenian hero; and both Athena and Hephaestus were fond of craft and of those who made things.

Athena's role in the battle of the gods and giants, too, appealed to the Athenians. Their patroness again showed her importance, not only among the deities but also as a strategist and as a warrior of uncommon skill. The popularity of the battle is attested by its prevalence as a theme on vases and as the subject of the pediment sculpture of the sixth-century temple of Athena and on the Parthenon's metopes. The battle is prominently featured, too, inside the shield of Phidias's great cult-statue of Athena. Perhaps its significance is best understood, however, by recalling that the battle of the gods and giants was the theme woven into the decorative pattern of the robe offered every four years to Athena, the ritual gift central to the celebration of the Panathenaea, the most important religious festival of the Athenians.

ATHENA CELEBRATED BY ATHENIANS

Festivals, like other arts, gave public expression and form to Greek religion. And, again like the popular arts of Athens, festivals both honored the gods and entertained the people. All festivals throughout ancient Greece combined processions, sacrifices, and feasting; but since festivals embodied the values and attitudes of their communities, Athenian festivals—like Athenian arts—were singularly styled by and characteristic of Athens and the city's relationship to its goddess.

Descriptions of Athenian festivals have come to us from ancient sources. Rooted in the same soil that produced myth, the various festivals preserved mysteries, beliefs, and rituals related to the gods, but, as they were practiced in Athens, the festivals often served to bridge the secular and divine. Not surprisingly, Athena occupied a prominent position in the festivals. The most important of these, of course, was the Panathenaea, but several less-known and smaller-scale festivals provide telling glimpses of Athena's relationship to the people of Athens, specifically the Arrephoria, Chalkeia and Plynteria—all with unique purposes and qualities that made them self-contained, yet all with direct bearing on the Panathenaea.

ARREPHORIA

The archon basileus—an official of kingly powers—selected two well-born young girls, aged about seven years, from four nominated by the people of Athens, to participate in a secret rite, the *Arrephoria*. The young girls, called *arrephoria*, lived in special quarters near Athena's temple and assisted her priestesses. At the time of the festival, in midsummer, the young girls were required to carry baskets containing holy objects placed in them by the priestesses of Athena. Neither the priestesses nor the young girls, it is told, knew what the holy objects were.

On the night of the main ceremony the girls carried the baskets through a secret underground passageway that took them from the top of the Acropolis to a place below known as the sanctuary of Aphrodite in the Gardens. There they deposited the baskets, and returned with another set of baskets, which they gave to Athena's priestesses. Once this sacred duty was performed and the secret objects exchanged, the young girls were dismissed and another set chosen the following year.

The meaning of the festival of the *Arrephoria* is unknown, but a rite of passage is seen by some in the actions described: young girls on the threshold of puberty carry secret objects from the higher precinct of Athena, goddess of wisdom, to the lower precinct of Aphrodite, goddess of erotic love. It is also tempting to speculate whether these baskets and their contents might in some way have recalled the hiding place Athena chose for Erichthonius and, for the citizens of Athens, would surely have recalled the strong relationship of their ancient kings to their patron goddess.

CHALKEIA

Named after copper and bronze, the *Chalkeia* involved both Athena and Hephaestus, colleagues in support of artisans; and it also involved the *arrephoria*. Unlike the festival of that name, however, the *Chalkeia* invited the people of Athens to a splendid public feast.

The *Chalkeia*, celebrated every fourth year before the Panathenaea, required *Ergastinai*—"female workers"—to weave a giant garment (*peplos*) for Athena. They worked diligently at a loom to produce a work that included images of the Gigantomacy, and that had to be completed in nine months; and everyone knew that it also had to please the goddess. The two young girls selected by the archon basileus from four nominated by the people of Athens, the *arrephoroi*, were dressed in white and assigned to assist the weavers.

A sacrifice and feast accompanied the presentation of the *peplos* to the heroic sculpture of Athena in her temple. While we do not know the precise purposes or significance of the *Chalkeia*, it appears to have been a celebration of craft and craftworkers under the protection of Athena and Hephaestus, those overlords of artistry who were themselves craftworkers.

Athena *Ergane*, inventor of the ceramic vase and an abiding patron of the potmakers at the foot of the Acropolis, was goddess of all handicraft, with a special affinity for women (such as Helen and Penelope) who executed fine work with fiber and fabric. Athena's pleasure in craft was not limited to weaving and pottery, but extended to all the other materials mortals chose to form for useful purposes. And it was remembered by Athenians that she had a special fondness for the lame smith-god Hephaestus, who, it was told, produced magnificent works in metal. By honoring the two gods together, acknowledging their special bond of friendship, the

Athenians gave themselves opportunity to recall the story of Erecthonius and the importance of one of their city's most famous heroes to the Olympians.

Not just aristocrats claimed immortal ancestors; *all* Athenians descended from the gods; that, of course, required gifts to the gods, and regular celebrations.

PLYNTERIA

The feast of the bath, or *Plynteria,* occurred on the day when the statue of Athena Polias was taken to the sea and washed. Rooted in Ionian custom, the festival also called for the washing of Athena's temple, so that the cleansed cult image returned to a suitably pristine dwelling.

It is believed that the particular cult statue involved in the ritual bathing was a seated figure without weapons, probably carved from olive wood, and probably dressed in real garments and adorned with real jewelry.

On the day of the bath, women belonging to a special clan, the Praxigeridai, undressed the statue and, accompanied by dashing Athenian horse soldiers, the ephebes, carried the goddess in a procession to the shore at Phaleron. No one save the women who bathed the statue were allowed to see the goddess naked; they remembered what had happened to Tiresias and, no impiety intended, they thought natural vision more desirable than god-sight into the future.

Athenians not only wanted to pay tribute to their goddess and keep her comfortable in her home on the Acropolis, but also enjoyed an intimacy with her that was denied others. Athena, it was said, allowed her chosen people the privilege of caring for her, keeping her images fresh and beautiful.

PANATHENAEA

Greek sculpture represents the life of the Greek mind rather than that actually experienced by the people of the age. Nowhere is this more apparent than in the sculptures on the Parthenon, where, among other depictions of myth and Athenian life, the procession of the Panathenaea are the best-known and arguably most important of the Athenian festivals, is presented.

The procession occurred on Athena's birthday, her miraculous emergence from the head of Zeus, and venerated in the sculpture on the east pediment of the Parthenon. There are numerous other evidences of the event, however, to be found on vases and in inscriptions detailing the prizes offered and won in the games associated with the celebration. The first Great Panathenaea, according to archaic inscriptions found on the Acropolis, was celebrated in honor of Athena, "the girl with the owl eyes," and occurred in 566.*

The Panathenaea is thought originally to have been called merely the *Athenaea* and, as the Athenians tell it, to have been founded by Erichthonious, but to have been renamed in honor of the unification of Attica at the time of Theseus. It is probably the most ancient and surely the most important of Athenian festivals: it is also dedicated solely to the patron goddess of the city, with all sacrifices, processionals, offerings, and rituals in her honor.

An annual, or lesser, Panathenaea was celebrated from the time of Pisistratus, but the *great* Panathenaea was held every fifth year, in the third year of each Olympiad, from the 24th to the 29th of Hecatombaeon (July–August), the date on which Athena was believed to have been born from Zeus's head. In 566 Peisistratus added horse and chariot races to the ancient athletic contests. It is uncertain whether he or his son Hipparchus introduced the recitation of the Homeric epics at each Panathenaea, at a special feast, thereby causing references to Athens in the epics that may not have appeared in the original works, but may have been added to please the proud Athenians.

Pericles added musical contests in 446. On the first day of the festival musicians gathered in the Odeum, one of the many architectural works sponsored by Pericles, and competed for honors in dancing and choral works, and for the golden crown that

---

*A. Raubitshek, *Dedications from the Athenian Akropolis*, Cambridge, Mass. 1949. Nos. 326–28.

designated the first prize. Like musicians, athletes also were crowned with a garland of olive leaves from Athena's sacred tree and presented with enormous and beautiful vases filled with oil from the same source. Typically these vases, dating from the fourth century, show the figure of Athena on one side and, on the other, a depiction or design related to the contest for which they were the prize.

Ten elected stewards oversaw these events, as well as torch racing and other splendid activities associated with the great festival. All events, however, led to the focus of the celebration, to the 28th day of the month, Athena's birthday. On that day the grand procession moved solemnly through the city to carry the richly embroidered saffron *peplos* to Athena in her sanctuary on the Acropolis.

Woven during the preceding nine months by women in Athens, decorated with scenes from the battle of the gods and giants, the *peplos* was set like a sail on a wheeled cart and paraded before all the people of Athens. Then it was taken by the solemn procession to the statue of Athena Polias.

The Panathenaic procession is the subject of the venerated frieze of the Parthenon, and shows priests and their religious attendants leading a long line of animals destined for sacrifice. Women carry baskets containing sacrificial implements; old men carry olive branches; warriors decked out with shields and spears, young men in armor, and the splendid cavalry add to the excitement of the procession. Women carry waterpots; men carry cakes for offerings; and maidens carry sunshades and stools. Other citizens and celebrants, some thought to represent other cities, join the march.

The procession ended with the offering of the *peplos* to Athena, and then with the sacrifice of oxen and a citywide feast.

ATHENA'S ACROPOLIS

As Athenians in the age of Pericles celebrated festivals in honor of their goddess, no one doubted that Athena occupied the splendid residence prepared by her people for her, the Parthenon on the

Acropolis. And of course Athena is still recalled in that most important of her ancient precincts; people today go there in crowds, walk among the ruins, and recall the glory of ancient Athens.

The Acropolis in Athens is a limestone table that rises over five hundred feet from the floor of the surrounding city and, for centuries, was the site of rituals, festivals, architecture, and sculpture dedicated to the goddess. Now the buildings are in various stages of ruin, the great sculpture lost or removed to safekeeping in museums, and the festivals and rituals only dim shadows in the works of ancient writers. Even so, with appropriate information and the exercise of imagination, we can infer from the battered stones the presence of Zeus's daughter, the goddess of wisdom, a personification of the Greek genius.

A person alive in fifth-century Athens knew the Acropolis in its splendor, and knew its altars, statuary, and architecture as embodiments of history, stories, and ideas associated with Athena, eponymous goddess of their city. The rituals and festivals celebrated around the altars, the sacrifices and offerings, the attributes of the sculptural images and the stories they depicted, and the grand marble buildings were familiar and necessary parts of civic life for the fifth-century Athenian. In brief, someone alive at the time of Pericles could read and understand the Acropolis as the people of the Middle Ages read and understood cathedrals, or as we might read the documents that define our government or the texts that sustain our religious beliefs.

We still find it possible to begin the long, complicated search for Athena on the Acropolis. It is true that we can only presume to envision the original grandeur of the Acropolis and can only hope to grasp the potency of the stone messages and meanings that crowned the rocky table in the center of Athens. Nonetheless, the Acropolis is precisely the point of departure for the intellectual journey in search of Athena. The goddess took shape in the minds, words, and works of mortals, and nowhere more powerfully than on the Athenian Acropolis. And there, if anywhere, we can imagine ancient people in the process of creating Athena—imagining her role in the cosmos, forming ideas and images of her to explicate the nature and scope of her powers, and making her visible, knowable, in real material and real space.

Despite the current state of the Acropolis we are able to see a plinth where a great bronze figure of the goddess once stood, the remains of several altars, the Temple of Athena Nike, the Erechtheum, and the Parthenon—altogether perhaps the greatest arts project ever undertaken at public expense, and certainly one of the most effective in promoting civic pride and loyalty. The buildings and sculpture in their dazzling prime exceeded the requirements of propaganda, however; they embodied the Greek consciousness, and all testified to the presence of Athena.

There was no doubt as to the purpose of the Acropolis in the days of its glory. It was dominated by a thirty-foot-high sculpture of Athena the Champion—*Athena Promachos*, which stood overlooking a processional way used by people making sacrifices and offerings to the goddess who was known to guarantee protection to Athens. Visible for miles, the heroic figure, masculine in style and stance, wore a warrior's helmet and carried a shield and spear, reminding all who saw her that she had given Athens victory over enemies.

Although she shared the temple with Poseidon and Hephaestus, Athena influenced the Erechtheum, a sanctuary on the north side of the Acropolis, where her olive tree grew as a reminder that she had won the contest with Poseidon for control of Attica. The site was said to have been chosen by the virgin goddess's surrogate son, Erichthonius, himself a link to her earlier powers as a fertility goddess, and to the snakes who served as familiars to the ancient earth goddess. Some say that Erichthonius lived in a house not far from the temple, and that Athena was a frequent visitor in his banquet hall. Today the Erechtheum's porch, its roof supported by caryatids, recalls stories about the relationship of Athena to Hephaestus and Poseidon, as well as the history of the early Athenian kings.

The jewel of the Acropolis, however, is the Parthenon, a magnificent residence for Athena the Virgin—*Athena Parthenos*—built on orders from Pericles, and with public funds in support of the greatest architects of the time, Ictinus and Callicrates. Phidias created sculpture to enhance the architecture and to remind people of the magnificent history of Athens and of their patron goddess Athena, an aspect of the goddess celebrated in the Parthenon frieze, with its heroized representation of the Athenian polis, description of the Panathenaic procession, and rituals and sacrifices made to Athena.

The east pediment told in lucid sculpture the story of Athena's birth from Zeus's head, an event that helped establish Zeus as the most powerful god in the pantheon and as the overlord of an ordered cosmos. The birth of Athena, solely from her male parent, also represented a theological sleight-of-hand that transmogrified an ancient and powerful-over-all female deity into a daughter goddess subservient to the all-powerful father god.

The sculpture of the west pediment of the Parthenon depicted the contest between Athena and Poseidon for possession of Athens. Poseidon has been allied with barbarity through his display of mercurial temperament, rebellion against Zeus' authority, and quick and terrible vengeance against mortals. Athena's struggle with Poseidon is both a challenge to male power and to barbarity. Winning Attica contributed to Athena's power, and therefore to the perception of her masculine personality; in defeating Poseidon in a political conflict, Athena established herself as a powerful female within a male hierarchy.

The sculptural sequences of the Parthenon remind us of contradictions, complications, and confusions surrounding Athena throughout the long millennia of her story. Perhaps the primary dichotomy is between her male character and female form. We know, for example, that she remained a virgin, refusing both lovers and marriage, a blatant rejection of the female role in society. Moreover, she displayed male characteristics in her love of war and political machinations, her inspiration and protection of heroes who combined the skills of leadership and action, and exercise of her will through both force and cunning. It is remarkable to find any female—even a goddess—in such discord with the prevailing attitudes of her time.

But Athena was extraordinary in every respect. To begin with, she was next to Zeus in power and therefore not limited by the usual constraints defining females; rather, through her association with male deities and mortal heroes, Athena became an honorary male who gloried in battle, championed heroism, and seemed to waste little affection on female mortals or deities.

In the presence of the Parthenon sculptures, it must be noted that other females who adopted a masculine lifestyle were punished severely, but Athena triumphed. For example, Athena, unlike the masculine Amazons depicted in the metopes below the pediment of the Parthenon, was not punished, but celebrated, for her adoption of masculine attitudes and postures.

A fifth-century Athenian would have known that the sculptural chronicle of the war between the Amazons and the giants pitted female against male, and would have identified the Amazons with barbarity because of their denial of marriage and family ties, and their refusal to submit to male domination and male-defined social codes; they were well known for their repudiation of marriage and their preference for the masculine lifestyle of hunting and fighting. The metopes show the Amazons being defeated and severely punished by males for their violation of social norms. Yet the Parthenon is evidence that Athena—who also engaged in masculine pursuits and who so thoroughly rejected the female womb that she was born from her father's head—was honored and worshiped by men, and was known to be welcomed into the company of warriors and heroes.

Moreover, in challenging her father's brother Poseidon for authority over Athens and Attica, and in winning the contest with her gift of the olive tree—deemed superior to Poseidon's offering of a spring of salt water on the Acropolis—Athena further validated her power and her successful renunciation of male authority. In the process, of course, she also secured Poseidon's eternal enmity.

By the time the Parthenon was erected, Athena had put aside her warrior ways in favor of order and prudence in human affairs. By then she resided in the Greek consciousness as a symbol of civility, a force for wisdom and against barbarity. Civic virtue and social order are preached on the south metopes, in the subject of the war of the Lapiths and centaurs, where a conflict rages between rational-man and animal-man, between order and chaos, between stable marriage and rape, between socially sanctioned behavior and sexual wantonness. The centaurs, a race of half-men soldiers/half-horses, were known for their savagery. Invited to a wedding, the centaurs drank wine and began to rampage and rape, thus displaying their brutish nature by violating hospitality that had been offered to them. Violation of hospitality was a desecration of civility, a near-sacrilege that had traditionally incited the wrath of Athena.

The north metopes recall the Trojan War, which, on one level at least, was fought as a defense of marriage and hospitality against barbarous foreigners. The Trojans provoked the Greeks to war by stealing a wife rather than abiding by the rules by which fathers, uncles, and brothers exchanged daughters, nieces, and sisters for treasure.

We find in these sculptural passages on the Parthenon Athena's social and spiritual themes: order and chaos, civility and barbarity, male and female, and mortality and immortality. These same issues punctuate the Homeric epics, as Athena promotes the war between Priam's Troy and Agamemnon's Greece, and negotiates the heroes' fates. In the *Iliad* she is a fierce and vengeful warrior-goddess, a supreme strategist who maneuvers her Greek heroes toward victory as she manipulates Zeus to issue the decrees she favors. As a prime mover of the war and one of its chief executioners, Athena, arguably, controls both her fellow gods and mortals: in the end, she has her way with the war and with the heroes. In the *Odyssey*, however, Athena concentrates on bringing about the homecoming of her favorite warrior, Odysseus, in routing uncivilized men from his home and bringing them to vengeance for their barbarity. Thus, the warrior-goddess in the *Iliad* becomes the champion of civility and peace in the *Odyssey*. Still, Athena's story is not confined to the bounds of the Homeric epics: it begins long before the Trojan War, in the dim recesses of Minoan and Mycenaean prehistory; it grows into myth in the fertile soil of human imagination; and it is given shape by the Greek genius in quest for civilization.

ATHENA PARTHENOS: IN THE SHADOW OF A
LOST MASTERPIECE

The most famous sculpture of Athena, the *Athena Parthenos,* a colossal sculpture by Phidias (ca. 460–455), no longer exists. Just as we probe the ancient texts for words about Athena, so we must infer from copies the glory of the original great sculpture. By all accounts, the *Athena Parthenos* was the image of the goddess most profoundly satisfying to the Hellenic mind, the one work of visual art that most profoundly summarized the history, attributes, dignity, and beauty of Zeus's gray-eyed daughter.

We can only imagine what she looked like to the people of the city. We know that she stood looming more than thirty feet high, at home and at rest in the city that shared her name, on the Acropolis where her greatest temple stood.

Today we can revivify the sculptor's vision of the gold and ivory—*chryselephantine*—summary image of Athena from several marble copies, as well as gem carvings and descriptions from ancient writers. *Athena Parthenos* was not merely a depiction honoring a powerful goddess; it was a civic portrait of the patron of the city that gathered and identified the ingredients of Western civilization. This dual function of the sculpture is rehearsed in the image of the goddess and in the iconography employed in the decorative schemes of the work; here, the goddess's history and identity, her aspects, powers, and epiphanies, were combined to remind Athenians—and those who have come after them—of her grandeur and of her ancient roots.

The gigantic sculpture stood on a base adorned with depictions of Athena greeting and dressing Pandora, the enchanting female created by Hephaestus at Zeus's command to fill men's lives with misery and lust. As presented by Phidias, *Athena Parthenos* is a tall, muscular woman, with handsome features and bearing; she wears a long, graceful gown and a warrior's helmet; her signature snake-bordered aegis shields her breast. In one hand she effortlessly carries a long spear; in the other she holds a six-foot-high Nike, goddess of victory. Her shield, an independent work of art itself, depicts scenes from the battles of the giants and

Amazons and, under the heavenly oversight of the sun and moon, Helios and Selene, the bas-relief on the shield describes the separation of gods from giants.

Almost hidden behind the golden shield, Athena's two most renowned familiars, her house snake and her round-faced owl, recall in their presence the goddess's long mysterious past before her membership in the Olympian pantheon. All of the images included in the *Athena Parthenos*—helmet, spear, shield, aegis, owl, snake—as well as the references to Athena's role in great episodes in the chronicle of the Olympian pantheon—are rooted in very ancient legends, and together constitute a system of symbols and signs that had the mythic power to enliven human imagination.

Athena Parthenos was not the goddess's final form, however; it is known that—taking intelligence, love of arts, and wisdom— she was transformed, this time into a less visible, perhaps more powerful force among those mortals who honored her. She moved as one aspect of the Greek genius into Western consciousness, into aspirations toward beauty, intelligence, and wise justice; she became embedded in human striving toward harmony.

IMMORTAL GODDESS

Just when Hellenic brilliance was being dimmed by the spread of Christianity, the last of the ancient great philosophies, Neoplatonism, developed. A strong intellectual force from the third century until 529, when Justinian closed the Academy at Athens, Neoplatonism was destined not only to influence Western metaphysics and mysticism but, in so doing, to serve as the means by which Athena solidified her place in human consciousness and civilization. Long before Saint Augustine, who was a Neoplatonist before he converted to Christianity, echoed the earlier brilliance of the Greek thinkers in his influence on the Christian church, Athena was assured a steady influence on human efforts to make art, know truth, and confer justice.

As much as any single identifiable human, Proclus assured Athena continuing life in the shared intelligence and cultural consciousness of Europe. According to his biographer, Proclus was born in Constantinople (probably around C.E. 410) and educated in Alexandria and Athens, where he became a teacher and a major Neoplatonist. As a mere lad, however, he told how he had been led to philosophy through Athena's interest in him; she drew him close to her and led him into the Platonic tradition, instructing him in the oneness of truth and beauty, in the nature of being, and in the steps by which an earnest student might gain knowledge.

Once settled in Athens, Proclus wrote hymns to Athena; and as a philosopher he identified her as the first pure god, the daughter of Zeus who is always represented as being armed and warlike. But her real attribute, he believed, is mind—she was, as Proclus knew her, the emblem of intelligence capable of knowing both truth and beauty.

Proclus argued that those who seek to know the nature of truth and being must first have been awakened to the distinction between mind and body, and must regard the body as the home of the mind or would; the seeker must then join Athena's domain in the universe, by residence in which the soul becomes, not surprisingly, the spectator of the primary realities themselves; then, through knowledge of the primary realities, the seeker can obtain a mystical vision of being.

It is told that sometime before his death in C.E. 485, Proclus often affirmed his debt to Athena, praising her for leading him to the life of philosophy. The goddess, it is said, let it be known that she indeed had chosen Proclus. The philosopher told how one night she visited him in a dream and stood before him as a beautiful woman. My image, she told him, that has stood so long in the Parthenon—he knew she meant her great sculpture—has been taken away by those people [Christians] who move things that should not be moved. Prepare your house, she said to Proclus, for the lady of Athens wishes to come to live with you.

And that is how Athena moved into the house of the mind, where since that time she has made herself available to those who share her love of beauty, truth, and justice.

ANCIENT WRITERS

Aeschylus (525–456). Greek tragic playwright. Many works lost; among extant: *Seven Against Thebes, Agamemnon, The Orestia.*

Apollodorus (b. ca. 180). Lived in Athens, Alexandria, Pergamum. His *Bibloteca* exists in part. Wrote on various subjects—myth, history, religion, geography.

Apollonius Rhodius (b. ca. 295). Greek epic poet. Best known for *Argonautica,* story of Jason and the Golden Fleece.

Diodorus Siculus (active ca. 60–30) Greek historian. Wrote history of Mediterranean world; fifteen books survive of the forty he wrote.

Euripides (ca. 480–ca.406). Tragic playwright, known for *Trojan Women, Helen, Orestes, Iphigenia at Aulis, Hecuba,* and other works.

Hesiod (probably lived in eighth century). Greek. Wrote poems, *Works and Days,* and *Theogony.*

Homer (probably lived in ninth–eighth century). Greek epic poet identified with *Iliad* and *Odyssey,* as well as collection of "Homeric" Hymns: the authorship of all, however, remains contested.

Hyginus (ca. 64–C.E. 17). Spanish ex-slave, librarian in Rome. *Genealogies* and *Fabula* attributed to him, along with work on astronomy, *De Astronomia,* which is probably not from his pen.

Ovid (43–C.E. 17). Latin poet. Wrote *Metamorphoses* and other epic and elegiac poetry.

Pausanias (second century C.E.) Greek writer and traveler. Recounted stories he heard and described religious and historical sites. Wrote *Description of Greece,* 10 vols.

Pindar (ca. 518–438). Greek lyric poet.

Virgil (70–19). Roman poet, known for *Georgics, Aeneid,* and *Eclogues.*

This Roman marble copy of the Athena Parthenos suggests Phidias's gold and ivory original (ca. 447-439), made for the Parthenon.

NOTES BIBLIOGRAPHY

Unless otherwise noted, the Loeb Classical Library was used as the source for ancient writers. Reference, secondary material, and general background sources include the following:

Adkins, Arthur W. H., *Merit and Responsibility: A Study of Greek Values,* Oxford, Clarendon Press (1960).

Austin, N., *Meanings and Beings in Myth,* University Park: Pennsylvania State University Press (1990).

Autenreith, G., *Homeric Dictionary,* translated Robert P. Keep; rev. Isaac Flagg Norman, University of Oklahoma Press (1958).

Barthes, Roland, *Mythologies,* trans. Annette Lavers, New York: Noonday Press (1972).

Bell, R. E., *Women of Classical Mythology,* Santa Barbara, CA: ABC-CLIO. (1991).

Bianchi, U., *The Greek Mysteries,* Leiden: E. J. Brill (1976).

Boardman, John, Jasper Griffin, and Oswyn Murray (eds.), *The Oxford History of the Classical World: Greece and the Hellenistic World,* Oxford; New York: Oxford University Press (1988).

Bremmer, J. (ed.), *Interpretations of Greek Mythology,* London: Croom Helm (1987).

Brunnel, P. (ed.), *Companion to Literary Myths, Heroes and Archetypes,* (1993).

Burkert, Walter, *Ancient Mystery Cults,* Cambridge: Harvard University Press (1987).

Burkert, W., *Creation of the Sacred,* Cambridge: Harvard University Press (1996).

Burkert, Walter, *Greek Religion,* trans. John Raffan, Cambridge: Harvard University Press (1985).

Burkert, Walter, *Homo Necans: The Anthropology of Ancient Greek Sacrificial Ritual and Myth,* trans. Peter Bing, Berkeley: University of California Press (1983).

Burkert, W., *Structure and History in Greek Mythology and Ritual,* Berkeley: University of California Press (1982).

Burn, L., *Greek Myths,* Austin: University of Texas Press (1990).

Buxton, R. (ed.), *Imaginary Greece,* Cambridge; New York: Harvard University Press (1994).

Campbell, Joseph, *The Masks of God,* New York: Viking Press (1953-68).

Carpenter, T. H., *Art and Myth in Ancient Greece,* London: Thames and Hudson (1992).

Childe, V. Gordon, *The Dawn of European Civilization,* New York: A. A. Knopf (1958).

Detienne, M., et al., *The Creation of Mythology,* trans. by Margaret Cook; Chicago, IL: University of Chicago Press (1986).

Detienne, Marcel, *The Cuisine of Sacrifice Among the Greeks,* trans. Paula Wissing, Chicago: University of Chicago Press (ca. 1989).

Detienne, Marcel, and Jean-Pierre Vernant, *Cunning Intelligence in Greek Culture and Society,* trans. Janet Lloyd, Chicago: University of Chicago Press (1978).

Detienne, M., L. Gernet, J. P. Vernant, and P. Vidal-Nacquet, *Myth, Religion and Society: Structural Essays,* ed. R.L. Gordon, New York: Cambridge University Press (1982).

Diel, P., *Symbolism in Greek Mythology,* trans. Vincent Stuart and Rebecca Folkman, Boulder, Shambala (1980).

Dillistone, F. W. (ed.), *Myth and Symbol,* London, S.P.C.K. (1966).

Dodds, E. R., *The Greeks and the Irrational,* Boston, MA: Beacon Press (1957).

Dowden, K., *The Uses of Greek Mythology,* London; New York: Routledge (1992).

Drews, Robert, *The Coming of the Greeks,* Princeton, NJ: Princeton University Press (1988)

Edmunds, L. (ed.), *Approaches to Greek Myth,* Baltimore, MD: John Hopkins University Press (1989).

Esterling, P. E., and J. V. Muir (eds.), *Greek Religion and Society,* Cambridge; New York: Cambridge University Press (1985).

Fine, John V. A. *The Ancient Greeks: A Critical History,* Cambridge, MA: Belknap Press of Harvard University Press (1983).

Finley, M. I., *The Ancient Greeks,* New York: Penguin (1977).

Finley, M. I. (ed.), *The Legacy of Greece,* Oxford: Clarendon Press (1981).

Finley, M. I., *The World of Odysseus,* revised edition, New York: Viking (1958).

Gernet, L., *The Anthropology of Ancient Greece,* trans. by J. B. Hamiliton and Blaise Nag, Baltimore, MD: Johns Hopkins University Press (1981).

Graf, F., *Greek Mythology: An Introduction,* trans. Thomas Marier, Baltimore, MD: John Hopkins University Press (1993).

Grant, M., and J. Hazel, *Gods and Mortals in Classical Mythology,* Springfield, MA: G. & C. Merriman Co. (1973).

Graves, R., *The Greek Myths,* 2 vols. Hammondsworth: Penguin Books (1955).

Griffin, J., *The Mirror of Myth,* London; Boston: Faber and Faber (1986).

Guthrie, W. K. C., *The Greeks and Their Gods,* Boston, MA: Beacon Press (1968).

Harrison, Jane Ellen, *Ancient Art and Ritual,* New York: H. Holt (c. 1913).

Harrison, Jane Ellen, *Epilegomena to the Study of Greek Religion and Themis,* Hyde Park, NY: University Books (1962).

Harrison, Jane Ellen, *Mythology,* Boston, MA: Marshall Jones Co. (c. 1924).

Harvey, Paul, *The Oxford Companion to Classical Literature,* 2nd ed. ed. M. C. Howaston, Oxford; New York: Oxford University Press (1946).

Herington, C. J., *Athena Parthenos and Athena Polias: A Study in the Religion of Periclean Athens,* Manchester: Manchester University Press (1955).

Homer, *The Iliad,* trans. Richmond Lattimore, Chicago and London: University of Chicago Press (1951).

Homer, *The Odyssey of Homer,* trans. Richmond Lattimore, New York: Harper & Row (1968).

Kerenyi, K., *The Gods of the Greeks*, trans. Norman Cameron, New York: Grove Press (1951).

Kirk, G. S., *Myth: Its Meanings and Functions in Ancient and Other Cultures*, Cambridge: University Press; Berkeley, CA: University of California Press (1970).

Kirk, G. S., *The Nature of Greek Myths*, Woodstock, N.Y.: Overlook Press (1974).

Leach, E. (ed.), *The Structural Study of Myth and Totemism*, London: Tavistock Publications (1967).

Leeming, D. A. (ed.), *The World of Myth: An Anthology*, New York: Oxford University Press (1991).

Lefkowitz, M. R., *Women in Greek Myth*, Baltimore, MD: John Hopkins University Press (1990).

Lerner, Gerda, *Women in History: The Creation of Patriarchy* New York: Oxford University Press (1986).

Levy, Gertrude Rachel, *Religious Conceptions of the Stone Age*, New York: Harper & Row (1963).

Metzger, H., *Recherches sur l'imagerie Athénienne*, Paris: E De Boccard (1965).

Morford, M. P. O., and R. J. Lenardon, *Classical Mythology*, 2nd ed., New York: McKay (1971).

Murray, Gilbert, *Five Stages of Greek Religion*, New York: Colombia University Press (1925).

Murray, H. A. (ed.), *Myth and Mythmakings*, New York: Braziller (1960).

Mylonas, G. E., *Mycenae and the Mycenaean Age*, London and Princeton, NJ: Princeton University Press (1966).

Nagy, G., *Greek Mythology and Poetics*, Ithaca, NY: Cornell University Press (1990).

Nilsson, M. P., *Griechische Feste,* Leipzig: B. G. Teubner (1906).

Nilsson, M. P., *Geschicte der griechischen Religion,* Munchen Beck (1941–50).

Pomeroy, Sarah B., *Goddesses, Whores, Wives, and Slaves. Women in Classical Antiquity* New York: Schochen Books (1975).

Pomeroy, Sarah B.(ed.), *Women's History and Ancient History,* Chapel Hill: University of North Carolina Press (ca.1991).

Puhvel, J., *Comparative Mythology,* Baltimore: Johns Hopkins University Press (1987, 1992).

Richter, Gisela M., *A Handbook of Greek Art,* London and New York: PHaidon (1959).

Rose, H. J., *Handbook of Greek Mythology,* New York: Dutton (1928).

Scully, Vincent, *The Earth, the Temple, and the Gods,* New York: Frederick A. Praeger (1969).

Seyffert, Oskar, *Dictionary of Classical Antiquities,* rev. Henry Nettleship and J. E. Sandys, New York: Meridian Books (1961).

Talbert, Richard J. A. (ed.), *Atlas of Classical History,* New York: Macmillan (1985).

Vernant, Jean-Pierre, *Myth and Society in Ancient Greece,* trans. Janet Lloyd (1980).

Vernant, J. P., *Myth and Thought Among the Greeks,* London; Boston: Routledge & Kegan Paul (1983).

Vernant, Jean-Pierre, *The Origins of Greek Thought,* Ithaca, NY: Cornell University Press (1982).

Vernant, Jean-Pierre, and Pierre Vidal-Naquet, *Myth and Tragedy in Ancient Greece,* trans. Janet Lloyd, New York: Zone Books (1988).

Veyne, P., *Did the Greeks Believe in Their Myths?* Chicago: University of Chicago Press (1988).

PHOTO CREDITS

Athenian silver coin. Courtesy, Agora Excavations, The American School of Classical Studies, Athens

Archaic head. Courtesy, Acropolis Museum, Athens

Athena with helmet and spear. Courtesy, Louvre, Paris

Mourning Athena. Courtesy, Acropolis Museum, Athens

Bronze figure of Athena Promachos. Courtesy, National Archaeological Museum, Athens

Athenian vase. Courtesy, Agora Excavations, The American School of Classical Studies, Athens

Athena holding the head of Medusa. Gift of Robert E. Hecht, Jr. Courtesy, Museum of Fine Arts, Boston

Athena Lemnia. Courtesy, Museo Civico, Bologna

Athena Parthenos. Courtesy, National Archaeological Museum, Athens

NOTES

PART I S*EVERAL* B*EGINNINGS*

O*UR BEGINNING: RACISM, SEXISM, AND CULTURE WARS*
    Bernal, Martin, *Black Athena*
    Keuls, Eva C., *The Reign of the Phallus: Sexual Politics in Ancient Athens*
       (1985).
    Lefkowitz, Mary, *Not Out of Africa* (1996)

I*N THE BEGINNING, MYTH*
    Burn, Andrew R., *The World of Hesiod*, 2nd ed. (1966).

I*N THE BEGINNING, DARKNESS*
    Hesiod, *Theogony, Works and Days, Shield*, trans. Apostolos N. Athanas-
      sakis (1983).
    Hesiod, *Theogony*, ed. M. L. West (1966).
    Hesiod, *Poems of Hesiod*, trans. R. M. Frazer (1983).

I*N THE BEGINNING, EROS*
    Hesiod, *Theogony* 211–232.
    Hyginus, *Fabulae, Poem*.
    Apollodorus: 1.7.1.
    Lucian: *Prometheus on Caucasus* 13.
    Pausanias: x.4.3.

ZEUS IN THE BEGINNING
Hyginus, *Poetic Astronomy* ii.13.
Aratus, *Phenomena* 163.
Hesiod, *Orphic Fragment* 58.
Apollodorus, i.3 1–2.

ZEUS, LORD OF THE UNIVERSE
Hesiod,
Hyginus, *Fabula* 188.
Apollodorus, i.1.7 and i.2.1.
Callimachus, *Hymn to Zeus* 52ff.
Diodorus Siculus, v.70.
Pausanias, viii.8.2.
Plutarch, *Why Oracles Are Silent* 16.

IN THE BEGINNING: PREHISTORY AND HISTORY
Chadwick, John, *The Decipherment of Linear B* (1958).
Fine, John V. *The Ancient Greeks* (1983).
Gimbutas, Marija, *The Civilization of the Goddess* San Francisco: Harper San Francisco (1991).
Gimbutas, Marija, *The Language of the Goddess* (1989).
Levy, Gertrude Rachel, *Religious Conceptions of the Stone Age* (1963).
Neumann, Erich, *The Great Mother*, trans. Ralph Mannheim (1974).
Vermeule, Emily, *Greece in the Bronze Age* (1964).
Warren, Peter, *The Aegean Civilization* (1975).

IN THE BEGINNING, RITUAL
Burkert, Walter, *Greek Religion* 10.
Apollonius Rhodius, iv.1310.
Plato, *Timaeus* 5.

OTHER BEGINNINGS: ATHENA IN CRETE
Scully, Vincent, *The Earth, The Temple, and the Gods* (1962).
Marinatos, Nanno, *Minoan Sacrificial Culture, Practice, and Ritual.* Stockholm: Swedish Institute, 1986.
Streep, Peg, *Sanctuaries of the Goddess.* Boston: Bulfinch, 1994.

THE MINOAN PALACES
Branigan, Keith, *The Foundations of Palatial Crete* (1970).
Evans, Sir Arthur, *The Earlier Religion of Greece in the Light of Cretan Discoveries* (1931).
Evans, Sir Arthur, *The Palace of Minos at Knossos*, 4 vols. (1921–23).
Graham, J. W., *The Palaces of Crete* (1962).
Hood, Sinclair, *The Minoans: The Story of Bronze Age Crete* (1971).
Hutchinson, R. W., *Prehistoric Crete* (1962).
Kenna, V. E. G., *Cretan Seals* (1960).

Levy, Rachel, *The Gate of Horn* (1948).

Marinatos, S. *Crete and Mycenae* (1960).

Palmer, Lenonard R., *Mycenaeans and Minoans*, 2nd ed. (1965).

Vaughan, Agnes Carr, *The House of the Double Axe* (1960).

THE MYCENAEAN CITADEL

Chadwick, John, *The Mycenaean World* (1976).

Mylonas, George E., *Mycenae and the Mycenaean Age* (1966).

Nilsson, M. P., *Homer and Mycenae* (1933).

Nilsson, M. P., *The Minoan-Mycenaean Religion and Its Survival in Greek Religion* (1950).

Nilsson, M. P., *The Mycenaean Origin of Greek Mythology* (1983).

Samuel, A. E., *The Mycenaeans in History* (1966).

Schliemann, Heinrich, *Mycenae* (1878).

Simpson, Richard, *Mycenaean Greece* (1982).

Taylour, William, *The Mycenaens*, rev. ed. (1983).

Ventris, Michael, and John Chadwick, *Documents in Mycenaen Greek* (1956).

Homer, *Iliad* iv.297ff.

PART II ATHENA AND THE OLYMPIAN PANTHEON

Hesiod, *Theogony* 886–8900.

Pindar, *Olympian Odes* vii. 34ff.

Apollodorus, i.3.6.

Herodotus, iv.180.

HERA AND HEPHAESTUS

Slater, Philip Elliot, *The Glory of Hera*

ATHENA, ZEUS, AND DIONYSUS

Diodorus Siculus, v.75. 4.

Nonnos, *Dionysica* vi.296 and xxvii.228.

Tzetzes, *On Lycophron* 355.

Eustathius on Homer's *Iliad* ii.735.

Euripides, *The Cretans*, Fragment 475.

Orphic Fragments (*Kern* 34).

PART III ATHENA, GODS, AND MORTALS

Hyginus, 166.

Apollodorus, 3.14.6.

A PROUD AND JEALOUS GODDESS

Euripides, *Ion* 995, 989ff.

Hesiod, *Theogony* 270ff. and 333ff.

Apollodorus, ii.4.3.

Ovid, *Metamorphoses* iv.1–145, 780, 792–802.

Scholiast on Apollonius Rhodius iv.1899.

Hyginus, *Poetic Astronomy* ii.12

Pindar, *Pythian Odes* x.31.

Virgil, *Georgics* iv.246.

PART IV EROS AND ERIS: MARRIAGE AND WAR

PART V WARRIOR-GODDESS

Homer, *Iliad*, trans. Robert Fagles (1990).

Homer, *Iliad*, trans. Richmond Lattimore (1951).

Homer, *The Odyssey*, trans. Richmond Lattimore (1968).

Homer, *Homeric Hymns*, trans. Thelma Sargent (1973).

Beye, Charles R., *The Iliad, the Odyssey, and the Epic Tradition* (1966).

Bowra, C. M., *Homer* (1970).

Ceram, C. W., *Gods, Graves, and Scholars*, 2nd rev. ed. (1986).

Clarke, Howard, *Homer's Readers: A Historical Introduction to the Iliad and the Odyssey* (1980).

Kirk, Geoffrey, *Homer and the Epic* (1965).

Mireaux, Emile, *Daily Life in the Time of Homer*, trans. Iris Sells (1959).

Nagy, Gregory. *The Best of the Achaeans: Concepts of the Hero in Archaic Greek Poetry* (1979).

Owen, E. T., *The Story of the Iliad* (1947).

Redfield, James M., *Nature and Culture in the 'Iliad': The Tragedy of Hector* (1975).

Vivante, Paolo, *The Homeric Imagination* (1983).

Wace, A. J. B., and F. H. Stubbings (eds.), *A Companion to Homer* (1962).

Wood, Michael, *In Search of the Trojan War* (1986).

*ATHENA, WARRIOR-GODDESS OF THE **ILIAD***

Boston Museum of Fine Arts, *The Trojan War in Greek Art* (1965).

Frazer, Richard M., *The Trojan War; The Chronicles of Dictys of Crete and Dares the Phrygian* (1966).

ACHILLES, PRINCE OF SULK

Iliad (hereafter I.) I.490–620.

Benardete, Seth, "Achilles and the *Iliad*," *Hermes* 91 (1963), 1–16.

ACHAEAN HONOR

I. I. 180–230; 525–570.

I. II. 878–900.

I. II. 523–545.

I. II. 555–560.

TROJAN HONOR

I. II. 921–926.

I. III. 15–22.
I. III. 45–60.

ATHENA, *LOVER OF WAR*
I. IV. 1–80.
I. IV. 81–99.
I. IV. 100–140.
I. IV. 148–167.
I. IV. 170–200.
I. IV. 212–218.

GODS *AND WAR*
I. IV. 510–530.

ATHENA *AND* **D**IOMEDES
I.V. 1–39.
I. IV. 40–43.
I. IV. 110–155.
I.V. 200–220.
I.V. 266–340.

APHRODITE, *SEX, AND WAR*
I.V. 360–494.

ATHENA *AMONG THE HEROES*
I.V. 480–508.

ARES
I.V. 816–1050.

THE **T**ROJANS *APPEAL TO* **A**THENA
I.VI.

ATHENA *AND* **A**POLLO; **A**JAX *AND* **H**ECTOR
I.VII.

ZEUS *DECREES*
I.VIII. 1–50.
I.VIII. 50–350.

HERA *AND* **A**THENA *AGAINST* **Z**EUS
I.VIII. 400–470.

GREEK *STRATEGY*
I. IX. 1–210.
I. IX. 220–550.

ATHENA, *QUEEN OF PLUNDER*
I. X.

Hyginus, *Fabula* 107.
Apollodorus, *Epitome* v.3., v.5.
Homer, *Odyssey* XXIV.43–84.

ATHENA PUNISHES GREAT AJAX
Homer, *Odyssey* xi.543ff.
Hyginus, *Fabula* 107.
Sophocles, *Ajax*, trans. John More; ed. David Grene and Richmond Lattimore (1957).
Knox, Bernard M. W., "The *Ajax* of Sophocles," *Harvard Studies in Classical Philology,* 65 (1961), 1–37.

ATHENA AND THE PALLADIUM
Apollodorus, *Epitome* v.13.
Sophocles, *Fragment* 367.

THE WOODEN HORSE
Hyginus, *Fabula* 108.
Tzetzes: *On Lycophron* 219ff., 344, 347, 930.
Apollodorus, *Epitome* v.14; v.16–17, v.19.
Homer, *Odyssey* viii.493.
Virgil, *Aeneid* ii.13–249, ii.256ff.
Homer, *Odyssey* xi.523–532 and iv.271–289.

MENELAUS RETRIEVES HELEN
Apollodorus, *Epitome* v.10, v.21, v.22.
Euripides, *Hecabe* 23.
Euripides, *Trojan Women* 16–17.
Virgil, *Aeneid* ii.506–557.
Homer, *Odyssey* viii.517–520.
Hyginus, *Fabula* 240.
Pausanias, v.18.

THE HOLOCAUST OF TROY
Arctinus of Miletus: *Sack of Ilium.*
Virgil, *Aeneid* ii.406.
Apollodorus, *Epitome* v.22, v.23.
Tzetzes, *On Lycophron* 365.
Pausanias, x.31.1; i.15.3 and x.26.1.
Homer, *Odyssey* iv.99.
Homer, *Iliad* vi.402.
Euripides, *Trojan Women* 719ff.
Hyginus, *Fabula* 109, 111.

PEACE AND PUNISHMENT
Euripides, *Trojan Women.*

ATHENA AND LITTLE AJAX
Hyginus, *Fabula* 116.

PART VII ATHENA AND THE ODYSSEY
Homer, *The Odyssey*, trans. Richmond Lattimore (1968).
Homer, *The Odyssey*, trans. E. V. Rieu, Penguin, rev. ed. 1991.
Dimock, G. E., *The Unity of the Odyssey* (1989).
Finley, Moses I., *The World of Odysseus* (1958).

ATHENA VISITS TELEMACHUS
Odyssey (hereafter O.) I. 1–106.
O. I. 107–270.

ATHENA INSTRUCTS TELEMACHUS
O. I. 270–446.

TELEMACHUS OBEYS THE GODDESS
O. II. 1–260.
O. II. 261–300.

ATHENA AND TELEMACHUS AGAINST THE SUITORS
O. II. 300–381.
O. II. 382–393.
O. II. 393–430.

ATHENA LEADS TELEMACHUS TO NESTOR
O. III. 1–395.
O. III. 329–497.

ATHENA WATCHES TELEMACHUS VISIT MENELAUS AND HELEN
O. IV. 1–625.

ATHENA AND PENELOPE
O. IV. 625–770.
O. IV. 795–845.

ATHENA APPEALS TO THE OLYMPIANS
O. V. 1–57.

ATHENA WATCHES OVER ODYSSEUS
O. V. 59–165.
O. V. 245–380.
O. V. 382–493.

ATHENA, ODYSSEUS, AND NAUSICAA
O. VI. 1–50.
O. VI. 110ff.
O. VII. 1–81.
O. VIII.

O. XIII. 1–186.

O. XIII: After an argument with Zeus, Poseidon punished the Phaecians for their courtesy to Odysseus by turning one of their
returning ships into stone. It is said that a great rock in the harbor
of Corcyra (Corfu) is that ship, and proof that Odysseus's Phaecia
was Corcyra.

ATHENA AND ODYSSEUS PLOT AGAINST THE SUITORS
O. XIII. 187–440.

ODYSSEUS FOLLOWS ATHENA'S PLAN
O. XIV.

ATHENA BRINGS TELEMACHUS HOME
O. XV. 1–300.
O. XV. 301–555.

ATHENA REUNITES FATHER AND SON
O. XVI. 1–321.

ODYSSEUS RETURNS TO HIS PALACE
O. XVI. 322–451.
O. XVI. 453–481.
O. XVII. 1–100; XVII. 105–605.

PREPARATIONS FOR BATTLE
O. XIV.
O. XVIII. 150–429.

THE SUITORS ARE DOOMED
O. XX. 1–394.
O. XXI. 1–430.

SWEET REVENGE WITH THE HELP OF A GODDESS
O. XXII.

REVENGE UPON REVENGE
O. XXIII.
O. XXIV.

PART VIII WISE GODDESS OF LAW AND JUSTICE

ATHENS, HOME OF THE GODDESS
Joint Association of Classical Teachers, *The World of Athens*, (1974).

ATHENS: HISTORY AND MYTH
Plutarch, *Solon* XVII 2.
Demosthenes, XIX 255.
Aristotle, *Constitution of Athens* XVI 2, XVI 9.
Bothmer, Dietrich von. *Amazons in Greek Art*. Oxford: Oxford Uni-
versity Press, 1957.

Harrison, A. R. W., *The Law of Athens I: The Family and Property* (1968).

Herington, C. J., *Athena Parthenos and Athena Polias: A Study in the Religion of Periclean Athens* (1955).

Princeton Symposium, *Athens Comes of Age: From Solon to Salamis.* Papers of the symposium sponsored by the Archaeological Institute of America (1978).

Wycherley, R. E., *The Stones of Athens* (1978).

ATHENS AND MYTH

Tyrrell, Wm. Blake, *Amazons: A Study in Athenian Mythmaking* (1984).

ATHENA AND THE FURIES

Apollodorus, *Epitome* vi.25.

Pausanias: viii.34.2.

Aeschylus, *Eumenides* 397, 470ff., and 681ff.

Euripides, *Iphigeneia Among the Taurians* 961ff.

Chesler, Phyllis, *Women and Madness* (1972).

Gargarin, Michael, "The Vote of Athena," *American Journal of Philology,* 96 (1975), 121–127.

ATHENA, ART AND CIVIC LIFE

Harrison, Jane Ellen, *Mythology and Monuments of Ancient Athens* London, 1890.

Thompson, H. A., and R. E. Wycherley, *The Athenian Agora* (1972).

Patterson, Cynthia. *Pericles' Citizenship Law of 451–50 B.C.* New York: Arno Press, 1981.

ATHENA CELEBRATED BY ATHENIANS

Parke, H. W., *Festivals of the Athenians.* London: Thames and Hudson, 1977.

Raubitshek, A., *Dedications from the Athenian Akropolis* (1949).

ATHENA'S ACROPOLIS

Robertson, Martin, *The Parthenon Frieze* (1975).

Robertson, Martin, "The Sculptures of the Partheon." *Greece & Rome* 10 (1963), 46–61.

ATHENA PARTHENOS: IN THE SHADOW OF A LOST MASTERPIECE

Hooker, G. T. W. (ed.), *Parthenos and Parthenon,* Oxford (1963).

Richter, Gisela M. A., *Handbook of Greek Art* (1959).

IMMORTAL GODDESS

Marinus, *Life of Proclus.*

Morrow, Glenn R., and John Dillon, *Proclus' Commentary on Plato's Parmenides* (Princeton, 1987), 654.

INDEX